TOURING BEYOND THE NATION:
A TRANSNATIONAL APPROACH TO
EUROPEAN TOURISM HISTORY

Touring Beyond the Nation: A Transnational Approach to European Tourism History

Edited by

ERIC G.E. ZUELOW
University of New England, USA

ASHGATE

Published by
Ashgate Publishing Limited
Wey Court East
Union Road
Farnham
Surrey, GU9 7PT
England

Ashgate Publishing Company
Suite 420
101 Cherry Street
Burlington
VT 05401-4405
USA

www.ashgate.com

British Library Cataloguing in Publication Data
Touring beyond the nation : a transnational approach to
   European tourism history.
   1. Tourism--Europe. 2. Transnationalism.
   I. Zuelow, Eric.
   338.4'7914-dc22

Library of Congress Cataloging-in-Publication Data
Zuelow, Eric G. E.
   Touring beyond the nation : a transnational approach to European tourism history / Eric G. E. Zuelow.
      p. cm.
   Includes index.
   ISBN 978-0-7546-6656-1 (hardcover) 1. Tourism--Europe--History. 2. Transnationalism--Europe. I. Title.
   G155.E8Z83 2010
   338.4'7914--dc22

2010032079

ISBN 9780754666561 (hbk)

MIX
Paper from
responsible sources
FSC® C013056

Printed and bound in Great Britain by
TJ International Ltd, Padstow, Cornwall.

Contents

List of Figures

List of Contributors

Stephen L. Harp is Professor of Modern French History at the University of Akron. He is the author of *Marketing Michelin: Advertising and Cultural Identity in Twentieth-Century France* (2001) and *Learning to Be Loyal: Primary Schooling as Nation Building in Alsace and Lorraine, 1850–1940* (1998). He is currently working on two book projects: "From Coolies to Consumers: A Cultural History of Rubber" and "Au Naturel: Naturisme, Nudism, and Beachfront Tourism in Modern France."

Christian Noack is a Lecturer on East European History at the National University of Ireland, Maynooth. He has published extensively on nationalisms in the Russian Empire, and mass tourism in Russian-speaking countries. He is co-editor (with Hasso Spode and Wiebke Kolbe) of *Tourismusgeschichte(n): Voyage – Jahrbuch für Reise- & Tourismusforschung, Vol. 8* (2009). His current research focuses on mass tourism during the Brezhnev era.

Angela Schwarz is Professor of Modern and Contemporary History at Universität Siegen. She has written extensively in German and English on World's Fairs, nationalism, national parks, media history, and interwar Germany. Her monographs include *Die Reise ins Dritte Reich: Britische Augenzeugen im nationalsozialistischen Deutschland (1933–1939)* (1993), *Der Schlüssel zur modernen Welt: Wissenschaftspopularisierung in Großbritannien und Deutschland im Übergang zur Moderne (ca. 1870–1914)* (1999), *Vom Industriebetrieb zum Landschaftspark* (2001), *Der Park in der Metropole: Urbanes Wachstum und städtische Parks im 19. Jahrhundert* (2005), and *"Wollten Sie auch immer schon einmal pestverseuchte Kühe auf Ihre Gegner werfen?" Eine fachwissenschaftliche Annäherung an Geschichte im Computerspie* (2010).

Kristin Semmens is a Lecturer in European and German History at the University of Victoria, Canada. She is the author of *Seeing Hitler's Germany: Tourism in the Third Reich* (2005) as well as several articles on commercial tourism in Nazi Germany.

Michelle Standley is completing work on a dissertation in Modern European History at New York University. Her project examines the relationship between the Cold War and mass tourism in East and West Berlin during the 1960s and 1970s. She is the former Book Review Editor of H-Travel@h-net.msu.edu. Her writing and reviews have appeared in such publications as *Pulse-Berlin Magazine*, *Left History*, and *Artdish*.

Laurent Tissot is Professor of Contemporary History at the University of Neuchâtel. He is the former president of the executive committee of the Swiss Economic and Social History Society and member of the Swiss National Research Council. His main themes of research are: history of transport and tourism, history of sports, and history of industrialization (business history, regional history). He is the author of *Naissance d'une industrie touristique: Les Anglais et la Suisse au XIXème siècle* (2000), *Construction of a Tourist Industry in the 19th and 20th Centuries: International Perspectives* (2003), (with Gijs Mom) *Road History: Planning, Building and Use* (2007), and (with Gijs Mom and Gordon Pirie) *Mobility in History* (2009).

Alexander Vari is Assistant Professor of Modern European History at Marywood University in Scranton, PA. He has published articles on tourism and nation-building in Hungary, and the experience of Hungarian travelers in Paris in the *Austrian History Yearbook* and *Journeys: The International Journal of Travel and Travel Writing*, and book chapters in Anne Gorsuch and Diane Koenker (eds) *Turizm: The Russian and Eastern European Tourist under Capitalism and Socialism* (2006), and Judith Schachter and Stephen Brockmann (eds) *(Im)permanence: Cultures in/out of Time* (2008). He is currently working on a comparative history of city marketing, nationalism, and urban-tourism promotion in Budapest and Bucharest.

John K. Walton is IKERBASQUE Research Professor in the Basque Foundation for Science in the Departamento de Historia Contemporánea, Universidad del País Vasco, Bilbao. He has published extensively on regional history, regional identities, popular culture, sport, and seaside resorts, especially in Britain and Spain in the nineteenth and twentieth centuries, as well as on proto-industrialization, Victorian insanity, Chartism, and Benjamin Disraeli. His major publications include *The Blackpool Landlady: A Social History* (1978), *The English Seaside Resort: A Social History 1750–1914* (1983), *Fish and Chips and the British Working Class, 1870–1940* (1992, 1994, 2000), *The British Seaside: Holidays and Resorts in the Twentieth Century* (2000), (with Gary Cross) *The Playful Crowd: Pleasure Places in the*

Twentieth Century (2005), and *Riding on Rainbows: Blackpool Pleasure Beach and its Place in British Popular Culture* (2007). He is editor of the *Journal of Tourism History*.

Patrick Young is Assistant Professor of Modern European History at the University of Massachusetts–Lowell. His current research focuses on the role of modern tourism in France as a medium for regional preservation and development. He is currently completing a book manuscript, entitled *Looking for the Last Bretons: Tourism, Preservation and Loss in Brittany, 1890–1937*, which explores how dilemmas over cultural value, preservation and loss played out in the tourist development and consumption of the French region of Brittany during the transition from elite to early mass tourism.

Eric G.E. Zuelow is Assistant Professor of European History at the University of New England, Special Graduate Faculty at the University of Guelph, Ontario, and Adjunct Graduate Faculty at Union Institute and University. He is the author of *Making Ireland Irish: Tourism and National Identity since the Irish Civil War* (2009) and co-editor (with Mitchell Young and Andreas Sturm) of *Nationalism in a Global Era: The Persistence of Nations* (2007). He serves as reviews editor for the *Journal of Tourism History* and is the editor/creator of *The Nationalism Project* (http://nationalismproject.org).

Acknowledgements

The idea for this book is a result of an email exchange between Michelle A. Standley and myself. During the course of our correspondence, we started to toy with the idea that tourism history might be as much about transnational, and especially pan-European, discourse as it was about discrete national developments in any one state. Inspired, I began to ask other historians, many of them suggested by Michelle, about their findings. Exchanges with the contributors to this collection, as well as with Sasha D. Pack and Shelley Baranowski, ultimately generated the idea for this book as well as for a panel presentation at the American Historical Association annual conference.

I am tremendously grateful to all of those who contributed their work to the collection. Not only is their scholarship first rate, they displayed extraordinary patience with me as we collectively negotiated the challenges of doing pan-European history. We weathered differing grammar conventions and spellings, language barriers, and the simple difficulty of writing about a very large geographic and chronological space.

Over the past several years I have benefited tremendously from my ongoing friendship with Kevin James of the University of Guelph. Frequent conversations, joint participation in the advising of Guelph graduate students interested in tourism history, and the opportunity to take part in a conference that Kevin organized in Londonderry continue to shape and expand my understanding of and interest in the historical evolution of tourism.

My colleagues at the University of New England also deserve thanks. Elizabeth De Wolfe, Paul T. Burlin, Robert Alegre, Jeff Ball, Ali Ahmida, Anouar Majid, and Linda Sartorelli, among many others, were generous with their advice and kind words. The staff of the UNE library was very helpful with tracking down various materials. I am especially grateful to the UNE College of Arts and Sciences for its ongoing support of my research.

I would also like to thank my parents for the opportunities and inspiration that they give me on a daily basis. My partner, Catherine M. Burns, deserves special recognition and thanks, not only for her day-to-day support but also for her willingness to comment on drafts of my writing. I dedicate my contributions in this volume to her.

Chapter 1

The Necessity of Touring Beyond the Nation: An Introduction

Eric G.E. Zuelow

Although tourism history is still in its infancy, the bird's-eye narrative of the story is relatively well established, even as it is also somewhat problematic. Most scholars agree that modern tourism started to take shape as a product of the eighteenth-century Grand Tour, a coming of age ritual for English gentlemen. These young men ventured to continental Europe for between a few months to a few years and were expected to learn languages, form relationships, and improve their aesthetic sensibilities.[1] At roughly the same moment, notions of landscape attractiveness and desirability changed profoundly when Edmund Burke, a transplanted Irishmen who later made a name in British politics, published *A Philosophical Inquiry into the Origin of Our Ideas of the Sublime and Beautiful* in 1757. When combined with scientific advances that prompted many Enlightenment-minded tourists to seek new discoveries in the natural classroom of the outdoors,[2] and the burgeoning Romantic movement which encouraged an emotional, solitary, and semi-spiritual relationship with aesthetically pleasing landscapes,[3] Burke's essay soon convinced tourists to visit places that were once deemed frightening and ugly but which now allowed visitors to experience the sublime.[4] Within the next 150 years, the seaside

---

[1]   Jeremy Black, *The British Abroad: The Grand Tour in the Eighteenth Century* (New York: St. Martin's Press, 1992) and James Buzard, "The Grand Tour and After (1660–1840)," in Peter Hulme and Tim Youngs (eds), *The Cambridge Companion to Travel Writing* (Cambridge: Cambridge University Press, 2002), pp. 37–52.

[2]   Robert Macfarlane, *Mountains of the Mind: How Desolate and Forbidding Heights were Transformed into Experiences of Indomitable Spirit* (New York: Pantheon Books, 2003), pp. 22–65. See also: Alain Corbin, *The Lure of the Sea* (Berkeley and Los Angeles: University of California Press, 1994).

[3]   John Urry, *The Tourist Gaze* (London: Sage Publications, 2002), pp. 42–3.

[4]   Gerhard Stilz, "Heroic Travellers—Romantic Landscapes: The Colonial Sublime in Indian, Australian and American Art and Literature," in Barbara Korte, Hartmut Berghoff, Ralf Schneider, and Christopher Harvie (eds), *The Making of Modern Tourism: The Cultural History of the British Experience, 1600–2000* (Basingstoke: Palgrave, 2002), pp. 85–107.

emerged as a leading attraction for tourists: starting with elites and gradually filtering down to the working classes.[5]

Technological advances added to a growing desire to escape from the work-a-day world into leisure pursuits. Initially, engineers and investors imagined that railways would carry coal, lumber, iron, and steel. Passengers were, if anything, an afterthought. Even so, less than a year after the famous Rainhill Trials prompted the emergence of a more efficient steam engine, the Liverpool and Manchester Railway launched a passenger service. That first year 460,000 travelers experienced mobility at a blistering 17 miles per hour. Leisure rail travel soon expanded still more.[6] Teetotaler Thomas Cook led his first excursion on July 5, 1841 and within only a few years he transported leisure travelers all across England, then Scotland, and soon the world.[7] Trains made travel more affordable and efficient.

Henceforth, resorts developed,[8] cruise lines stepped up trans-Atlantic tourism opportunities,[9] the number of guidebooks mushroomed,[10] and companies in the

---

[5]   For example, see: John K. Walton, *English Seaside Resorts: A Social History, 1750–1914* (Basingstoke: Palgrave, 1983).

[6]   P.J.G. Ransom, *The Victorian Railway and How it Evolved* (London: Heinemann, 1990), pp. 56–7. See also: Jack Simmons, *The Victorian Railway* (London: Thames and Hudson, 1991) and Wolfgang Schivelbusch, *The Railway Journey: The Industrialization of Time and Space in the 19th Century* (Berkeley and Los Angeles: University of California Press, 1986).

[7]   Piers Brendon, *Thomas Cook: 150 Years of Popular Travel* (London: Secker and Warburg, 1991).

[8]   John K. Walton's *Blackpool* (Edinburgh: Edinburgh University Press, 1998) offers an invaluable history of the most popular of working-class English resorts. Ellen Furlough's "Making Mass Vacations: Tourism and Consumer Culture in France, 1930s to 1970s," *Comparative Studies in Society and History* 40 (1998): pp. 247–86 includes interesting material about the rise of commercial tourism in France, including a discussion of the creation and early development of Club Med. John Beckerson and John K. Walton's "Selling Air: Marketing the Intangible at British Resorts," in John K. Walton (ed.), *Histories of Tourism: Representation, Identity, and Conflict* (Clevedon, Buffalo, and Toronto: Channel View Publications, 2005), pp. 55–70 examines how fresh air was marketed as a primary selling point at British seaside resorts between the late nineteenth and mid-twentieth centuries.

[9]   Tarry Coleman, *The Liners: A History of the North Atlantic Crossing* (Middlesex: Penguin, 1976). See also: Lorraine Coons and Alexander Varias, *Tourist Third Cabin: Steamship Travel in the Interwar Years* (New York: Palgrave Macmillan, 2003).

[10]   For a useful discussion of tourist guidebooks, see: Rudy J. Koshar, "'What Ought to Be Seen': Tourists' Guidebooks and National Identities in Modern Germany and Europe," *Journal of Contemporary History* 33/3 (1998): pp. 323–40. See also: Jan Palmowski, "Travels with Baedeker: The Guidebooks and the Middle Classes in Victorian and Edwardian England," in Rudy Koshar (ed.), *Histories of Leisure* (Oxford and New York: Berg, 2002), pp. 105–30.

United States and across Europe catered more and more to largely middle-class clients anxious to pursue "what ought to be seen." Later, during the second half of the twentieth century, the advent of jet aircraft inserted the final piece of the puzzle.[11] Costs dropped, time investment decreased, and all at once even many members of the working class could realistically dream of traveling the world. The age of mass tourism dawned.[12]

There are a number of striking things about this account. First, it tends to be fairly Anglocentric. The narrative posits that the Grand Tour, railways, seaside resorts, and mountaineering were all English inventions that spread easily to the rest of the world; the vectors of distribution were straightforward and uncomplicated. It follows that much (though certainly not all) of the scholarship on tourism history focuses disproportionately on Great Britain.[13] Second, and perhaps as an outgrowth of the extraordinary preponderance of class analysis in English historiography, social class dominates as a focus of scholarly enquiry.[14] While many studies adopt a top-down narrative for tourism development, other accounts, such as Susan Barton's excellent *Working-Class Organisations and Popular Tourism, 1840–1970*, suggest a more bottom-up course of events in which workers increasingly defined leisure patterns in Britain.[15] Either way, class stands as a driving force behind the evolution of tourism. Third, and perhaps most striking, the narrative of tourism history is largely contained within national borders. Without singling out specific studies, histories of

---

[11]   Kenneth Hudson, *Air Travel: A Social History* (Totowa: Rowman and Littlefield, 1972).

[12]   Orvar Löfgren offers a very readable account that discusses many of these developments in *On Holiday: A History of Vacationing* (Berkeley: University of California Press, 1999).

[13]   John K. Walton, "Prospects in Tourism History: Evolution, State of Play, and Future Developments," *Tourism Management* 30 (2009): pp. 783–93. See especially p. 787.

[14]   See Eric G.E. Zuelow, "The Making of the English Traveling Class: A Review of Susan Barton's *Working-Class Organisations and Popular Tourism, 1840–1970*," *H-Travel*, March 2007. Available online at: http://www.h-net.org/~travel [accessed November 16, 2009].

[15]   Susan Barton, *Working-Class Organisations and Popular Tourism, 1840–1970* (Manchester: Manchester University Press, 2005) stands as the principal example of a bottom-up narrative. Top-down narratives are more numerous. Rudy J. Koshar's excellent study of German travel guidebooks, *German Travel Cultures* (Oxford and New York: Berg, 2000), for example, is concerned with guidebook authors/publishers rather than with any broader dialogue about German tourism. Shelley Baranowski's superb study of Nazi leisure policy, *Strength through Joy* (Cambridge and New York: Cambridge University Press, 2004), addresses policymakers and their objectives. Irene Furlong's study of tourism in Ireland, *Irish Tourism: 1880–1980* (Dublin: Irish Academic Press, 2009) is overwhelmingly focused on agencies, governments, and prominent tourism developers rather than community-led development efforts.

American, French, German, Spanish, English, and Irish tourism function within geographically bounded areas. Even when developments are understood within a larger context, the relationships between actors are surprisingly limited. For example, Irish tourism is almost always imagined in terms of the Anglo-Irish relationship; little space is allowed for larger transnational connections—with Germany or France, for example—by Irish developers.[16]

It is not that scholars completely ignore transnational relationships. Shelley Baranowski's superb book on *Kraft durch Freude* [*Strength through Joy*], the Nazi leisure organization, places National Socialist leisure policy into the context of the international push toward Fordist production techniques and clearly acknowledges connections between Nazi and Italian fascist leisure regimes.[17] Sasha D. Pack's excellent account of tourism development in Spain under Francisco Franco certainly positions developments on the Iberian Peninsula within a larger European context.[18] Likewise, Harvey Levenstein's entertaining two-book treatment of American tourists in France from the eighteenth century to the present clearly addresses a relatively simple bi-dimensional transnational relationship.[19] The issue is that the self-conscious focus on specific national cases or on discrete two-way tourist flows almost always fails to ask whether there are still more complicated dynamics at work. Are there broader transnational discourses, developments, or trends that drove the history of tourism, both in terms of tourist practices and in terms of the evolution of national tourist movements?

There is considerable evidence that suggests the growth of tourism occurred amid a complicated matrix of transnational forces. Consider what happened in the immediate aftermath of World War II. Europe was in dire shape. Many British and German cities were little more than piles of debris that were so vast that even Germany's hardworking *Trümmerfrauen* [rubble women] and their British equivalent could only make a start with the cleanup. More daunting, some 70 percent of Europe's industrial infrastructure was destroyed. Vital transportation networks were broken into so many occasional patches of roadway or bits of track. Supplies were scarce and rationing nearly ubiquitous. Worse still, many

---

[16]   William H.A. Williams, *Tourism, Landscape, and the Irish Character: British Travel Writers in Pre-Famine Ireland* (Madison: University of Wisconsin Press, 2008) and Melissa Fegan, "The Traveller's Experience in Famine Ireland," *Irish Studies Review* 9/3 (2001): pp. 361–72.

[17]   Baranowski, *Strength through Joy*.

[18]   Sasha D. Pack, *Tourism and Dictatorship: Europe's Peaceful Invasion of Franco's Spain* (New York: Palgrave Macmillan, 2006).

[19]   Harvey Levenstein, *Seductive Journey: American Tourists in France from Jefferson to the Jazz Age* (Chicago: University of Chicago Press, 1998) and *We'll Always Have Paris: American Tourists in France since 1930* (Chicago: University of Chicago Press, 2004).

in the West saw the specter of totalitarian rule waiting in the wings yet again. For Winston Churchill, Russia's failure to "co-operate"[20] was akin to an "iron curtain" descending across the continent. Faced with a new autocratic threat, he demanded close collaboration because "the safety of the world ... requires a unity in Europe."[21] These were urgent times requiring dramatic measures. Another Adolf Hitler must not be allowed to rise; Joseph Stalin must be blocked from spreading his red menace to the West. If only the dire economic conditions of the inter-war years could be avoided, principally by assuring that American dollars flowed into Europe while also increasing the corresponding export of European products to America,[22] peace and stability might yet reign.

The European Recovery Program (ERP), or Marshall Plan, with its millions of dollars in aid, was one solution to the crisis. Agricultural and industrial redevelopment was obviously a major part of the story—perhaps the most famous part—but for those anxious to rebuild Europe, tourism was a core component of any revitalization program. The industry was particularly intriguing because it offered twin benefits: "dollar-earning capacity of the tourist services proper" (including the purchase of European products while traveling) and the prospect of "stimulating the export of commodities to America" after the "American tourist traveling in Europe gets to know European goods, for which, on his return to America, he may help to create a demand."[23] With so much to add to reconstruction, both Marshall Plan officials and the member countries of the Organisation for European Economic Co-operation (OEEC) saw tourism as a cornerstone of a sound economic future. Both groups had working committees devoted to tourism policy. The OEEC Tourism Committee and the Marshall Plan's "Travel Development Section" cooperated with a third group, the European Travel Commission (ETC), to conduct an international marketing campaign, to make it easier to cross borders, to assure adequate facilities for tourists, and even to devise ways to smooth the path for working-class people into the tourist ranks.

Officials launched their collaborative efforts in early February 1949, anxious to tackle tourist problems from "every angle." From the OEEC perspective the

---

20 Mary Saran, "Europe and the Marshall Plan," *The Antioch Review* 8/1 (Spring, 1948): pp. 26–32.

21 Winston Churchill, "Iron Curtain Speech," March 5, 1946. Available online from *The Modern History Sourcebook*. Available online at: http://www.fordham.edu/halsall/mod/churchill-iron.html [accessed February 8, 2009].

22 National Archives of Ireland [hereafter NAI], Tourism, Transport, and Communications, 3/1/3 vol. 1, Letter from the Swedish Tourist Association, November 28, 1952.

23 Ibid.

goal was primarily "coordination and inspiration," but as time passed, officials expected the group's remit to grow. Above all else, the Organisation recognized the need for extensive cooperation and "close contact with the other technical committees and the specialized bodies outside the OEEC" including the International Hotel Federation, the ETC, and other such groups. It would be necessary to be flexible and to adopt the best ideas wherever they came from.[24]

In keeping with this collaborative spirit, one of the first ideas floated by Marshall Planners was the composition of an international group of tourism officials who would travel to the United States to "examine on the spot the arrangements and services which an American tourist expects when he travels in his own country." Following this trip, American officials would be invited to Europe in order to "assist in whatever reorganization it is decided to effect."[25] By the first months of 1950, teams of experts from Belgium, Ireland, the Netherlands, the United Kingdom, France, Greece, Italy, Germany, Austria, Luxembourg, Switzerland, Denmark, Norway, and Sweden traveled to the United States to study hotel development and other tourism infrastructure questions.[26]

During the spring of 1949, a sub-committee of the ETC successfully launched a joint advertising campaign in the United States. The program included the United Kingdom, France, Italy, Belgium, Switzerland, Denmark, Norway, Sweden, Austria, and Luxembourg, each contributing funds ranging from $30,000 each for Britain, Italy, and France to just $1,000 from Luxembourg. Ordinarily the massive market represented by the United States was available only to countries with significant economic muscle; now even smaller countries got the word out. This joint advertising campaign continued into at least the mid-1960s before financial concerns expressed by countries such as France, who paid a disproportionate amount of the cost while seeing little obvious benefit, decided to withdraw from the program.[27]

The impressive post-war development effort proved remarkably successful; tourism in Europe grew steadily. Perhaps more intriguing, however, the Europeans provided more impoverished geographic regions with a strategy for selling a tourist product to middle America. Specifically, various combinations of

---

24   NAI, Department of Foreign Affairs [hereafter DFA], 305/57/128 pt. 1, "Tourism Working Party, Minutes of the 1st Meeting held on Thursday 27th and Friday 28th January 1949," February 7, 1949.

25   NAI, Department of the Taoiseach [hereafter DT], S5472B, "Tourist Traffic with USA: Development," 1949.

26   NAI, DFA, 305/57/128 pt. 1, E.C.A., "Dispatch of Teams of Experts to Study Tourist Equipment in the United States," December 16, 1949.

27   NAI, DFA, 2005/4/665, "Position of France in Relation to European Travel Commission," March 31, 1965.

countries adopted the ETC as a model and created their own travel organizations in order to carry out the type of advertising campaign in the United States that was conducted by the Europeans. Thus, by 1959 there was a Pacific Area Travel Association (PATA) that included 22 countries such as Japan, Indonesia, and Australia. The South American Travel Association (SATA) included Panama, Chile, Peru, Colombia, and Bolivia. A Central American organization called the Caribbean Tourist Association conducted publicity campaigns in the United States. As an OEEC report noted, "joint publicity is becoming increasingly the custom" and it "can be handled best by a group of countries forming a geographical unity, rather than by any one country on its own."[28]

Towards a Transnational History of Tourism

The above story is obviously transnational, pan-European, and trans-Atlantic. More importantly, it is not an isolated example of wide-ranging connections that resulted from or even prompted tourism promotion efforts. Tourism development in Europe was seldom, if ever, contained within national borders. Tourism was bigger than a series of discrete national stories; it was hardly ever entirely the domain of specific state actors but was often the result of a larger current of developments. Obviously each individual country or tourist movement has its own unique story, but the argument put forward in this volume is that truly understanding the history of tourism requires moving beyond national boundaries. Simply stated, it is essential to recognize that the history of tourism unfolded across a broad, transnational canvas.

The present book offers ten case studies that collectively make the argument for the development of a transnational history of European tourism. The authors address cases ranging from the development of tourist practices and types of tourism to more traditionally "national" stories placed within a much larger framework. Their studies span geographic territory from the Soviet Union in the east to Ireland in the northwest to the Mediterranean in the south while also addressing a good deal of what falls in between.

Part I: Transnational Spaces: From Mountains to World's Fairs

The collection opens with four chapters that explore how transnational relationships play a vital role in the creation and perpetuation of tourist spaces

---

[28]   NAI, DFA, 305/57/128/1 pt. 4, "Joint Publicity in the United States for the Development of American Tourism in Europe," October 16, 1959.

such as beaches, mountains, and world's fairs. Tourists and historians alike often correlate these places with specific national, or at least regional, settings or characteristics. Beach tourism is associated with tropical or Mediterranean settings, mountain resorts take on a Swiss appearance, and world's fairs showcase the host country, even as they provide a vast display of world cultures. Yet, as John K. Walton, Stephen L. Harp, Laurent Tissot, and Angela Schwarz demonstrate, these places both developed through transnational dialogues and grew to provide a setting for further transnational exchange.

In Chapter 2, John K. Walton surveys some of the issues and impacts that resulted from interaction and development at the seaside. Although essentially an eighteenth-century English invention, seaside resorts soon emerged as a truly global phenomenon. From the Mediterranean to the United States, from Africa to Latin America, the seaside attracted "international seekers after health, pleasure, fashion, and display." Beaches prompted international middle- and working-class tourist flows, drawing social classes and national cultures together in a way that was not common during day-to-day existence. High-level diplomatic activity took place at the beach. Backpacker tourism drew young people to the world's coasts in greater and greater numbers from the 1960s. By surveying all of these interactions, Walton suggests that truly understanding the seaside resort and its global impact requires recognizing it as a transnational space that virtually demands a truly wide-angle perspective.

In Chapter 3, Stephen L. Harp picks up on the idea of the beach as transnational space by examining the evolution of nude tourism at the French Mediterranean resort at Cap d'Agde. According to Harp, the development of this prominent nudist destination is unthinkable without placing the site into a larger European context. During the 1950s, a small number of reportedly German nudists asked for permission to use a beach owned by a local vintner. Over the next several decades, extraordinary demand led to the creation of more and more amenities that, although not entirely popular with municipal authorities, were too lucrative to abandon. By the 1990s, Cap d'Agde was the "most heavily visited tourist center in all of France." International tourists made the resort, transformed the site, and constantly challenged local authorities to keep up with ever changing tourist demands. As Harp notes, "the 'naked city' has been a victim of its own rapid and wild success, adequately controlled neither by the municipality nor by the developers" but instead shaped principally by much larger international forces and demands.

Beyond beaches, mountains are perhaps the only geographic feature that inspires a comparable level of devotion. The various intellectual developments that prompted a reassessment of mountains during the eighteenth century, and which included thinkers from both Britain and continental Europe, are well known.[29] The fact that mountain resorts and hotels nearly all have a distinctive Swiss character is far more mysterious. In Chapter 4, Laurent Tissot explains that the process behind the "Swissification" of mountain tourism is a complicated one. "Scientific, technological, economic, political, social, physical, medical, geologic, symbolic, educational, and cultural dimensions joined and blended in the development of this new tourist model." Some developments were unique to the Swiss context, but others, such as the sport of mountaineering itself, emerged from a much larger transnational framework. Ultimately, Tissot illustrates that the Swiss-style resorts found in the United States, Canada, and even Latvia would not have developed at all without the larger transnational environment of European tourism development.

Like mountains and beaches, world's fairs serve as a distinctive transnational space that both shaped and was shaped by discourse that extended well beyond national borders. In Chapter 5, Angela Schwarz examines this phenomenon, tracing the transnational nature of world's fairs from the first such event in 1851 to the interwar period. Like beach and mountain resorts, fairs brought together "people, goods, technologies, ideas, and values." The events allowed people to travel the world without venturing further than a single city, and they inspired enterprising businessmen to create exhibitions and infrastructure that ushered in "the age of tourism as an industry." Between 1851 and 1937, more than 200 million people attended world's fairs, venturing into a collective experience in which pavilions showcased unique cultures using common approaches. The result was the establishment of many universal tourism tropes that included both practices and modes of display.

Part II: Selling the National in a Transnational Context

Part II changes direction to focus explicitly on the marketing of more distinctly regional or national tourism products. When people travel, they often seek to encounter something different (though perhaps not too different) from what they know at home. An American traveling to France, for example, certainly expects to find a different experience from what she would see in the United States. An Englishman traveling to Budapest undoubtedly hopes that the "Queen of the Danube" is markedly different from London. It follows that one of the great challenges facing tourism developers is to carefully brand their product as distinctive. The Hungarians must sell what is uniquely Hungarian and the French must present something definitely French. It is unfathomable to imagine an Irish marketing scheme that reads: "Come to Ireland, very much like

---

[29]   Macfarlane, *Mountains of the Mind*.

England but in the Eurozone and with darker beer!" One might imagine that development of a distinctive brand is almost entirely inward looking, prompting promoters to ask: "What makes us different?" The truth is therefore somewhat surprising. As Alexander Vari, Patrick Young, and Eric G.E. Zuelow illustrate in the three chapters comprising Part II, it turns out that the creation of national tourist products often (maybe always?) involves a much broader dialogue that necessitates moving beyond the nation.

According to Alexander Vari, city-marketing in Budapest between 1885 and 1939 involved frequent debate about whether to sell the city as the embodiment of the Magyar past, as nationalists wanted, or as the "Paris of the East" as profit-minded tourism developers wished. Those in favor of "Paris of the East" hoped to establish a city that was truly cosmopolitan, so they introduced Spanish-style bullfights and casino gambling. The result was heated conflict. In Chapter 6, Vari details the evolution of city marketing, taking us from the late-nineteenth-century "Paris of the East" campaigns, with their self-consciously international flare, to the twentieth-century "Queen of the Danube" idea that merged less offensive foreign gimmicks (fireworks, boat parades, and lit crosses) with more traditional Magyar imagery. Put another way, foreign ideas merged with national ones through fierce debate, creating a unique tourist product in Budapest.

The challenge of balancing national aspirations toward distinctiveness with external pressures, demands, and influences ran far beyond Hungary. In Chapter 7, Patrick Young explores how French tourism developers, starting in the 1890s, strove to create a unique French tourist product while repeatedly encountering the need to engage with others. On the one hand, tourism advocates held an "Estates General of Tourism" in 1913 that symbolized French difference, while on the other hand they found themselves faced with the need to adapt to larger trends. Over time, the French adopted more international approaches to advertising, followed the lead of others toward state-sponsored tourism development and away from private initiatives, and began to base their hotels on Swiss, Austrian, and German models. As developers sought to offer growing legions of visitors something that was uniquely French, "they also brokered a more complicated interface with a touring public that was not only significantly larger but also in some ways still largely unknown." It was necessary to balance national and international pressures. Tourism necessitated crossing borders and demanded a truly transnational view of the industry and its various tropes.

The Irish story is similar. According to Eric G.E. Zuelow, Irish tourism promoters endeavored to sell a vision of Ireland that was at once unique and familiar. The Emerald Isle offered a place where visitors would find recognizable amenities, even as they experienced a culture and landscape that was distinctive. Without denying that an extraordinary amount of internal dialogue helped to create tourist Ireland, the end product was every bit as much a result of larger forces. In Chapter 8, Zuelow argues that the transnational discourse that ultimately shaped Ireland's global persona were present from the very first. From the initial sense that tourism was a desirable national interest to the marketing and presentation of specific tourist products and amenities, Irish tourism evolved within a broad pan-European and trans-Atlantic context. The way in which all of the ingredients were combined ultimately made Ireland different, but the notion that they should be pieced together at all came from much further a field.

Part III: The Politics of Transnational Tourism

In Part III, Christian Noack, Kristin Semmens, and Michelle Standley make clear that tourism did more than shape practices or market specific places, the industry held potential for regimes anxious to distinguish themselves politically and economically from the rest of the world. Whether examining Soviet Russia where many dreamed of creating a class-free world that benefited all equally, studying Nazi Germany where the National Socialists looked forward to demonstrating their superiority, or investigating the German Democratic Republic where tourism offered a means of educating citizens and visitors alike about the positive strengths of the East German state, one finds that tourism promised an opportunity to remake society itself.

In the wake of the 1917 Bolshevik Revolution, some among the intelligentsia dreamed of further distinguishing the Soviet state from the West by creating a new type of tourism. For some intellectuals, *Kurort*, an eighteenth- and nineteenth-century leisure regime born of the aristocracy that defined pre-Soviet Russian tourism, had to be abandoned in favor of something altogether new and class free. In Chapter 9, Christian Noack details the rise and fall of such endeavors. Soviet leaders, it turns out, were steeped in "cultural outlooks" informed "by ideas prevalent among the late imperial intelligentsia that were solidly rooted in noble lifestyles and habits developed during the nineteenth century." Therefore, it was up to other intellectuals to endeavor to originate something special. As it happens, the task of building a new type of tourism proved to be nearly impossible. No matter how hard idealists tried, Western tourist ideas simply would not die.

However revolutionary Hitler and his cronies imagined the Nazi Party to be, they too were trapped within the larger context of tourism. In Chapter 10, Kristin Semmens demonstrates that Nazi tourism developers responded to the outside world not by trying to escape from larger tourist discourse, but rather by actively engaging with it. By examining three tourism conferences that were held in Germany under Nazi auspices, Semmens illustrates that even during the Third Reich, conferences "became vehicles for cross-border conversations, which though carried out in different languages, were easily understood because notions about the problems of workers' leisure time, the challenges of commercial tourism, and the trials of the hotel industry were shared by many participants." The Nazis certainly sought to use tourism conferences to present their unique organization, *Kraft durch Freude*, to the world, but at the same time, they could not help but borrow from others.

Although there was unquestionably a politics to the presentation of virtually every tourist destination regardless of the type of government, the political motivation of tourism marketers in East Berlin was even more pronounced. In the final chapter, Michelle Standley illustrates that promoters had to show East Germany to be modern and successful, while eschewing capitalist corruption. They had to demonstrate to outsiders how successful their country was, while minimizing the grim reality that East Berliners experienced every day: that just over the Berlin Wall there were bright lights and endless consumer goods, while at home all was monotone, bleak, and often under-stocked. It was not enough to create mountains of plastic household items as a means of proving East German success,[30] tourism had to be employed to sell the country itself. The T.V. Tower Information Center was one way to accomplish this objective and the various actors involved thus worked tirelessly to use this facility not only to show visitors what ought to be seen, but how to see it.

Tourism: Beyond the Nation

Tourism scholars should not be surprised by the existence of transnational and pan-European tourism development links such as the ones described in this volume. After all, tourism is inherently a transnational phenomenon. Scholars who examine tourist behavior and experience often note the omnipresent interaction between hosts and guests—interaction that has economic, cultural, political, and social implications.[31] Tourism necessarily places people from disparate backgrounds into contact with one another. When tourists travel, they seek the exotic. The further they venture, the more unique the cultures they gaze upon, the greater the prestige accrued; cross-cultural contact is virtually inherent in tourist practice.[32]

---

[30]   Eli Rubin, *Synthetic Socialism: Plastics and Dictatorship in the German Democratic Republic* (Chapel Hill: University of North Carolina Press, 2008).

[31]   Valene L. Smith, *Hosts and Guests: An Anthropology of Tourism* (Philadelphia: University of Pennsylvania Press, 1989), pp. 6–17.

[32]   Michel Peillon, "Tourism: The Quest for Otherness," *Crane Bag* 8 (1984): pp. 165–8.

Until recently, scholars focused disproportionately on the impact of these guests on host cultures. Each tourist season, a "golden horde" invades less dynamic societies, turning them into a "pleasure periphery" and demanding that tourist regions provide a product suited to tourist demands.[33] According to some scholars, faced with the need to make money, as well as a very human desire to please, host cultures do their best to behave for the benefit of the tourist. They play a role, acting out stereotypical regional or national parts, eventually forgetting that they are acting. They become what hosts *think* the tourist wants, little more authentic than the "little hyper-real celluloid animal deities" that inhabit Disneyland. The tourist gaze thus creates cultures rather than offering visitors the chance to see something "real."[34]

There is a certain amount of truth to the influence exerted by guests. Consider an Irish example. As tourists venture to distant places, they bring with them preconceptions about what they will find that ultimately shape not only the tourist experience, but the place visited. As William H.A. Williams points out in his wonderful book on tourism, landscape, and identity in pre-Famine Ireland, travelers apply ideas drawn from their own lived experience to the places they go to see. These guests make value judgments about the sites that they view and sometimes they even make a conscious effort to recast these sites in their own image. Williams, for example, describes how English tourists grew convinced that the Irish must be morally deficient because they had not created a landscape in Western Ireland that resembled England. How could beautiful land not be productive? When the west of Ireland was suddenly depopulated in the wake of the mid-nineteenth-century Potato Famine (1845–51), English entrepreneurs attempted to resettle the area with English farmers—farmers who quickly discovered that morality was hardly the problem in a boggy, rock-strewn landscape not suited to economically viable agriculture. Despite this failure, according to Williams, the English tourists did manage to present the

---

[33]   Louis Turner and John Ash, *The Golden Hordes: International Tourism and the Pleasure Periphery* (New York: St. Martin's Press, 1976); Jost Krippendorf, *The Holiday Makers: Understanding the Impact of Leisure and Travel* (Oxford: Butterworth Heinemann, 1987); C. Michael Hall and Alan A. Lew, *Understanding and Managing Tourism Impacts: An Integrated Approach* (London and New York: Routledge, 2009); and, Catherine A. Palmer, "Tourism and Colonialism: The Experience of the Bahamas," *Annals of Tourism Research* 21/4 (1994): pp. 792–811.

[34]   Dean MacCannell, *Empty Meeting Grounds: The Tourist Papers* (London and New York: Routledge, 1992): pp. 74–5 and 158–71. The tension between the respective interests of hosts and guests is well covered in Hazel Tucker, "The Ideal Village: Interactions through Tourism in Central Anatolia," in Simone Abram, Jacqueline Waldren, and Donald V.L. Macleod (eds), *Tourists and Tourism: Identifying with People and Places* (Oxford and New York: Berg, 1997), pp. 107–28.

west as "real Ireland," facilitating late-nineteenth-century Irish nationalist land agitation in western counties.[35] Put another way, the image of "Ireland" used by travel writers and later by Irish nationalists did not develop in Ireland among a collection of Irish-Irelanders, Fenians, and others; *it emerged from a transnational dialogue.*

While it is undoubtedly true that the tourist industry and the demands placed by guests can and sometimes do play a devastating role in destroying native culture—one need only look at the "socioeconomic apartheid" found in what some call "Cancún's Soweto"[36]—a growing number of scholars now point out that the relationship between hosts and guests is not nearly as one-sided as the traditional view suggests. Anthropologists such as Simon Abram and Moya Kneafsey, studying France and Ireland respectively, clearly show that host cultures do not lack agency nor are they so daft as to forget who they are, anymore than an actor like Meryl Streep or Robert De Niro forgets her or his identity following a film shoot. There is no "one-way process" whereby guests permanently alter their hosts; there is always a complex dialogue.[37]

Tourism developers endeavor to provide visitors with what they believe guests will want to see or do, but they also try to create a positive image of themselves. Consider, for example, what happened when *Holiday* magazine, an American publication, released a story about Ireland that was less than flattering. The story spoke about domestic pigs, tyrannical priests, horrendous slums, the oppression of pregnant girls and courting couples, and a host of other evils. To read the article was to discover an Ireland that was somewhat less than appealing. The response was immediate and dramatic. The Old IRA, Church authorities, Irish-American groups, county councils, and the Department of External Affairs in Ireland all protested. The Irish government even demanded an explanation from the magazine. Although the story was not retracted, only one year later *Holiday* released a second feature on Ireland that painted a much more idyllic picture. The Irish government vetted the new story prior to publication. As noted in

---

[35]   Williams, *Tourism, Landscape, and the Irish Character.*

[36]   In Mexico, much of the problem stems from top-down government policy that, over time, handed much of the development and perpetuation of tourism over to transnational corporations. The result was an ever-widening gap between those who administer tourism services and those who toil on the bottom rungs of the industry, often with few benefits and almost nonexistent salaries. See: Tamar Diana Wilson, "Economic and Social Impacts of Tourism in Mexico," *Latin American Perspectives* 35/3 (May 2008): pp. 37–52, especially pp. 46–50.

[37]   Simone Abram, "Performing for Tourists in Rural France," in Jacqueline Waldren, Simon Abram, and Donald V.L. Macleod (eds), *Tourists and Tourism: Identifying with People and Places* (Oxford and New York: Berg, 1997), pp. 29–50; and Moya Kneafsey, "Tourism and Place Identity: A Case-Study in Rural Ireland," *Irish Geography* 31/2 (1998): pp. 111–23.

Chapter 8, throughout the history of tourism development, Irish planners worked tirelessly to decide who they thought they were and what they thought Ireland should be. They certainly considered the tourist viewpoint in these deliberations, but domestic concerns and ideas of self were always part of the equation.

Neither a story of purely hosts or guests, the development of tourist images and products turns out to be a story of dialogue.[38] *Any* such interaction between people causes what Stuart Schwartz describes as "readjustments and rethinking as each side [is] forced to reformulate its ideas of self and other in the face of unexpected actions and unimagined possibilities."[39] This process is not a one-way thing; all sides play an active role in it. All sides make conscious decisions. All sides are fully involved actors.

If both hosts and guests are active in shaping tourism, it is hardly surprising to discover that the creation of tourist products, the manufacture of tourist practices, or even the effort to mold society, government, and economic systems through tourism is also shaped by widespread interaction—much of which is carried out by tourist agencies or governments anxious to create the best possible product. Stated simply, it is important to look across national borders and to place national movements into transnational contexts. To understand the history of tourism, we must not just acknowledge the big picture or the host/guest relationship we must make a larger transnational analysis a core component of our analytical frameworks. The histories of tourism in England, France, Germany, Russia, Italy, Spain, Ireland, Hungary, and beyond, to say nothing of the histories of touristic activities such as nude tourism, seaside tourism, mountain tourism, or world's fair tourism are parts of something bigger.

The ten scholars whose work makes up this volume adopt often very different approaches to their respective subjects. While some of the authors focus overwhelmingly on specific cases and primary documents, others adopt a much broader, more social science-oriented perspective. Furthermore, some explore totalitarian regimes while others study democracies. And yet, despite differences, the overwhelming message contained here is the need to adopt a transnational focus. It is not enough for scholars of tourism to study German, Italian, or Latvian tourism, totalitarian or bourgeois tourism regimes, urban adventures or remote and wild rambles, they must place those histories into a

---

[38]   Eric G.E. Zuelow, *Making Ireland Irish: Tourism and National Identity since the Irish Civil War* (Syracuse: Syracuse University Press, 2009).

[39]   Stuart B. Schwartz, "Introduction," in Stuart B. Schwartz (ed.), *Implicit Understandings: Observing, Reporting, and Reflecting on the Encounters Between Europeans and Other Peoples in the Early Modern Era* (Cambridge: Cambridge University Press, 1994), p. 3.

larger context. They must self-consciously ask: what did my actors know about the rest of the world? Who did they talk with? What fact-finding trips did they take? What models did they mimic or replicate? Historians are always concerned with context, of course, but, as this volume demonstrates, for tourism scholars, that context must be truly transnational in scope.

PART I
Transnational Spaces:
From Mountains to World's Fairs

Chapter 2
Seaside Resorts and International Tourism

John K. Walton

Coastal, seaside or beach resorts, constituting a distinctive kind of tourist destination (but with a wide range of variations around the theme), have been meeting points for international seekers after health, pleasure, fashion, and display for more than two centuries, beginning in north-western Europe.[1] Sea-bathing as the basis for a commercial tourist season is an English invention of the early to mid-eighteenth century, probably originating at Scarborough and Whitby on the North Sea coast, although the visual and artistic attractions of the beach were already drawing affluent visitors to Scheveningen in the Netherlands from the mid-seventeenth century.[2] The extension of coastal tourism from domestic to international markets, and the emergence of coastal locations as gathering points first for international high society, and ultimately for popular tourist industries whose reach spans continental as well as national boundaries, has been a long and complex process.[3] Alongside the pioneering role of the English in the early development of coastal tourism, they have been important on the international stage as tourists to, and expatriate residents on, European and later more distant shores: but the English (and indeed the British) seaside has drawn its holidaymakers overwhelmingly from the domestic market, which has made it less visible on the international stage. We should emphasize that the growth of international coastal tourism is not just a matter of the development and dynamics of international visiting publics: it also extends to the provision of services in the tourist economy, which entailed the development of international markets, migration flows, and communities of provision as well as consumption within the resorts in question.

---

[1] John K. Walton, "The Seaside Resorts of Western Europe, 1750–1939," in Stephen Fisher (ed.), *Recreation and the Sea* (Exeter: University of Exeter Press, 1997), pp. 36–56; Alain Corbin, *The Lure of the Sea* (Cambridge: Polity, 1994).

[2] Allan Brodie and Gary Winter, *England's Seaside Resorts* (Swindon: English Heritage, 2007).

[3] Louis Turner and John Ash, *The Golden Hordes: International Tourism and the Pleasure Periphery* (London: Constable, 1975); Lena Lencek and Gideon Bosker, *The Beach: A History of Paradise on Earth* (London: Secker and Warburg, 1998).

The coastal resort is clearly an international phenomenon in the sense that it has spread across most of the temperate and tropical globe during the nineteenth and twentieth centuries; but since its original migration across the English Channel, bringing together French and British users of summer bathing beaches in and around Boulogne and Dieppe in the intervals between wars from the late eighteenth century onwards, it has also had international dimensions in the sense of bringing people from different countries into propinquity and contact, whether in cordiality or conflict, in pursuit of health, pleasure, fashion, and display.[4] This applies both to international visiting publics and to relations between external visitors, local service providers, and agencies of the host government. The coastal resort was not the first modern international commercial leisure phenomenon to have such an impact: the European Grand Tour and the spa resort, named after the small Ardennes town which helped to pioneer the concept, offered related opportunities for international cultural mixing both in established centers and in newer settlements built around mineral springs, at a time when many European national polities were themselves in an emergent state.[5] The international spa resort, with its grand hotel, pump room, dancing, sociability, woodland walks, and (sometimes) roulette, might provide its own cosmopolitan microcosm of high society, and this remained the case across the European mainland into the twentieth century, especially in Central Europe where the sea was a long way away.[6] But although the coastal resort emerged later, it proved to be a particularly durable, expansive, and adaptable incarnation of the rapidly-developing tourism industries of Europe and the modern world; and in the twentieth century some coastal resorts, beginning on western Europe's Channel, Atlantic, and Mediterranean coasts, began to extend the role of the seaside as international melting-pot beyond the aristocratic and moneyed elites to embrace the lower middle and working classes in a process of democratization that the spas could not emulate.

---

[4]   Walton, "Seaside Resorts of Western Europe."

[5]   Jeremy Black, *The British Abroad: The Grand Tour in the Eighteenth Century* (Stroud: Sutton, 2003).

[6]   Roy Porter (ed.), *The Medical History of Waters and Spas*, *Medical History*, Supplement no. 10 (London: Wellcome Institute, 1990); Jill Steward, "The Spa Towns of the Austrian-Hungarian Empire and the Growth of Tourist Culture: 1860–1914," in Peter Borsay, Gunther Hirschfelder, and Ruth Mohrmann (eds), *New Directions in Urban History* (Munster: Waxmann, 2000), pp. 87–126; Douglas Peter Mackaman, *Leisure Settings: Bourgeois Culture, Medicine and the Spa in Modern France* (Chicago: University of Chicago Press, 1998); Annick Cossic and Patrick Galliou (eds), *Spas in Britain and France in the Eighteenth and Nineteenth Centuries* (Newcastle: Cambridge Scholars Press, 2006).

The "coastal resort" category is blurred at the edges, as inland resorts on lakes, rivers, or even reservoirs may share some characteristics with their coastal counterparts, while the attractions of beaches, harbors, and waterfronts are often combined with those of distinctive landscape features such as mountains or forest, of historical or cultural assets, or of mineral springs.[7] The concept is necessarily inclusive and expansive, but it does require that access to, use of and views across a substantial area of water should form a significant, indeed identifying component of the attractions of a city, town, or village whose main livelihood comes from attracting and welcoming tourists.

Many coastal resorts have been overwhelmingly, or even exclusively, dedicated to the satisfaction of regional or national demand flows: indeed, some have grown to considerable size on the basis of almost exclusive relationships with individual cities or restricted hinterlands. Examples would include Morecambe, in north-west England, whose growth from the mid-nineteenth century until World War II depended overwhelmingly on two industrial cities in West Yorkshire; or Atlantic City, whose close relationship with Philadelphia and industrial Pennsylvania and New Jersey was the making of the resort; or Coney Island, above all a bathing place and playground for the lower middle and working classes of Brooklyn and New Jersey.[8] Moreover, until the rise of Florida as an international destination (in which guise the Disney resorts were more important than the beaches) in the late twentieth century, almost all demand for ocean coastal tourism within the United States was domestic and (Florida apart) regional, apart from a regular Canadian presence, especially in the north-east.[9]

We need to remember that not all destination resorts have passed through all the imagined stages of Butler's Tourism Area Life Cycle, from "discovery" to over-development and the need for regeneration or reinvention; and that international "mass tourism," a multi-faceted concept in itself, is only a late stage in the working out of a much longer and more complicated array of histories, an important issue which is often ignored or glossed over in work in tourism

---

[7]   For reservoir tourism see, for example: Allan Williams and Vladimir Balaz, *Tourism in Transition* (London: I.B. Tauris, 2000).

[8]   Roger Bingham, *Lost Resort: The Fall and Rise of Morecambe* (Milnthorpe: Cicerone Press, 1991); Nelson Johnson, *Boardwalk Empire: The Birth, High Times and Corruption of Atlantic City* (Medford: Plexus Publishing, 2002), Chapter 4; Bryant Simon, *Boardwalk of Dreams: Atlantic City and the Fate of Urban America* (New York: Oxford University Press, 2004); Gary Cross and John K. Walton, *The Playful Crowd: Pleasure Places in the Twentieth Century* (New York: Columbia University Press, 2005).

[9]   Cindy S. Aron, *Working at Play* (New York: Oxford University Press, 1999).

studies or cultural studies.[10] Moreover, some international beach resorts, such as Biarritz (and even more so St Jean-de-Luz or Antibes), made a virtue out of remaining relatively small and exclusive, avoiding the pressures associated with over-development.[11]

Such destinations took their place among the most important and influential of those coastal resorts which developed into meeting places for international high society and its hangers-on: royalty (whether ruling or in exile), aristocrats, financiers, industrialists, property developers, company promoters, arms dealers, professional gamblers, prostitutes, and confidence tricksters. As such they became centers for the diffusion of new fashions and ideas within their own countries, and between the different parts of the world that came into contact with each other in what became, from at least the late nineteenth century, melting pots whose catchment areas (especially in Europe) were often intercontinental as well as transcontinental, as a cursory survey of the lists of visitors to Ostend, Biarritz, or San Sebastián confirms. Visitors from the United States and Latin America were conspicuous, alongside Russian aristocrats and international arms dealers of cosmopolitan extraction, in the casinos and grand hotels of these resorts. A similar intercontinental reach would apply to (for example) the Lido at Venice (with a strong representation from Germany and Central Europe), and to Nice, Cannes, and Monte Carlo (a coastal resort, but only in the sense that it was on the coast: it had no beach worth speaking of) from the 1870s to the 1930s.[12] In this respect such resorts were at least as important as capital cities, spa towns, or centers of cultural tourism in bringing together royalty, aristocrats, plutocrats, and adjacent circles of aspiring affluence.

In 1930 the English travel writer and gossip columnist Charles Graves, brother of the poet Robert, provided an insider's account of the kind of

---

[10]   Richard W. Butler (ed.), *The Tourism Area Life Cycle* (2 vols, Clevedon: Channel View, 2006).

[11]   Michel Chadefaud, *Aux origines du tourisme dans les pays de l'Adour* (Pau: Université de Pau, 1987).

[12]   John K. Walton, "'The Queen of the Beaches': Ostend and the British, from the 1890s to the 1930s," *History Today* 51/8 (August 2001): pp. 19–25; John K. Walton, "Tourism and Politics in Elite Beach Resorts: San Sebastián and Ostend, 1830–1939," in Laurent Tissot (ed.), *Construction of a Tourism Industry in the 19th and 20th Century: International Perspectives* (Neuchatel: Alphil, 2003), pp. 287–301; Chadefaud, *Aux origines*; Jenny Smith and John K. Walton, "The First Century of Beach Tourism in Spain: San Sebastián and the 'Playas del Norte' from the 1830s to the 1930s," in John Towner, Mike Barke, and Michael T. Newton (eds), *Tourism in Spain: Critical Issues* (Wallingford: CAB Publications, 1996), pp. 35–61; Helen Meller, *European Cities 1890–1930s* (Chichester: John Wiley, 2001), Chapter 5; John Pemble, *Venice Rediscovered* (Oxford: Clarendon Press, 1995); Mary Blume, *Côte d'Azur: Inventing the French Riviera* (London: Thames and Hudson, 1994).

cosmopolitan international high society that frequented such places at that time, and sustained their casino and grand hotel economies. He suggested that, "The various casino towns subsist on the comings and goings and gamblings and flirtings of ... not more than 30,000 people." He offered his perspective on the most influential nationalities in European elite resorts of all kinds:

> Even to-day, with the exception of Switzerland, there are infinitely fewer Englishmen at the regular continental resorts than you would imagine. The people you meet are the Armenians like Michael Arlen, the Greeks like M. Zographos and M. Vlasto, the Argentines like M. Uriburu, the Spaniards like the Duchess of Peneranda (*sic*: Peñaranda) or the Duchess of Alba, the Americans like Mr Laddy Sanford and Mr A.K. Macomber ... and the French like Baron de Jumilhac, and the Belgians like M. Pierre Wertheimer. They, indeed, are the only people who can consistently afford the prices of the villas and yachts and hotels and casinos.

It is noteworthy that these "known names" and their associations were part of the expected cultural capital of Graves' intended readership, offering the essential attraction of fashion in the resorts concerned, to go with gambling, golf and bathing (often at private beaches or rock pools), whose importance is particularly signalled at Juan-les-Pins, Antibes and Brioni, the exclusive resort on the pre-war "Austrian Riviera" which was then in Italy and subsequently in Yugoslavia and then Croatia, a reminder of shifting definitions of national boundaries and therefore of the "international" in this and other parts of the world.

Graves also provides a perspective on change over time, pointing out the post-war decline of the Russian Grand Dukes ("all penniless except the Grand Duke Dmitri, who married an American"), the "poverty-stricken" Austrian and Hungarian aristocracy who had formerly been the mainstay of Brioni, and the disappearance of the Germans and Italians, though the former were apparently returning. "Their places at the high table have been taken by the Americans, the Greeks, the Argentines, and a few Egyptians." He takes us round the table with the highest minimum stake at the Deauville casino, in a resort in Normandy which was famous for its horse-racing, and whose visiting public was dominated by wealthy Parisians but enjoyed a top-dressing of international high society, which Graves proceeds to anatomize: an oil millionaire from Chicago, a "department store king" from the same city, a French stockbroker, a Wall Street broker, the Aga Khan, a wealthy and sophisticated Frenchwoman, an Egyptian banker "rich beyond the dreams of Mr Churchill," the "dark and hook-nosed" nephew of an English tobacco millionaire, and the young mistress of a French silk manufacturer. Graves offers us a great deal more in this vein, salted with allusions to Jewish and Middle Eastern ancestry, and bringing out the declining British presence in this "big league" of international politicians, industrialists, financiers, and people of mystery. Testing these playful impressions more systematically, and analysing change over time in the distribution of elite resorts and the nature of their patrons, would form the basis for a fascinating research project, not least because of the external importance of the transactions that might be originated and developed in these distinctive and alluring environments.[13]

Where, as at San Sebastián, Ostend, or Abbazia/Opatija, elite beach resorts of this kind were also summer capitals, they would act more overtly as centers for political intrigue, cabals, and official and unofficial diplomacy, as in the case of Bismarck's visits to Biarritz or the *tertulias* or conversational gatherings of the leaders of political factions on La Concha beach at San Sebastián, within sight of the royal summer palace.[14] As indicated above, the role of seaside grand hotels and casinos as focal points of international dynastic, diplomatic, and economic activity also merits examination, as well as the ways in which such projects themselves attracted international finance.[15] The role of coastal locations, if not always conventional beach resorts, in the development of international artists' colonies and cosmopolitan gatherings of literary expatriates is also a significant theme.[16] Beyond this, the development of international middle- and working-class tourist flows, starting from at least the 1920s and gathering momentum rapidly in Europe after World War II, was also particularly in evidence at the seaside, as was the phenomenon of "backpacker tourism" in search of new destinations and experiences, which helped to extend the "pleasure periphery" from the 1960s onwards and was again disproportionately, though certainly not exclusively, attracted to the beaches. How far the resulting interactions promoted international amity and understanding, and how far they perpetuated and helped to construct stereotypes and even enmities, constitutes an important set of questions.[17] This chapter surveys these issues on a global stage, although it will pay particular attention to those seaside destinations in western Europe that

---

[13]   Charles Graves, *And the Greeks* (London: Bles, 1930), pp. 20–22, 44–8, 56.

[14]   Walton, "Tourism and Politics in Elite Beach Resorts"; Sandra Covak and Irena Ateljevik, "Colonization and 'Taking the Waters' in the Nineteenth Century," in Philip Long and Nicola J. Palmer (eds), *Royal Tourism* (Bristol: Channel View, 2008), pp. 128–41.

[15]   John K. Walton, "Grand Hotels and Great Events: History, Heritage and Hospitality," in Nadja Maillard (ed.), *Beau-Rivage Palace: 150 Years of History* (Lausanne: Payot, 2008), pp. 102–12.

[16]   Nina Lübbren, "North to South: Paradigm Shifts in European Art and Tourism, 1880–1920," in David Crouch and Nina Lübbren (eds), *Visual Culture and Tourism* (Oxford: Berg, 2003), pp. 125–46.

[17]   Turner and Ash, *Golden Hordes*; Waleed Hazbun, *Beaches, Ruins, Resorts: The Politics of Tourism in the Arab World* (Minneapolis: Minnesota University Press, 2008); Kevin Hannam and Irena Ateljevik (eds), *Backpacker Tourism* (Clevedon: Channel View, 2007).

pioneered these phenomena and displayed them to the fullest advantage during the nineteenth and twentieth centuries.

The first international beach resorts were those that brought British (especially), German (increasingly), French, Austrian, and Russian visitors to European locations outside their own countries during the nineteenth century, as the aesthetic and health-promoting attractions of the coast became more firmly established in the wake of the dramatic positive reassessment of coastal (as well as mountain) environments that took place across much of western Europe during the second half of the eighteenth century.[18] The arrival of comfortably-off British sea-bathers on the coast of northern France in the late eighteenth century, and especially after the end in 1814–15 of the continental wars which had interrupted this process, brought the British and French landed and upper middle classes (especially those of Paris and London) into regular contact in a different setting from fashionable Paris, the Grand Tour, or the European spas.[19] The British summer presence, increasingly augmented by expatriate residents in search of cheap prices, escape from creditors or the law, or the opportunity to run illicit bookmaking businesses, spread southwards to Normandy and Brittany, and further south to Biarritz, during the course of the nineteenth century, while British aristocratic and moneyed demand played a key part in initiating and sustaining the rise of the French Riviera, although here climate and the relief of tuberculosis were more important than sea-bathing until the 1920s.[20] Meanwhile the seaboards of several countries in north-west Europe were attracting sea-bathers from their own nationals, without developing significant international dimensions to their trade.[21]

Simona Pakenham provides a useful and entertaining account of the British community in nineteenth-century Dieppe, with implications for other places. Here, the British and French regarded each other with a mixture of curiosity and acceptance, and the otherness of the bathing customs and the sociability of the beach casino were additional dimensions of the differences in dress, architecture, religion, festivals, language, food, public health, and customs that the cross-channel voyager encountered. Painters, beginning with Robert Haydon and David Wilkie at the end of the Napoleonic Wars, were attracted by

---

[18] Corbin, *The Lure of the Sea*; Walton, "Seaside Resorts of Western Europe"; John K. Walton, "Seaside Resort Regions and their Hinterlands in Western Europe and the Americas, from the Late Eighteenth Century to the Second World War," *Storia del Turismo* 4 (2003): pp. 69–87.

[19] Walton, "Seaside Resorts of Western Europe."

[20] Gabriel Désert, *La vie quotidienne sur les plages normandes du Second Empire aux années folles* (Paris: Hachette, 1983); Chadefaud, *Aux origines*; Blume, *Côte d'Azur*.

[21] Walton, "Seaside Resort Regions and their Hinterlands."

the quality of the light and the novelty of the ambience, and a resident English community grew up alongside the French, mixing tentatively with Parisian summer visitors and enjoying the regular proximity of Bourbon and Napoleonic royalty until the advent of the Third Republic in 1870. Many of these features of the Channel coast resorts were repeated further south, and a hybrid seaside fantasy architecture of exotic villas and terraces developed, which is beginning to attract sustained research.[22]

Like Dieppe, many coastal resorts did not have international visiting publics in the fullest cosmopolitan sense, but brought together home demand with a strong presence from a single other country. Coastlines, and individual resorts, where one neighbouring country dominated the visiting public alongside the "locals," have been vulnerable to the development of tensions and exploitation wherever the "visiting" nation is more powerful or culturally assertive than the hosts, especially in the social melting pot of beach or promenade. This has applied most obviously to the centrally important role played by United States demand in the development of beach resorts in Mexico and parts of the Caribbean, especially in Puerto Rico, and in Cuba before the Castro revolution took hold.[23] As already mentioned, the United States, on the other hand, was conspicuously lacking in international beach resorts until Florida became important in that guise in the late twentieth century, although Miami was already attracting Cuban and other Latin American tourists at mid-century.[24] Elsewhere the only discernable international presence was Canadian, although twentieth-century Coney Island catered for the full, shifting spectrum of New York's ethnic groups, who arranged themselves by beach and bath-house in ways that minimized potential conflict.[25] Another very clear example of international development based mainly on two neighbouring countries was the Uruguayan side of the River Plate estuary from the late nineteenth century,

---

[22]   Simona Pakenham, *60 Miles from England: The English at Dieppe, 1814–1914* (London: Macmillan, 1967); Yves Perret-Gentil, Alain Lottin, and Jean-Pierre Poussu (eds), *Les villes balnéaires d'Europe occidentale du XVIIIe siècle a nos jours* (Paris: Presses de l'Université Paris-Sorbonne, 2008).

[23]   Dina Berger, *The Development of Mexico's Tourism Industry: Pyramids by Day, Martinis by Night* (London: Palgrave Macmillan, 2006); Michael Clancy, *Exporting Paradise: Tourism and Development in Mexico* (London: Pergamon, 2002); Dennis Merrill, "Negotiating Cold War Paradise: United States Tourism, Economic Planning and Cultural Modernity in Twentieth-Century Puerto Rico," *Diplomatic History* 25 (2001): pp. 179–21; Rosalie Schwartz, *Pleasure Island* (Lincoln: University of Nebraska Press, 1997).

[24]   Dennis Merrill, *Negotiating Paradise* (Raleigh: University of North Carolina Press, 2009), p. 121.

[25]   Joseph Heller, *Now and Then: From Coney Island to Here* (London: Simon and Schuster, 1998).

which attracted large numbers of tourists from the prospering and increasingly populous economy of Argentina, especially Buenos Aires, although the beaches of Montevideo and its neighbors also drew to a much lesser extent on other neighbouring Latin American states.[26] The British presence at the Irish seaside was also significant as the only external market, not only during the nineteenth century while Ireland was constitutionally part of the United Kingdom, but also, after the dust of partition and civil war had settled, in the Republic. The importance of British tourists to the seaside economy of Bray, County Wicklow, is a case in point: it was reinforced in the aftermath of World War II when the British enjoyed escaping from the domestic regime of food rationing.[27] Elsewhere in Europe we might also consider the German presence at twentieth-century Rimini, the Finns mixing with the Russians at their resort of Terjoki in the inter-war years, or the various and shifting mixes of Germans or Russians and local people in the coastal resorts of the Baltic states during the twentieth century.[28]

Over and above such specific international exchanges between neighbouring states, some resorts (like the European elite mineral spas before them) were already developing in the nineteenth century into the centers of international high society that were introduced above. This process originated on the coasts of Atlantic and Mediterranean Europe, beginning with the French Riviera, extending in the late nineteenth century to Deauville and Trouville, Biarritz (whose strong Spanish presence was part of a much wider international public, from the British and Russian aristocracies to Latin America),[29] San Sebastián (with its popular French presence at the August bullfights from the 1870s onwards), Ostend, and the Venice Lido. The latter two resorts became more "open" and popular from the early twentieth century, as the "salariat" descended on the Lido alongside increasingly scantily-clad Austrians and Hungarians.[30] Meanwhile new elite haunts rose, fell and sometimes rose again, at the whim of

---

[26]   Elisa Pastoriza (ed.), *Las puertas al mar: Consumo, ocio y política en Mar del Plata, Montevideo y Viña del Mar* (Buenos Aires: Biblos, 2002).

[27]   Mary Davies, *That Favourite Resort: The Story of Bray, Co. Wicklow* (Bray: Wordwell, 2007).

[28]   Patrizia Battilani and Maurizio Mussoni, "Il turismo a Rimini," in Lionello F. Punzo and Stefano Usai (eds), *L'estate al mare* (Milan: McGraw-Hill, 2007), pp. 97–110; Auvo Kostiainen, "A Northern 'Riviera': Tourism in Terjoki in the 1920s and 1930s," *Scandinavian Journal of Hospitality and Tourism* 7 (2007): pp. 328–46; Barry Worthington, "Change in an Estonian Resort: Contrasting Development Contexts," *Annals of Tourism Research* 30 (2003): pp. 369–85.

[29]   Michel Pinçon and Monique Pinçon-Chartet, *Grand Fortunes: Dynasties of Wealth in France* (New York: Algora, 1997), pp. 202–3.

[30]   Smith and Walton, "First Century"; Pemble, *Venice Rediscovered*, p. 16.

speculation and fashion as it interacted with the interventions of individuals, businesses, and local government in the "tourism area life cycle," from "Paris Plage" at Le Touquet through to Sitges, Marbella, and then, especially as the "pleasure periphery" became more elastic in the wake of long-haul air travel, to exclusive Mediterranean or Caribbean islands, sometimes owned by individuals who could filter out undesirables by making access dependent on invitation.[31]

The idea of the French Riviera as the archetypal international coastal playground, which gathered momentum as its summer beaches became more fashionable than its winter climate in the inter-war years (although it is high time that the myth that Coco Chanel invented the sun-tan as fashion accessory was laid to rest: its origins were much earlier and its history more complex than a focus on the Riviera and the late 1920s might lead one to believe), led to the diffusion of the label as an international ideal.[32] From the end of the nineteenth century the French and adjoining Italian Rivieras were joined by a sequence of more or less convincing global aspirants to a brand identity that instantly conjured up international high fashion, sophisticated beaches and beachwear, night life, luxury villas, yachts, and exciting maritime scenery. So, as the twentieth century progressed, the idea of the Riviera was claimed and promoted on coastlines in northern and eastern Europe (Finland, the Baltic, Bulgaria, the Crimea), and later South Africa, Mexico (the "Mayan Riviera"), the Red Sea, Australia's "Gold Coast," Pondicherry in India, and Turkey, as well as the Cornish variant created by the publicity machine of the Great Western Railway for domestic consumption in England. This widespread desire to appropriate the aura of the term was often accompanied by progress down-market towards versions of international "mass tourism," not least in the original French setting from the 1950s; and changing ideas about and uses of the label "Riviera" would merit further examination.[33]

The international seaside might also have its unconventional aspect, over and above the eccentricities that were tolerated and even celebrated among the aristocracies of title and wealth. Certain coastal locations attracted international communities of artists and writers, for whom the liminal status of beach and shoreline, together with the transient and exotic aspects of seaport as well as seasonal resort life and the customs and superstitions of fishing and other seafaring communities, all provided (or were thought to provide) creative stimulation for individuals, which was reinforced by the arrival and company

---

[31]   Lencek and Bosker, *The Beach*; Mimi Sheller, *Consuming the Caribbean: From Arwaks to Zombies* (London: Routledge, 2003).

[32]   Simon Carter, *Rise and Shine: Sunlight, Technology and Health* (Oxford: Berg, 2007).

[33]   Roger Burdett Wilson, *Go Great Western: A History of G.W.R. Publicity* (Newton Abbot: David and Charles, 1970).

of like-minded others. Islands, first in the Mediterranean, then in the tropics, conjured up notions of the "island paradise" which were also particularly attractive to international communities of artists, writers, dreamers, and lotus-eaters in this context. The attractions of coastal locations for artists had their origins in the very reappraisals of seaside landscape and society that made the seaside attractive to tourists as well as invalids during the eighteenth century: they were part and parcel of the new trends, marched in step with them, and carved out their own niches within the proliferating variety of seaside destinations and refuges. Some artistic colonies were national or even regional in membership, like the predominantly northern English Staithes Group in North Yorkshire, or the groups in Cornwall at St Ives and Newlyn, part of a much wider pattern of artists' colonies that coalesced and sometimes took lasting root in picturesque fishing settlements on rugged and "unspoilt" parts of the coastlines of late Victorian England.[34] But others, especially in Mediterranean locations, were international in scope: the "Mediterranean passion" that drew northern Europeans to warm climates, ancient civilizations and the enticements of relaxed and exotic sexual mores was already displaying a coastal dimension by the later nineteenth century, especially in Italy.[35] Tangier in the twentieth century became a particular haunt of Bohemian visitors and expatriates, drawn to its liminal status as a gateway between land and sea, continents and cultures, and forbidden experiences with sex and drugs. It became a haven for British, American, French, and Spanish expatriates: Paul Bowles, William Burroughs, the Beats, Jean Genet, Juan Goytisolo, disporting themselves on the beaches as well as enjoying the Arab city. Hammamet in Tunisia attracted a less challenging international intellectual coterie in the inter-war years, long before it became a conventional package tour destination in the 1970s.[36] Then there was the Mediterranean "island paradise" of Mallorca, which was already attracting its artistic and hedonistic coteries of international visitors and expatriates (English, American, Swedish, German, and many others) in the 1920s and 1930s. The ebb and flow of the bohemian gatherings around Robert Graves at the north-western

---

[34]   Bernard Deacon, "Imagining the Fishing: Artists and Fishermen in Late-Nineteenth Century Cornwall," *Rural History* 12 (2001): pp. 159–78; Peter Phillips, *The Staithes Group* (Nottingham: Phillips and Sons, 1993).

[35]   Lübbren, "North to South"; John Pemble, *The Mediterranean Passion: Victorians and Edwardians in the South* (Oxford: Clarendon Press, 1987).

[36]   Michelle Green, *The Dream at the End of the World: Paul Bowles and the Literary Renegades in Tangier* (New York: Harper-Collins, 2002); Brian T. Edwards, *Morocco Bound: Disorienting America's Maghreb* (Durham: Duke University Press, 2005); Ridha Boukraa, *Hammamet: Le paradis perdu* (Aix-en-Provence: CHET, 1993); Waleed Hazbun, *Beaches, Ruins, Resorts*, Chapter 2.

coastal village of Deià constituted the most visible and well-documented of the many coastal communities of writers, artists, and hangers-on to emerge at this time, while the hundreds of visitors and residents in the Palma seaside suburb of Terreno had fewer pretensions and remained closer to a notional mainstream, although still displaying aspirations to their own less demanding versions of the earthly seaside paradise.[37]

But, of course, a further new dimension was added to the idea of the international coastal resort by the democratization and spread of international beach holidays to lower-middle- and working-class markets, especially after World War II.[38] We can trace the beginnings of this in Europe to the 1930s and even the 1920s, especially among Britons, as the distinctive accents of the skilled working classes of the northern industrial counties of Lancashire and Yorkshire's West Riding began to be heard in accessible North Sea resorts on the European mainland, especially Ostend.[39] As is familiar, the major developments in this regard came after World War II, through (mainly) middle-class package tours by coach in the 1950s supplemented by, and steadily giving ground to, air charter tourism from the 1960s; but the big breakthrough in working-class family tourism from northern Europe to the Mediterranean was a product of the later 1970s onwards, building on earlier more up-market growth.[40] A great deal of historical research remains to be conducted on the phenomena associated with the rise, consolidation, and (in some cases, such as Benidorm and Magalluf) regeneration within a generation of the international package tour destination resort, first for northern Europeans in Spain and Italy, then eastwards and southwards across the Mediterranean to Greece, Tunisia, and Turkey, while long-haul destinations in Florida, the Caribbean, the islands of the south Pacific, the Indian Ocean, and south-east Asia came into the frame, and beach resorts in Thailand (to take only the most prominent example)

---

[37]   Jacqueline Waldren, *Insiders and Outsiders: Paradise and Reality in Mallorca* (Oxford: Berghahn, 1996); John K. Walton, "Paradise Lost and Found: Tourists and Expatriates in El Terreno, Palma de Mallorca, from the 1920s to the 1950s," in John K. Walton (ed.), *Histories of Tourism* (Clevedon: Channel View, 2005), pp. 179–94.

[38]   Christopher M. Kopper, "The Breakthrough of the Package Tour in Germany after 1945," *Journal of Tourism History* 1 (2009): pp. 67–92; Julian Demetriadi, "The Golden Years: English Seaside Resorts 1950–1974," in Gareth Shaw and Allan Williams (eds), *The Rise and Fall of British Coastal Resorts* (London: Mansell, 1997), pp. 52–5; Susan Barton, *Working-Class Organisations and Popular Tourism 1840–1970* (Manchester: Manchester University Press, 2005), pp. 199–204; Roger Bray and Vladimir Raitz, *Flight to the Sun* (London: Continuum, 2001).

[39]   Walton, "'Queen of the Beaches.'"

[40]   Demetriadi, "The Golden Years"; Barton, *Working-Class Organisations*; Kopper, "The Breakthrough of the Package Tour in Germany after 1945."

became zones of intercontinental tourist encounter for Europeans, Americans, Australians, and Japanese. Historians must avoid the conjoined dangers of regarding all resorts constructed for these markets as generically the same and over-generalizing about them, of distorting our view of power relationships by focusing on international tour operators and development corporations as if they were the only actors worthy of consideration (to the detriment of national and local governments and of indigenous individuals and businesses in the resorts themselves), and of denying agency and the power of choice among so-called "mass tourists" who might actually display considerable pertinacity and ingenuity in constructing the holiday experience they wanted.[41] Benidorm, for example, is often regarded (especially through the narrowing and distorting lens of the popular British media) as the archetypal package tour resort, all concrete and lager louts; but it is actually a compact planned town with a distinctive history, taking its international visitor trade mostly from England, with an admixture of Dutch and Scandinavians, hardly any Germans, and staple domestic tourism flows from Madrid and the Basque Country, the last of these being highly visible to those who can read the signs in the names and lettering of bars, shops, and street advertising.[42] Even if we confine ourselves to Spain, the case of Benidorm is very different from those of (for example) Torremolinos, Marbella, Lloret de Mar, Tossa de Mar, Sitges, and the various "mass tourism" resorts of the Balearic and Canary Islands. Each has its own distinctive trajectory, each caters for a different international mix in different ways, each has its own internal sub-divisions in terms of age, gender, cultural and sexual preference, and predominant nationalities; and local cultures (and languages, at least since the transition to democracy which began in the later 1970s) interact with globalizing tendencies and with the national characteristics of the varying and changing mix of visiting publics in complex and unpredictable ways. There is a very attractive research agenda here, on the way to constructing nuanced, workable, defensible generalizations about the rise of international package tourism that make sense of the issues while respecting complexity and change. A further dimension to this should be the representation of international tourism and the creation of tourism stereotypes in host country media. And of course there are alternative models, especially those involving the development of international beach tourism in the socialist

---

[41]   Sue Wright, "Sun, Sea, Sand and Self-expression," in Hartmut Berghoff, Barbara Korte, Ralf Schneider, and Christopher Harvie (eds), *The Making of Modern Tourism* (Basingstoke: Palgrave, 2002), pp. 181–202; Harry Ritchie, *Here We Go: A Summer on the Costa del Sol* (London: Hamish Hamilton, 1993).

[42]   Charles Wilson, *Benidorm: The Truth* (Valencia: Comunitat de Valencia, 1999); personal observations on site visit to Benidorm, March 2009.

states of eastern Europe and the changes that took place after the fall of the Berlin Wall and dismantling of the Iron Curtain.[43] The case of Yugoslavia and its successor states is particularly interesting here, as the relationships between state direction and private enterprise were negotiated through the emergence of a distinctive political and economic regime, an intermediate experience between the capitalist and socialist worlds. Conflicts of values and expectations in how to deal with growing international markets from the 1960s onwards, and in the balance of provision for Yugoslav and international tourists on contrasting assumptions about resources and preferences, generated revealing source material for historical engagement, as did the impact of the break-up of Yugoslavia and the concurrent dismantling of the socialist economic system.[44]

Where international tourism flows crossed cultural boundaries, problems of morality and regulation might come to the fore. This was especially the case on the liminal territory of the beach, where the conventions of everyday life might be set aside and replaced by more liberating expectations about (un)dress, informality, relaxation, and the limits of acceptable behaviour, although norms were hardly ever abandoned in any carnivalesque, "anything goes" sense: rather, they were eased consensually but to varying degrees, which could give rise to tensions about what was and was not acceptable. Questions of appropriate dress and deportment on the beach were particularly threatening to international holiday harmony, as examples from Spain and Germany illustrate.

When Franco's Spain began to pursue the development of international beach tourism on its Mediterranean and island coastlines, with gathering momentum from the arrival in power of a new generation of outward-looking technocrats in 1960, it soon encountered tensions between welcoming tourists, regulating them, and protecting local susceptibilities. These issues had their roots in the 1920s and early 1930s, as conflicts over what constituted appropriate and "moral" beachwear and behaviour erupted between religious puritans within the Roman Catholic Church, and more relaxed attitudes influenced by exposure to French and Latin American resorts. These were also, more immediately, conflicts over "fashion" versus "decency" between mothers and daughters, as the local press in San Sebastián made clear. By the 1960s all these issues were emerging more forcefully: visitors from France and northern Europe encountered

---

[43]   Diane P. Koenker and Anne E. Gorsuch (eds), *Turizm: The Russian and Eastern European Tourist under Capitalism and Socialism* (Ithaca: Cornell University Press, 2006); Kristen Ghodsee, *The Red Riviera: Gender, Tourism, and Postsocialism on the Black Sea* (Durham: Duke University Press, 2005), Chapters 1–2.

[44]   Karin Taylor, "Fishing for Tourists: Tourism and Household Enterprise in Biograd na Moru," in Hannes Grandits and Karin Taylor (eds), *Yugoslavia's Sunny Side: A History of Tourism in Socialism* (Budapest: Central European University Press, 2010).

entrenched opposition to bodily exposure, even on the beach, as the dominant Catholic ideology was enforced by Civil Guards and municipal police. Cartoons in the British popular press alluded to the problem, treating it with humor while recognizing the potential for humiliation and financial loss, and the gradual acceptance of the bikini was a saga of the 1960s in Benidorm and elsewhere. Ultimately the general relaxation of restrictions on behaviour that was necessary to sustain the flow of hard foreign currency must have played its part in the demise of the regime after Franco's death: tourism was economically necessary, but politically and socially damaging to an authoritarian and puritanical polity.[45]

A related issue was the export of German cultures of nudity on the beach to other parts of Europe, and reactions to them by visitors from elsewhere in Europe to (especially) the Baltic coast. The arrest of two German visitors to Ostend for walking nonchalantly along the beach in an unclad state provided a graphic illustration of the potential problems, which may have been exacerbated in this case by anti-German feeling in the Belgian resort, which made German visitors, who had been important to the local economy before World War I, unwelcome and few in number in the immediate post-war years. Beach nudity seems to have been more a Baltic than a pan-German phenomenon: at any rate, the return of West German visitors to beach resorts like Warnemuende after German reunification brought conflict between locals who defended their preference for nudity, and visitors from the West who made scandalized complaints and secured changes in laws and practices.[46] Muslim reactions to far less extreme beach behaviour generated conflict at (for example) Hammamet, where a secular

---

[45]   Sasha D. Pack, *Tourism and Dictatorship: Europe's Peaceful Invasion of Franco's Spain* (Basingstoke: Palgrave Macmillan, 2006); John K. Walton, "Consuming the Beach: Seaside Resorts and Cultures of Tourism in England and Spain from the 1840s to the 1930s," in Ellen Furlough and Shelley Baranowski (eds), *Being Elsewhere: Tourism, Consumer Culture and Identity in Modern Europe and North America* (Ann Arbor: University of Michigan Press, 2001), pp. 272–98; Fátima Gil Gascón, "Construyendo a la mujer ideal: mujer y censura cinematográfica durante el franquismo (1939–1963)," (Ph.D. diss., Universidad Complutense de Madrid, 2009), pp. 458–60.

[46]   Wiebke Kolbe, "Strandurlaub als Liminoides: Deutsche Seebadr im Spaten 19. und Frulen 20. Jahrhundert," in Hans-Jörg Gilomen, Beatrice Schumacher, and Laurent Tissot (eds), *Temps libre et loisirs, du 14e au 20e siècles* (Zurich: Chronos Verlag, 2005), Chapter 15; "I Grew Up Being Naked at the Beach," *Financial Express*, August 9, 2004; Walton, "Queen of the Beaches." It is interesting that Chad Ross, *Naked Germany: Health, Race and the Nation* (Oxford: Berg, 2005) has hardly anything to say about nudity on the German Baltic or North Sea coast: his focus is on policy, ideology and organizations, and perhaps the beach, especially between the late nineteenth century and World War II, was such uncontested or "natural" territory for nudity that it does not feature in his sources.

state bent on promoting tourism for economic reasons encountered religious and cultural opposition to the logic of the implementation of its policies, while the tense relationships between beach and other kinds of international tourism, Islam, and the state in Bali generated terrorist attacks on tourist targets, with particularly heavy casualties among visiting Australians.[47]

Less challenging, but difficult, was the kind of cultural encounter that led tourists to realize that, in the particularly demanding setting of the bathing beach, their otherness made them a target for the attention and curiosity of holidaymakers from other nations. Hazel Thurston, an Englishwoman who in the late 1950s took part in what she described as the first Mediterranean cruise to visit the Bulgarian Black Sea coast, conveyed the nature of this problem and her reactions to it very effectively:

> This place is called the Sunny Beach, but being so very new it may develop a less extempore name later on. The sands were extensive and the sea warm—not only because it was congested with superfatted bodies ... after we had coped with heterosexual bathing cabins ... it began to sink in that this was an International Resort within the limitations of the Iron Curtain, and that our fellow-wallowers in the sea were East Germans, Poles, Roumanians [sic], and everything except Bulgarians. What also sank in—even when we were in the sea—was that *we* were the exhibits. This came as a salutary shock to our arrogant national habit of what may be called vivispection ... (While bathing) people converged on us for conversation, in known and unknown languages and no language at all ... When we waded back to the beach there were small happenings of interest, like the excitement aroused by our nylon underclothes. In default of language, holidaymakers lifted up our skirts to feel and admire the beauties of our drip-dry petticoats and knickers ...

This reversal or redirection of the tourist gaze was always a potential hazard of the popular international resort, but in these circumstances and these forms it was particularly piquant and disturbing, challenging assumptions of superiority and reversing the right to direct an inspecting, orientalizing scrutiny at others, while invading physical privacy and turning the beach into a challenging arena of direct encounter and interaction rather than merely a crucible of intersecting, appraising, and evaluative gazes and glances.[48]

Under certain circumstances the rise of popular international tourism from the 1960s onwards, perhaps especially in those Mediterranean beach resorts that attracted air charter tourism and became the "playgrounds" of wide areas of

---

[47] Boukraa, *Paradis perdu*; Michael Hitchcock and Nyoman Darma Putra, *Tourism, Development and Terrorism in Bali* (Aldershot: Ashgate, 2007).

[48] Hazel Thurston, *From Darkest Mum* (London: Shenval Press, 1960), pp. 56–7.

northern Europe, could give rise more directly to the creation and reinforcement of negative national stereotypes, both in jest and in earnest. In the paradigmatic case of interaction between British and German tourists, this has given rise to a small academic industry, using cartoons and reports from the tabloid press to chart conflict over access to desirable space on beaches and at hotel swimming pools. The central focus in the British sources has been the use by German tourists of beach towels as markers to lay claim to the occupation of preferred sites, often from an early hour of the morning. This became an issue in popular newspaper wars in the spring of 1987, with *Bild* and the *Sun* acting as the most prominent protagonists, and acted as a symbol of enduring stereotypes associated with ideas about German arrogance and expansionist tendencies. The beach towel became a metaphor for German competitiveness and aggrandizement, and its use extended into representations of business, politics, and even the first invasion of Iraq. Insistence on the underlying jocularity of such engagement with stereotypes should not be allowed to disguise the negative aspects of these encounters and representations for international relations at a grassroots level.[49]

Since the 1960s backpackers have provided a further dimension to the development of international markets for seaside tourism, first within Europe, then across the globe. As with other forms of popular tourism, the diversity of experience covered by the general label has over-simplified academic perceptions and presentations of the phenomenon. Academics have tended, at least until very recently, to treat this as an undifferentiated variant on "mass tourism," and to miss out on the contrasting experiences of different nationalities and subcultures within it, as with the similarly over-generalized representations of post-1960s air charter "mass tourism" to international resorts.[50] Recent work on Bondi Beach shows an international backpacker "community" defined in relation to conflicts between locals over economic interests and amenity; but work on the internal dynamics of such shifting "communities," especially where they may be mapped on to national identities, might well prove fruitful.[51] There

---

[49]   Cedric Cullingford and Harald Husemann, *Anglo-German Attitudes* (Aldershot: Ashgate, 1995); Harald Husemann, "We Will Fight Them on the Beaches," in Rainer Enig (ed.), *Stereotypes in Contemporary Anglo-German Relations* (Basingstoke: Macmillan, 2000), pp. 58–78; Lachlan R. Moyle, "Drawing Conclusions: An Imagological Survey of Britain and the British and Germany and the Germans in German and British Cartoons and Caricature, 1945–2000" (Ph.D. diss., University of Osnabruck, 2004), pp. 146–8.

[50]   Darya Maoz, "Backpackers' Motivation: The Role of Culture and Nationality," *Annals of Tourism Research* 34 (2007): pp. 122–40, for the Israeli case.

[51]   Julie Wilson, Greg Richards, and Ian MacDonnell, "Intracommunity Tensions in Backpacker Enclaves: Sydney's Bondi Beach," in Hannam and Ateljevic (eds), *Backpacker Tourism*, pp. 199–214.

is also the South Asian dimension to backpacking, also involving travellers or tourists from all over the globe, and helping to extend the "pleasure periphery" at a grassroots level through the "discovery" of places like the island of Koh Samui in the Gulf of Thailand, which has since developed through a mixture of local, national, and international capitalist initiative, and in ways that threaten its own sustainability. Here are some interesting apparent paradoxes to work through.[52] What about the role of backpacker tourism since the 1960s in the development of Goa, which was already a rich international or intercultural society in heritage terms?[53]

Backpackers and "gap year" tourists have been particularly likely to bridge the gap between enjoying beach tourism as consumers and contributing to it as workers; and there is no space here to develop the important further theme of the role of the international workforce in tourism. Nor is there space to explore the vexed, and related, issues surrounding international sex tourism. On the consumer side, however, this chapter provides signposts and road maps for an extensive array of research projects which may help us to tease out, using the depth of field provided by rich contextualized historical analysis, the roles of international beach tourism in developing intercultural contact and conflict at a variety of social levels and in a variety of locations. What we need now is more case studies.

---

[52]   Chris Podwysocki and Gail Johnson, *Koh Samui, Gulf of Thailand: Paradise Found* (Brentford: Lascelles, 1992).

[53]   Arun Saldanha, "Identity, Spatiality and Post-colonial Resistance: Geographies of the Tourism Critique in Goa," *Current Issues in Tourism* 5 (2002): pp. 94–111.

Chapter 3

The "Naked City" of Cap d'Agde: European Nudism and Tourism in Postwar France

Stephen L. Harp

In his 1998 bestseller, novelist Michel Houellebecq recounts the trip characters Bruno and Christiane made to Cap d'Agde, the Mediterranean nudist resort dubbed the "naked city" by Anglophones and other Europeans. With a realistic description reminiscent of nineteenth-century French novelists, Houellebecq portrays Cap d'Agde as a milieu combining "traditional *naturisme*"[1] and a sexualized nudity of swingers' nightclubs. On their second day at the beach, Bruno and Christiane meet Rudi and Hannalore, a middle-class German couple who have been coming to Cap d'Agde for 10 years. Rudi is a satellite technician while Hannalore works in a bookstore in Hamburg. After a seafood dinner, they have group sex, as Rudi says mechanically "gut, gut [good, good]." Bruno, who is writing an article about the Cap, then describes the pornographic spectacles that take place daily in the dunes behind the beach. Emphasizing the northern European, particularly German, origins of many participants and the exceedingly polite, almost contractual, respectful, and even courteous approach of men hoping that women would accede to their joining in, Bruno proclaims that the Cap d'Agde is a sort of "sexual social democracy." In the end, Bruno writes that group sex at the Cap has "the same qualities of discipline and respect of a contract that permitted the Germans to conduct two horribly murderous world wars before reconstructing ... a powerful and export-oriented economy."[2]

---

[1]   In postwar France, the term *naturisme* has been largely synonymous with the English "nudism," to the extent that *naturisme* always included the practice of complete nudity by the 1950s. As a term, however, *naturisme* connotes a return to nature that *nudisme* does not. Moreover, participants and movement leaders tended to use *naturisme* because it seemed less controversial a word than *nudisme*. While I do use the terms "nude" and "nudism" in this chapter, particularly when nudity is being emphasized, they lack the connotations of the French *naturiste* and *naturisme*, so I often repeat the terms *naturiste* and *naturisme* as they appear in my sources.

[2]   Michel Houellebecq, *Les particules élémentaires* (Paris: Flammarion, 1998), pp. 265–76.

In portraying the dual nature of Cap d'Agde as a European tourist destination, first as a *naturiste* resort, second as a haven for swingers, Houellebecq captured the historical evolution of Cap d'Agde after World War II. Since the 1950s, European tourism has driven the establishment and expansion of nudist centers in France, including the rapid development of a *naturiste* campground and then the state-supported building of a resort at Cap d'Agde. Since the 1970s, the Cap has been transformed into a sexual mecca for swingers, exhibitionists, and voyeurs from across Europe. Despite the considerable changes at the Cap since the 1950s, one constant remains: the ever-increasing demand on the part of reasonably well-heeled Europeans for nude tourism. At the same time, Houellebecq implicitly attributed the sexual extremes of the Cap to the Germans by having the more experienced swinging couple of Rudi and Hannalore be German, by assuming German participation in the activities in the dunes, and especially in making a tie between German atrocities during both world wars and German sexual escapades at the Cap d'Agde. In the end, Houellebecq's novel reveals that contemporary Cap d'Agde cannot even be imagined by a French novelist without a European, and particularly a German, presence.

This chapter explores the reality of nude tourism to Cap d'Agde, which turns out to have been every bit as European in nature as Houellebecq implies, both before and after it became a destination for swingers. Given that the French nudist association, the Fédération Française du Naturisme (FFN), reported in 1970 that at least 40 percent of visitors to French *naturiste* centers were foreign, Cap d'Agde provides a case study of the critical role of other Europeans in the expansion of nude tourism in France. By examining the evolution of Cap d'Agde and its visitors, this chapter argues that neither postwar French tourism nor the stunning growth of postwar *naturisme* can be understood without reference to the fundamentally European—and not simply French—demand for nude tourism after World War II.[3]

---

[3]   Despite the large numbers of Europeans who have practiced nudism, particularly while on vacation, French *naturisme* has attracted comparatively little interest among historians. Two recent books, deriving from doctoral theses, have appeared in France, but both focus on *naturisme* in France before World War II, that is before it was practiced by many French or foreigners in France: Arnaud Baubérot, *Histoire du naturisme: le mythe du retour à la nature* (Rennes: Presses Universitaires de Rennes, 2004) and Sylvain Villaret, *Histoire du naturisme en France depuis le siècle des lumières* (Paris: Vuibert, 2005). Villaret does provide a general overview of the postwar years, though it lacks the more detailed analysis of his thesis, which focused on the earlier period. Anglophone and French historians of Germany have considered several different aspects of German nudism but have not considered German nude tourism outside Germany. See, for example, Matthew Jeffries, "'For a Genuine and Noble Nakedness'? German Naturism in the Third Reich," *German History* 24/1 (2006): pp. 62–84; Arnd Krüger, Fabian Krüger, and Sybille Treptau, "Nudism in Nazi Germany:

Establishing *Naturiste* Tourism at Cap d'Agde

Located along the Hérault River a few kilometers from the coast of the Mediterranean, the commune of Agde did not receive many tourists in the nineteenth or early twentieth centuries. The coast at the Cap d'Agde, about three kilometers from Agde proper, consisted mostly of mosquito-infested salt marshes, sand, and marginal vineyards. The region around Agde, like much of the Languedoc, had turned to widespread, largely low quality wine production in the wake of the phylloxera crisis of the late nineteenth century. Mediterranean tourism, by contrast, was concentrated on the French Riviera.

In the 1950s tourists began to find their way to the Languedocian coast. On the beaches near the Cap d'Agde, as elsewhere on the coast, German, French, and other nationalities pitched tents and parked tiny car-towed trailers along the beach, sometimes ignoring the municipal and private campgrounds not directly on the beach, at other times turning to makeshift camping when the campgrounds filled. At the beach, most wore some clothes. But several, later claimed to have been German, asked two local vintners with vines along an isolated stretch of the coast to the east of the Cap, René and Paul Oltra, if they might cross the brothers' property to get to the beach where they proceeded to undress.[4] Skinny-dipping was nothing new in isolated locales (though it had been tightly controlled at bourgeois resorts since the nineteenth century),[5] and even

---

Indecent Behavior or Physical Culture for the Well-being of the Nation," *International Journal of the History of Sport* 19/4 (December 2002): pp. 33–54; Josie McLellan, "State Socialist Bodies: East German Nudism from Ban to Boom," *Journal of Modern History* 79 (March 2007): pp. 48–79; Chad Ross, *Naked Germany: Health, Race and the Nation* (Oxford: Berg, 2005); and Karl Toepfer, *Empire of Ecstasy: Nudity and Movement in German Body Culture, 1910–1935* (Berkeley: University of California Press, 1997). See also Marc Cluet, "La libre culture: le mouvement nudiste en Allemagne depuis ses origines au seuil du XXe siècle jusqu'à l'arrivée de Hitler au pouvoir (1905–1933): présupposés, développements et enjeux historiques" (Thèse d'état, Université de Paris IV, Sorbonne, 1999). Among Anglophone, and particularly American historians, there has been even less interest, perhaps because of the tight North American associations of France with cultural tourism, a notion only partly shared by European travelers to France. The relatively small number of American nudists might also have caused Americans to miss the importance of nude tourism in twentieth-century Europe. The neglect is unfortunate, for we are ignoring a huge development within French and European tourism, as well as the nudist movement, after World War II.

4   Roger Frey, *Cap d'Agde, 1970–2000: L'histoire de la plus grande station touristique française* (Cap d'Agde: Editions Georges Renault, 2001), p. 132.

5   Alain Corbin, *The Lure of the Sea: The Discovery of the Seaside in the Western World, 1750–1840*, trans. by Jocelyn Phelps (New York: Penguin, 1994), pp. 262–3, 278–9.

the Oltra family had skinny-dipped at the beachfront.[6] Camping was, however, carefully regulated by the French state, so when nudists asked the Oltra brothers to camp, the Oltras needed municipal approval to set up a campground.

In 1956, René Oltra approached the mayor, Louis Valières, to ask for his support for the establishment of a *naturiste* campground near the beach. In the midst of a great deal of joking, the municipal council gave its approval, and the prefect also agreed to the plan. As had been the case at Montalivet (Gironde) in the late 1940s, a poor, cash-strapped municipality in an out-of-the-way place was given the option of increasing tourism by accepting nudism. As at Montalivet, the Oltra property was isolated—it was a few kilometers from the inland town of Agde and east along the coast from the sparsely populated village of Cap d'Agde.[7] Given the isolation of the locale, municipal approval evoked no significant local opposition. In return, the campground would bring in desperately needed revenue, in the form of taxes as well as the sale of goods and services to the largely foreign clientele.

By the summer of 1958, the Oltra brothers had established a *naturiste* campsite of six hectares (15 acres) a short walk through the dunes from the beach. One visitor, L. Clairval, described the new Centre Hélio-Marin (CHM) Oltra, a name obviously reminiscent of the Centre Hélio-Marin of Montalivet. Clairval noted in the pages of the *naturiste* periodical *Vie au Soleil* that conditions were a little crowded, and that the Oltras had to provide additional toilet facilities with some urgency. Above all, he emphasized the conviviality of nude visitors from Germany, England, Belgium, the Netherlands, Italy, and even North and South America.[8]

In 1959, *Vie au Soleil* featured a long article by Louis Marre about the CHM Oltra. He too concentrated on the fellowship of international nudists, particularly among Belgians, Swiss and Germans as well as French in the makeshift camp and at the beach, appreciating "the camaraderie and relaxation. Nowhere else besides among nudists have I found such an ambiance." In the evening, campers made a campfire on the beach, and sang German and French songs, told stories and played games. For Marre, this cosmopolitan gathering of nudists amounted to a veritable paradise: "Above all, we are in *naturiste* territory, and the daily contact of nude men, women and children gives birth to an ambiance of honesty and innocence without hypocrisy."[9] Not surprisingly,

---

6   B. Baraille, "Les deux visages du Cap d'Agde," *Midi Libre* (July 23, 1976), Section C: 1.

7   *Hérault-Tribune*, June 5, 1976; Jacqueline de Linarès, "Cap d'Agde: les nudistes en ville," *L'Express*, 1255 (July 28–August 3, 1975), Section *Méditerranée Vacances*: B.

8   L. Clairval, "Le Centre Helio-Marin d'Agde," *Vie au Soleil*, 64 (March–April 1959): p. 10.

9   Louis Marre, "La journée d'un nudiste moyen," *Vie au Soleil*, 71 (October 1960): pp. 8–9.

such reports, appearing in the most important nudist publication in France, did much to spur yet greater demand and the CHM Oltra grew to accommodate more visitors. These writers proclaimed the existence of a certain nude utopia, in which French, German, and other Europeans returned to "nature" by practicing "*naturisme*," and abandoning the "hypocrisy" of the clothed world. Of course, none of these tropes was new, having been widely used by both interwar accounts of nudist sites and among commentators in postwar nudist periodicals in France, Germany, and the United States; what was new was a relatively affordable nudist destination on the Mediterranean coast.

In the 1960s, as nude tourism grew in importance, so too did the CHM Oltra. Authorized to have 500 campers at a time in 1960, the campground had, in fact, about 3,500 in the high season by the mid-1960s, squeezed onto 12 hectares. By 1966 the campground had 800 campsites with electricity for tents or trailers, as well as 80 bungalows with electricity, gas, and water. Visitors could even get a full *pension* [meals] prepared by the Oltras.[10] More than half of visitors were foreigners, who represented approximately one half of the campers even in the French high season of July and August. More important, foreigners were much less attached to vacationing in July and August than were the French, and thus extended the all important tourist "season." Into the early summer and early fall, foreigners represented about 80 percent of visitors to the campground.[11]

In fact, the Oltras' campground was such a success that in 1961 Fournier and Malafosse founded a second *naturiste* campground, this one to the west at Cap d'Agde. In this case, the campground's name itself indicates the intended foreign clientele: the Centre Naturiste International de la Méditerranée (CNIM).[12] By 1967, it welcomed approximately 2,500 campers in high season on its 15 hectares.[13]

State-Sponsorship of Nude Tourism: The Racine Mission

In the course of the 1960s, demand for nude tourism grew quickly among northern Europeans. In 1958, the CHM Oltra, Montalivet, and the Île du Levant were the only nudist vacation destinations in France. By 1967, there

---

[10]   Ad for the "Centre Hélio-Marin Agde," in *Vie au Soleil* 105 (May–June 1966): p. 19.

[11]   Archives Départementales de l'Hérault [hereafter ADH], 1103 258 Mission Interministérielle, Letters from René Oltra to Pierre Racine, to Pierre LeRoy-Beaulieu and to the SEBLI, January 11, 1968.

[12]   ADH, 1103 258 Mission Interministérielle, Dossier #16, Campings naturistes au Cap d'Agde/intervenant M. Roger Sommer, 1967.

[13]   ADH, 1103 W 695 Mission Interministérielle, "Zone d'Action Directe du Cap d'Agde: Projet d'Extension de la DUP."

were 22. As a result of this demand, the Oltra brothers not only expanded their campground but were also able, ultimately, to insert nude tourism into the huge state-sponsored development of the Languedocian coast. Facing loss of their campground to the declaration of eminent domain ("Domaine d'Utilité Publique" [DUP]), the Oltras managed to convince authorities that a nude resort would be a draw for European tourists. In the end, it was the demand of Europeans for nude tourism that gave the Oltra brothers a strong position in their negotiations with the Racine Mission for the preservation and expansion of their nudist vacation center.

In 1963, de Gaulle's government created the Délégation à l'Aménagement du Territoire à l'Action Régionale (DATAR), attached to the office of the prime minister. Its purpose was to coordinate public and private initiatives to foster tourism, and thus economic development, within France.[14] On a more local level, the Mission Interministérielle pour l'Aménagement Touristique du Littoral Languedoc-Roussillon took charge. As an inter-ministerial mission, its director reported directly to the office of the prime minister. It quickly became known as the Mission Racine, named for Pierre Racine, the Mission's long-time chief. Its objective was to develop 210 kilometers of the Languedoc-Roussillon coastline in order to diversify and foster the local economy. French and other European tourists traveled along the coast of Languedoc and Roussillon, but few stayed in an area infested with mosquitoes and with very limited accommodations. The Mission Racine was to work with private developers to build affordable vacation centers that would keep tourists' hard currency in France.

Although numerous centers of varying sizes would ultimately emerge along the coast of Languedoc-Roussillon, the focus was initially on the five largest (of which Cap d'Agde would ultimately become the biggest), each of which was delegated to a single architect who could create and enforce a specific style. Jean Balladur took responsibility for the now famous pyramids at La Grande-Motte, the first center to be completed, in 1968.[15] Architect Jean Le Couteur received the commission for the project as a whole at Cap d'Agde.

---

[14]   Christophe Bouneau, "La promotion de l'économie touristique, lévier de la politique d'aménagement du territoire de France des années 1950 aux années 1980," *Entreprise et Histoire* 47 (2007): pp. 93–108, p. 97.

[15]   See Ellen Furlough and Rosemary Wakeman, "La Grande Motte: Regional Development, Tourism, and the State," in Shelley Baranowski and Ellen Furlough (eds), *Being Elsewhere: Tourism, Consumer Culture, and Identity in Modern Europe and North America* (Ann Arbor: University of Michigan Press, 2001), pp. 348–72; Antoine Picon and Claude Prélorenzo, *L'aventure du balnéaire: La Grande Motte de Jean Balladur* (Marseille: Editions Parenthèses, 1999).

Much of the financing and local decision-making at Cap d'Agde came from a public–private development partnership, the SEBLI (Société d'Equipement du Biterrois et de son Littoral).

Planning began immediately, and the Mission bought up properties within the area declared the Domain d'Utilité Publique (DUP) while Le Couteur designed and oversaw other architects' designs for a new vacation village on the hitherto largely deserted stretch of beach and salt marshes at Cap d'Agde. Draining of the marshes, canalization, and the creation of marinas began almost immediately. And chemical eradication of mosquitoes from local marshes with DDT was a priority here as elsewhere in Languedoc-Roussillon, gobbling up 11.7 percent of the total budget of the Mission, a category surpassed only by the investment in roads to facilitate access to the centers.[16] The Oltras' campground near the Cap d'Agde fell within the perimeter of the area declared a DUP, putting Mission authorities in the position of deciding the fate of the Oltra operation. As late as 1967, plans showed no provision for a nudist component in the development.[17] Rather, the development of Cap d'Agde was to be one unified vacation village. The nudist campgrounds of the CNIM and the CHM Oltra presented serious challenges. The CNIM was closer to the center of the development plan, so it would be impossible to create a largely clothed resort with a nude campground in the middle. The Oltra campground was near the edge, but there was still no clear divide between nude and clothed portions of the beach. Thus in both cases, the practice of nudism was solely on isolated stretches of beach, so that other tourists would not be offended, but development would eliminate that isolation. As important, Jean Le Couteur's vision of Cap d'Agde was of low-rise, permanent buildings; after all, it was precisely the helter-skelter of ever-increasing makeshift camping that was to be eliminated at the new vacation centers. The Oltra campground, whatever its modest improvements since the 1950s, looked to Le Couteur and other officials like little more than *camping sauvage* with nude bodies in close proximity.

By 1967, the Oltra brothers realized that the stakes were high, as they risked losing their campground because of its location within the new DUP. They began an extensive lobbying campaign with the SEBLI, the mayor of Agde, and even Mission authorities in Paris. In September 1967, while Paul Oltra met with Mission officials in Agde, his brother René was off to a meeting in the Ministry

---

[16]   Investment in roads made up 34.2 percent of the budget of the Mission Racine from 1964 to 1980, while *démoustication* [mosquito eradication] required 11.7 percent. Madeleine Giral and Etienne Brualla, *Le Grau d'Agde* (Nîmes: C. Lacour, 1994), p. 129.

[17]   ADH, 1103 W 345 Mission Interministérielle, Maps from 1967 in "Secteur Promotion: Cap d'Agde," 1967.

of Equipment in Paris.[18] After suggestions that they might not be allowed to maintain any *naturiste* campground, the Oltras played their strong suit—foreign as well as French tourists' demand for nude tourism. After extended correspondence and multiple meetings in 1967, René Oltra wrote the Mission on January 11, 1968. Oltra confirmed in the letter that the brothers had "firmly decided to be promoters of a campground and *naturiste* vacation village in the sector" where they had been for the past 12 years. He noted that the idea for the campground was "revolutionary at the time if you consider that there were only two large vacation centers for *naturistes*: the Île du Levant and Montalivet," whereas there were 22 by 1967 as the *naturiste* clientele was growing by about 20 percent annually. Then Oltra played his trump card by claiming that if "you judge the *naturistes* undesirable we could reconvert the operation into a normal campground and village but that this solution would be catastrophic for regional commerce and even for the development of the coast because it would eliminate" the 80 percent of visitors who are foreign who stretch the season out to six months per year. He further pointed out that the *naturistes*, who had obviously chosen their campground so that they could be nude, would not don clothing but rather flee to the grand Yugoslavian centers being built with German funds or to Spain where French developers supposedly had an agreement with Spanish authorities to build a "Grand Centre Naturiste" at the outlet of the Ebro.[19]

Moreover, word got out quickly among *naturistes* that they could lose Cap d'Agde. In 1967, as rumors circulated, Roger Sommer wrote worriedly (in excellent French) from Berlin. Identifying himself as the official German delegate to the FFN, Sommer wrote to learn whether it was true that at least one of the centers would be forced to close while the other might remain open. He received an evasive answer.[20]

The Oltras' position, backed by support from foreign nudists like Sommer, was simply that *naturiste* visitors were disproportionately foreign, which extended the otherwise quite short French tourist season of July and August, the bane of promoters of tourism in France, for it meant that facilities would remain idle the rest of the year. In contrast, the Oltra campground remained open year-round even if there were few visitors from November to April. Given that the very

---

[18]   ADH, 1103 W 258 Mission Interministérielle, "Visite à MM Oltra Frères, Agde, par MM de Rosnay et Astruc," September 7, 1967.

[19]   ADH, 1103 W 258 Mission Interministérielle, Letter from René Oltra to Bonnaud, copies sent to mayor of Agde, Mission headquarters in Paris, and the SEBLI in Béziers, January 11, 1968.

[20]   ADH, 1103 W 258 Mission Interministérielle, Roger Sommer to the Mission Interministérielle, July 22, 1967; ADH, 1103 W 258 Mission Interministérielle, Raynaud to Sommer, July 27, 1967.

objective of the Racine Mission was to improve and diversify the local economy through tourism, especially by Parisians and foreigners, the CHM was clearly an advantage for Agde that planners were reluctant to abandon. Soon the plans for the eastern end of the DUP changed to include a *quartier naturiste* [nudist neighborhood]. The CNIM would in essence be moved to the *quartier naturiste* and named Port Nature, a development with small villas as well as apartments and shops, distinct from the rest of the *quartier*. Nearby the Oltras obtained the right to build multi-storied apartment blocks for nude tourists.

In the ensuing years, negotiations continued between the Mission and the Oltras, as their early plans for a renovated campground met stiff resistance. Le Couteur had a vision of a built environment, with shops and apartments. In the meantime, the Oltras kept building, without permits, new facilities, thus expanding their campground on land adjacent to the new *quartier*. By 1969, they had built a cement open-air sanitary block with 30 sinks, 20 showers, 11 washbasins, a prefabricated clubhouse, and a prefabricated hangar to serve as a child care center. To the chagrin of the Mission, the Oltras had permission, since 1960, for a campground with two stars, with a capacity of 500. By 1967, they already had 3,500 campers in high season, and then continued after 1967 to make improvements on the very ground that now belonged to the state; now they were at it again. For Mission authorities, the Oltras were clearly bending the rules, and there were suggestions to keep them from participation in the *quartier naturiste* or to impose other sanctions. For the Oltras, who had been there before the creation of the Mission, and who had behind them a seemingly insatiable demand for nude tourism, it no doubt seemed like a safe bet to continue to present the Mission with *faits accomplis*.[21]

In the meantime, despite differences of opinion as to the wisdom of a *quartier naturiste*, Racine Mission officials could not deny its value in attracting foreign as well as French tourists. To avoid conflicts with other tourists, the *quartier naturiste* would be placed on the land occupied by the Oltra campground, at the eastern end of the DUP. It was isolated, separated to the west by a new canal and marina named Port Ambonne. To the north were mostly dunes and undeveloped land. To the east there was an unbroken stretch of isolated beach two kilometers in length, culminating with the commune's boundary with Marseillan.

The Oltras' architect, François Lopez, finally received the first commission for a multi-storied nudist apartment block, itself to be named Port Ambonne and completed in 1972. Facing the marina rather than the beach, and separated from the beach by Port Nature, Port Ambonne had a shopping center on the first

---

[21]   ADH, 1103 W 258 Mission Interministérielle, "Note pour Monsieur Bonnaud" by MM Lepetre, de Rosnay and Tessier, Direction Départementale de l'Equipement de l'Hérault (Bonnaud signed and transmitted to Reynaud), October 30, 1969.

floor with 200 apartments in a semi-circle above.[22] The style was modernist, and the placement was designed to maximize sunshine on the terraces of apartments while minimizing the wind, thus extending the season for comfortable nudity as long as possible.

Architect Claude Comolet's Port Nature, the second major building project, would be at the corner of the sea and the channel. The Centre Naturiste Internationale de la Méditerranée was a development separate from the rest of the *quartier naturiste*, including a shopping center on the ground floor and 600 apartments on upper floors. Three hundred individual villas with private gardens were also part of Port Nature.[23]

Fifteen hundred apartments were projected for the Oltras' Héliopolis, to be completed in stages during the 1970s. These, like the earlier dwellings at Port Nature, continued to sell briskly, reminding all that demand for nude tourism was outstripping supply.[24] Its name, meaning "city of sun," had been the name of the Durville brothers' *naturiste* settlement at Île du Levant since the 1930s, a reference no European *naturiste* would have missed. Héliopolis was a large, mostly enclosed circle with shopping on the ground floor and apartments above. The opening to the circle faced the beach and offered spectacular views from terraces. In all, the three apartment complexes and surrounding grounds occupied approximately 27 hectares.[25]

A small, naked city with a rather dense population thus emerged rather quickly. In addition to the apartments, shops provided much of what tourists would need to remain within the *quartier*, and thus nude, for an entire month of vacation. By 1978, the *quartier naturiste* had 60 small businesses. For food there were two groceries, four shops for fresh fruit and vegetables, a bakery, two *traiteurs* [caterer/grocer], two butchers, and two fish shops. There was a gas station, a bicycle rental store, a cinema. One *crêperie* [restaurant serving crepes] and seven restaurants fed those wanting to eat out. There were five clothing shops (see below for context), three banks, two nightclubs, two cafés, two doctors, a dentist, two photographers, two *librairies* [press/book shops], a perfume shop, and even a laundry.[26] Also in 1978, lobbying by the mayor of Agde, Pierre Leroy-Beaulieu, resulted in a branch post office set up at the entry to the *quartier*, so

---

[22]   Christian Camps, *Agde d'hier à aujourd'hui* (Péronnas: Editions de la Tour Gîle, 1999), p. 275.

[23]   ADH 1103 W 257 Mission Interministérielle, Typewritten manuscript by Diane Pensieri and Elysabeth Ebel, of Havas Conseil Relations Publiques, from the early 1970s.

[24]   Camps, *Agde*, p. 275.

[25]   ADH 1103 W 259 Mission Interministérielle, "Zone d'Action Directe du Cap d'Agde/Projet d'Extension de la DUP."

[26]   *Hérault-Tribune*, September 9, 1978.

that the approximately 20,000 inhabitants of the *quartier* during the high season could get their mail and use public telephones.[27]

Much to the chagrin of Racine Mission authorities, the Oltra brothers did not really accept that their campground should be replaced by Port Ambonne and Héliopolis. After much of their own land and the land they had leased had become part of the DUP, they simultaneously leased land just to the east of the DUP and continued to run their campground. Just beyond the beach, stretching one kilometer and thus most of the way to the boundary with the commune of Marseillan, the new campground benefited from the amenities of the *quartier* while offering campers lower prices and the more rustic environs that many associated with *naturisme*. By the early 1970s, the campground had the capacity to welcome more than 10,000 campers at a time, though the Oltras had received authorization for a campground with a capacity for only 1,200 campers.

Le Couteur and his colleagues were infuriated, particularly since the location of the new campground essentially blocked access to the beach from the area to the north, thus giving the Oltras a sort of monopoly near the beach. And after bending the rules in the 1960s and getting away with it, the Oltras were once again forcing the issue. Long memoranda and repeated meetings ensued. The Mission, now realizing the demand for nude tourism, foresaw a massive expansion of the DUP on 127 hectares to the east, including the land the Oltras were using for a campground. Their motive was simple; while being very concerned about the hygienic conditions of the Oltras' makeshift campground, particularly the issue of wastewater, as well as its presumed aesthetic shortcomings, they wanted to expand offerings for nude tourists in the *quartier naturiste*. As of 1972–73, Mission authorities considered a five-fold expansion of the number of nude tourists who could be accommodated.[28] Clearly, Mission authorities were quickly won over by the potential profits generated by nude tourism.

In the end, the proposed DUP ran into serious obstacles. The cost of appropriation was prohibitive. And the grand plan to develop the area north and east of the Oltra campground, with an artificial lake, roads, campgrounds, hotels, and apartment blocks, ran afoul of a new environmental consciousness and resistance to such grand development plans. But after years of wrangling with the Mission, which abandoned its plans, the Oltras managed to maintain a campground with nearly 2,500 campsites and bungalows, theoretically with a capacity of 10,000 or so nude tourists.[29] Including the dunes and undeveloped

---

[27]   *Hérault-Tribune*, July 1, 1978.

[28]   ADH 1103 W 259 Mission Interministérielle, "Zone d'Action Directe du Cap d'Agde/Projet d'Extension de la DUP."

[29]   This conflict is reflected in innumerable memoranda and minutes of meetings from the 1970s, ADH 1103 W 258 and 259 Mission Interministérielle.

land to the north-east of their campground, their campground, and developments of Port Ambonne, Port Nature, and Héliopolis, the Oltras could advertise that Cap d'Agde offered a huge sandy beach and 150 hectares in which tourists could live in "nature."[30]

By the early 1970s, in terms of the number of visitors, the *quartier naturiste* was the largest nudist tourist destination in France and the world, surpassing even Montalivet in importance. And while huge new centers would soon open in Aquitaine, such as Euronat (in which the name itself plays on the hoped-for European and *naturiste* clientele), Cap d'Agde remained the most visited destination.

Europeans in the "Naked City"

Despite the rapid expansion and building of Port Ambonne, Port Nature, and Héliopolis, demand remained strong. As René Oltra put it in 1975, "all the records were again beaten. ... Demand is growing much faster than supply. There is an extraordinary market."[31] Earlier investors, both foreigners and other nudists who used and sometimes rented out their apartments but also locals who purchased apartments solely to rent out, profited handsomely. In 1975, the Montpellier-based *Midi Libre* claimed that investors in the *quartier naturiste* had earned three times the profit of investors in "classic stations." An apartment for five persons purchased in 1973 for 80,000 francs was worth 240,000 in 1979. It could be rented out for a profit of 13,000 francs each year, a far higher profit than in the textile portion of Cap d'Agde.[32] In large part, this was due to the fact that the tourist season lasted more than six months in the *quartier naturiste*; whereas French vacationers were always concentrated in July and August, foreigners took vacations in other relatively warm months.[33] It was also due to the fact that European nudists were willing to pay more to vacation naked near the beach.

Foreigners were often buyers. At the new Port Nature, which would have nearly 1,000 dwellings once completed, only 45 percent of buyers were French (and even some of the French were purely investors, not vacationers). Among the non-French, 35 percent were German, 10 percent Belgian, with the others coming from the Netherlands, Britain, Czechoslovakia, Switzerland, and a few

---

[30]   Advertisement entitled "Le Paradis Naturiste International de la Méditerranée," in *Vie au Soleil* 29, special vacation edition (1974): frontmatter.

[31]   Cited in Jacqueline de Linarès, "Cap d'Agde," p. C.

[32]   *Hérault-Tribune*, May 19, 1979.

[33]   *Midi Libre*, August 17, 1975.

from Spain. And, as the *Midi Libre* pointed out, *naturistes* had a purchasing power well above that of the average tourist to the region.[34] Not surprisingly, when the cooperative association of Port Nature (l'Union Syndicale de Port Nature aux Copropriétaires) published the rules of the resort in Cap d'Agde's *Hérault-Tribune*, they were in both French and German. Here German as well as French owners and visitors were reminded that they must belong to either the French *naturiste* association (the FFN) or the international federation (the Fédération Naturiste Internationale [FNI]), that any person could be expelled for inappropriate behavior, that full nudity was obligatory whenever weather permitted, that films and photographs might be made only with the subjects' express permission, and that dogs had to be kept on leashes and were prohibited from the beach.[35] Presumably other Europeans were supposed to have adequate reading knowledge of French or German in order to follow the rules.

The accommodation of German speakers was the norm rather than an exception. Even the huge upright beachfront scrabble board set up by the Club Nature at the Café l'Horizon (of course with a view of the Mediterranean) had a German as well as a French version.[36] Businesses would post or advertise that "Man spricht Deutsch [German spoken here]." At times, whole advertisements would be in German without there being any French counterpart. For example, in the old bishopric in the city of Agde, called "Le Donjon" [the dungeon], there was a restaurant of some repute. In the pages of the *Hérault-Tribune*, an advertisement for the restaurant, solely in German, reminded German nudists that they were in the oldest city of the Mediterranean and must surely be thinking about excellent food, which France had always offered: they could find both excellent cuisine and a wonderful atmosphere at the "Donjon."[37]

Not surprisingly, the primary appeal of the *quartier naturiste* was that weeks of vacation might be spent on the Mediterranean entirely without clothes. Foreign nudists varied in their interest in cultural and regional tourism in the backcountry. In 1976, the local *Hérault-Tribune* did a series on the reasons that nudists flocked to Cap d'Agde. One article interviewed Théo, *un professeur de musique* (it is unclear whether he worked in higher education or a secondary school), and Hetty Vrydag, from the Netherlands. They had first gone, six years earlier, to Montalivet but then discovered the better weather of the Mediterranean. They had been coming to the Cap for six years with their three children, Marc (age 14), Désirée (11), and Aimée (5). The family proclaimed

---

[34]   Ibid.; Pierre Laurent Ortas, "Naturisme moderne et architecture," *Agde, Revue Municipale* (1975): p. 47.

[35]   *Hérault-Tribune*, June 5, 1976.

[36]   *Hérault-Tribune*, July 2, 1977.

[37]   *Hérault-Tribune*, June 22–8, 1974.

a love of French cuisine and regional specialties accompanied by fine wine, even if Hetty admitted to cooking traditional Dutch cuisine in their trailer at the CHM Oltra. Théo regularly undertook wine tasting in the region, hauling many bottles of wine back with him to Holland each year. Although the article implies that they spent most of their time with Dutch friends at the CHM—a potentially revealing fact about the national norms within the cosmopolitanism at the CHM—the Vrydag family appreciated French "food, wine, people and historic sights" as well as the "ambiance."[38]

By contrast, in the same series, Jacques and Marina Pitsch, both Wallons (French-speaking Belgians), expressed no interest in such cultural tourism. Instead, Jacques, a fireman, and Marina, a secretary, had been bringing their 16-year-old daughter Martine and 18-year-old son Marc, to the CHM for 12 years but did not bother to see the *arrière-pays* [backcountry]. Rather, they came for the sunshine, driving from cloudy Belgium to the Mediterranean each summer. They expressed some disappointment that the expansion of the campground had caused local prices to rise and that the conviviality of early *naturistes* had been replaced by anonymity. They clearly preferred more rustic camping, but they continued to adore the cicadas, the trees, sun, and sea of the south of France.[39] They also had reason to celebrate: their daughter Martine had just been elected "Miss CHM 1976."

As had been the case at Île du Levant, beauty contests were regular events at Cap d'Agde. They were clearly international. The jury that elected Mlle Pitsch in 1976 consisted of a couple of Czechs, a couple of Austrians, a couple of Germans and "old-timers from the camp."[40] In 1978, at the Port-Ambonne, contestants included "two French girls, two English, two Belgian, and eight German." A young Frenchwoman from Carcassonne, Françoise Dumez, won, while the runners-up were German. These international events were not marginal affairs; they carried the stamp of approval of local authorities as well as *naturistes*. "The contestants were dressed by the boutique Les Frusques before they undressed before a jury led by the mayor of Agde, Pierre Leroy-Beaulieu, and the director of the SEBLI, Jean Miquel."[41] In 1978, leading contestants were Belgian and Italian. Nathalie Dewere, an 18-year-old Wallon won, while the runners-up were the Flemish 15-year-old Katja Goethals, and the Italian 16-year-old Isadore Isr.[42] It was not unusual for contestants to be under 18, and they were almost always under 20. There were no comparable contests for young men and boys, and there appears to

---

38   *Hérault Tribune*, July 17, 1976.
39   *Hérault-Tribune*, July 24, 1976.
40   Ibid.
41   *Hérault-Tribune*, July 15, 1978.
42   *Hérault-Tribune*, August 28, 1982.

have been little consciousness, let alone controversy, that such contests might have undermined longstanding *naturiste* claims that going nude would lead to greater acceptance of bodily differences, erasing traditional notions of beauty. Nor did organizers seem aware that the contests of nude women but not nude men also undermined *naturiste* claims that *naturisme* would lead to greater gender equity. Yet it is clear that the contests, at least in the *quartier naturiste*, were very much international, being widely accepted by European vacationers to the Cap.

Although most of the tourist center at Cap d'Agde was "textile," the *quartier naturiste* was more profitable, in large part because of foreign demand for nude tourism. The commune of Agde quickly came to rely on revenues from the Cap generally, and the *quartier naturiste* with its more affluent and foreign visitors was the moneymaker. In 1979, as construction continued, *Le Monde* reported that of the six stations being built on the coast of Languedoc-Roussillon, Cap d'Agde was the most lucrative, creating between 1,500 jobs in the winter and 2,500 jobs in summer. According to Miquel, head of the SEBLI, the Cap did not cost the municipality of Agde anything; in fact, once expenses to the commune were covered, it produced between two and three million francs in profit for the municipality each year.[43] According to Miquel, much of that profit came from foreigners; he estimated that more than 100,000 people practiced *naturisme* at the Cap d'Agde in 1979, with "the foreign clientele reaching 75–80 percent in the low season and 50 percent in the high season." As important, the clientele is "young, with an elevated standard of living."[44]

The Challenges of Sexualized Nudism

Into the 1970s, though some *naturistes*, much like the Pitsch family above, complained that there was little that was "natural" in the new urban setting at the *quartier naturiste*, *naturisme* at the Cap was still largely familial. By the 1980s, however, the Cap became less familial and more sexually charged. Nightclubs became more risqué until the primary purpose was simply to host group sex. Clothing shops focused on selling sexual clothing, sex toys, and sado-masochistic equipment. And open sexual activity became the norm even on the beach itself. Increasingly, European swingers came to the Cap d'Agde, rather than the Île du Levant, for ease of access, lower cost, and greater numbers of like-minded sex tourists. This transformation presented serious challenges for the municipality at Agde.

---

[43]   *Hérault-Tribune*, May 19, 1979, reprinting an article from *Le Monde* of May 7, 1979.

[44]   *Hérault-Tribune*, January 10, 1981.

Legally, before the early 1970s there had been no authorization of nudity at the beach at the Cap, and in principle campers at the CHM Oltra were to cover themselves through the dunes on the trek to the beach and at the beach itself, though the municipality clearly knew what would be happening on that isolated stretch of beach in approving the Oltras' campground in 1956. There is no evidence in the archives or in *naturiste* publications, which carefully documented such cases elsewhere, of anyone from the campground being prosecuted for nudity on the beach, even though pictures and articles in the *Vie au Soleil* make clear that full nudity was the norm. Basically, the municipality was choosing to interpret Article 330 of the Napoleonic code rather loosely. That article set the parameters for nudity by prohibiting *outrage public à la pudeur* [public indecency]. It was being seen nude and offending the viewer that was illegal. The campground itself was private property and could thus be nudist, as it was isolated from prying eyes and thus eliminated the potential for complainants to invoke article 330.

Since nudists at the beach were also staying at the Oltra campground, the Oltras could easily police behavior and expel campers not respecting *naturiste* norms. All campers needed to join the FFN or the FNI, and subscribe to family-oriented *naturisme*—meaning nudity without sexual overtones. Although *naturistes* were of course human, and there were, according to old timers, the same private *histoires de fesses* [literally "butt stories," figuratively a gender-neutral way of referring to what Anglophones usually call "skirt-chasing"] as in the clothed community,[45] nudity was effectively distinct from sexuality on the beach and at the campground. Of course, beauty contests rested partly on sex appeal. At the same time, pictures of winners look much like Miss America contestants without the clothes. Winners sported no tattoos or body-piercings. Pubic hair was not shaved. They did not wear scarves, belts, leashes, chains, boots or any other accoutrements suggesting sex or sado-masochism. Poses were often nude but not particularly sexual.[46] The *naturiste* movement had long maintained that it was clothes and especially disrobing that were sexual, and that nudity and sexuality were in no way connected. While much of French society might not have accepted that cultural construction, *naturistes* knew the difference, a veritable leitmotif in the pages of the *Vie au Soleil*.

In the early 1970s, as the number of *naturistes* and other tourists increased, so too did the potential for conflict on the beach. *Naturistes* and non-*naturistes* not willing to pay the entrance fee complained that the Oltra brothers were

---

45   Anonymous source, interview by the author, Agde, July 16, 2006.

46   *Hérault-Tribune*, July 24, 1976; *Hérault-Tribune*, August 28, 1982; *Hérault-Tribune*, July 28, 1984.

blocking access to a public beach.[47] In June 1973, the mayor and municipal council attempted to remind everyone of French law and regulate the situation accordingly. In part, they wanted to define where *naturisme* could be practiced and prohibit it on "textile" portions of the beach. Above all, they wanted to "avoid that people not practicing *naturisme* find themselves mixed with those practicing it," and then get upset about it. The mayor began by reinforcing that on most of the beaches of the commune, a bathing suit was required for everyone, including children. He then expressly authorized *naturisme* in the *quartier naturiste*, provided that "good morality" [*bonnes moeurs*] and public order be respected. The *quartier naturiste* was to be defined officially by the channel of access to Port Ambonne to the west, the territory of the commune of Marseillan to the north-east, where signs would mark off the *naturiste* beach. The signs had a dual function. On the one hand, they signaled to *naturistes* that passing beyond a certain point could incur charges of public indecency; on the other, they informed other beachgoers that nudity was formally authorized in the *naturiste* zone. That is, any beachgoer entering the nudist area could not file charges against nudists for public indecency. *Naturisme* was also strictly forbidden on the water of Port Ambonne, on the channel of access, on the jetty between the *naturiste* beach and the channel, and "every point visible from the exterior of this zone."[48]

Enforcement fell to security guards to be paid for by the *naturiste* centers. They were charged solely with ensuring "respect of good morality [*bonnes moeurs*] and public order," without other powers which fell to the police. They were to ensure that *naturisme* would be practiced by *naturistes* without infractions "against morality on the part of *naturiste* campers and on the part of those not from the campground."[49]

The Oltras and other proprietors were thus charged with ensuring appropriate *naturiste* behavior on the beach and throughout the *quartier*. *Naturiste* centers did that by requiring FFN or FNI membership and adherence to their codes of conduct to practice non-sexualized nudism and to go nude whenever the weather permitted. Centers enforced these rules by limiting access and expelling offenders. So the guards at the Cap attempted to control behavior in the ways long accepted in *naturiste* circles. But then the mayor received more complaints. Non-*naturistes* complained that Oltra guards were blocking access to the public beach. *Naturistes* complained that the Oltras and

---

47   Archives Municipales d'Agde [hereafter AMA], document not yet catalogued, Complaint from "Mécontents d'un passage à Agde," in mayor's files, April 27, 1973.

48   AMA, document not yet catalogued, "Extrait du Registre des Arrêtés du Maire de la Commune d'Agde," June 14, 1973.

49   Ibid.

other co-proprietors were forcing them to pay a 10 franc fee for entry to the *quartier* and thus the beach, in violation of French law.[50] Moreover, guards appear to have told clothed beachgoers that they had to undress or leave,[51] long a practice in private *naturiste* grounds, as the best way to reduce the sense of voyeurism was perceived to be for everyone to be nude, but not a practice with any legal standing on public land.

So the municipality issued more regulations in 1978. Now the municipality specifically authorized pedestrian access (for a fee) to the *naturiste* beach; this rule stood for both clothed and unclothed since nudism was "authorized" on the beach, but not "required," which would have been illegal.[52] The barrier to the *quartier* would now be maintained by the SEBLI, not the centers, which would thus receive revenues for vehicular traffic and for parking outside the barrier for pedestrian visitors.[53] The beach itself remained theoretically public though inaccessible unless tourists paid the fee or went to the commune of Marseillan and walked south-westward along the beach to gain access.

The eventual difficulties in controlling sex at the Cap d'Agde resulted from the fact that the Oltras and other center directors thus lost any real authority to police behavior on the beach or in the *quartier*. Municipal authorities and the police, who were not *naturistes*, did not fully understand or apply *naturiste* ethics in the *quartier*. For example, other *naturiste* centers had preserved relatively traditional morality (no sexualized nudity) by drawing a clear distinction and expelling visitors who broke the norms. But how could "textile" police recognize and pursue voyeurism? For "textiles," nudism looked a lot like exhibitionism. Lingering glances on body parts were the norm on textile beaches, but they were usually strictly regulated in most *naturiste* clubs and centers; many police officers simply could not make such a distinction. Moreover, in the regulation of 1978 the *naturistes* clearly lost the right to require nudity when weather permitted. While the Oltras could continue to require adherence to the FFN or FNI and their principles within their campground, the brothers could not require adherence in the *quartier* as a whole.

---

50   AMA, document not yet catalogued, in the mayor's files, Jacques Dumont of the FFN to the mayor, June 12, 1974.

51   AMA, documents not yet catalogued, René Thomas to the mayor, September 9, 1974; AMA, documents not yet catalogued, the subprefect of Béziers G. Pigoullie to the mayor, October 2, 1974 in reference to an article in the *Midi Libre* of September 13; and AMA, documents not yet catalogued, the Procès Verbal of the meeting at the mayor's office in Agde, November 19, 1976.

52   AMA, document not yet catalogued, Arrêté du Maire de la Commune d'Agde, May 26, 1978.

53   *Hérault-Tribune*, May 1978.

The problem was aggravated as the number of proprietors multiplied. Interestingly, René Oltra himself realized the threat when he argued in a letter to the Mission in March 1970 that, contrary to his earlier plan to build apartments and sell some of them off to finance the rest of his investment in Port Ambonne, he wished to abandon the sales. Claiming he had had many discussions and contacts with "specialists," probably the FFN, he noted that it would be impossible to prohibit access to those visiting the proprietors of apartments, and noted that as a result "numerous abuses could be committed and that would risk compromising the naturist discipline in the center." Instead he argued that the Oltras wanted to remain fully responsible for their center because "our movement is evolving and all of Europe follows with grand interest the development of *naturisme* at Agde." In particular, he noted that "we don't want to commit the grand error of the Île of Levant," which, due to "a lack of discipline and organization, has become the European meeting place for persons of dubious morality" so that the "real *naturistes* don't frequent it any more." In short, Oltra specifically predicted that fragmented ownership and attendant disorganization would lead to a loss of control as at Île du Levant, where it had become impossible to control behavior of nudists.[54] Whatever his reservations, when Mission authorities proceeded with the plan without heeding his advice, Oltra did not sell out and abandon his investment, but he did work closely, though ultimately unsuccessfully, with the new owners' associations and the management of Port Nature to establish codes of conduct for the *quartier naturiste* as a whole and avoid the fate of Île du Levant.[55]

Eventually, however, René Oltra's prediction was fully realized. By the 1980s and 1990s, voyeurs, exhibitionists, and swingers from across Europe flocked to the *quartier naturiste*. M. Rouvier of the municipal police reported to the mayor in July 1992 that there had been "an increase in pederasty [*pédérastie* in the original, which indicated adult male homosexual activity, not sex with children], exhibitionism, [and] voyeurism in the dunes." He "had arrived, in the middle of the day, to find several couples having sex on the beach giving a spectacle to more than a hundred persons." At night, "pederasty takes over the totality of the beach."[56] Research notes of sociologist Daniel Welzer-Lang confirm the situation. He interviewed one small business owner in the mid-1990s who claimed that although a few "Germans and Dutch" had slipped off to the dunes for collective

---

54 ADH 1103 W 258 Mission Interministérielle, René Oltra to Raynaud, March 13, 1970.

55 *Hérault-Tribune*, October 1975.

56 AMA, document not yet catalogued, in the mayor's files, Brigadier Marc Rouvier to the mayor, July 10, 1992.

sex during the past 25 years (thus since about 1970), it had, according to him, only recently become the norm on the beach.[57]

The municipality of Agde had a serious dilemma. On the one hand, the *quartier naturiste* was a financial success. As the most frequented *naturiste* destination in the world, the *quartier* clearly generated revenue and employment for a municipality now dependent on tourism. On the other, its reputation as a destination for public and collective sexuality risked the reputation of the *quartier* among family-oriented *naturistes*, some of whom abandoned the Cap in favor of the ever-increasing alternatives for nude tourism in France and Spain. And of course the entire tourist center at the Cap could be affected. There was a real risk that French families, who dominated the "textile" areas, would not realize how isolated the *quartier naturiste* was and would simply choose another tourist destination.

In 1994, faced with an ever deteriorating situation, the municipality of Agde sought legal advice from M. André Brunel, their attorney in Montpellier. His detailed report, returned to the mayor's office on September 14, 1994, laid out the legal situation and the commune's options. According to Brunel, there was relatively little that Agde could do. Legally, non-owners (presumably many of the swingers in question) could not be prohibited from the *quartier*, and the various businesses relying on their trade would fight any move in that direction. The owners' association itself had no right to expel members, and thus could not force an owner of a nightclub or sex shop to sell and leave. The city did have the power to enforce both French law against exhibitionism and the city's 1973 law requiring public order and good morals ["*bonnes moeurs*"] in the *quartier*, but that could only be applied on the streets, beach, and open-air cafés. What proprietors, tenants, and private nightclubs hosted out-of-sight could not be banned. Brunel did suggest that members of the owners' association could collectively impose adherence to a *naturiste* association before allowing visitors to enter, but that would of course depend on a majority of the association's members. This could not apply to proprietors, many of whom were quite complicit with the new status quo at the Cap. In the end, Brunel provided little in the way of options for the municipality, beyond calling for a greater police presence on the beach and in the *quartier*.[58]

---

[57]   The anonymous small business person was, in effect, blaming the municipality's efforts to eliminate such activity in the dunes. This interpretation seems somewhat difficult to believe, given municipal reports and Welzer-Lang's other interviews; collective sexual activity was far too widespread at the Cap for its presence on the beach to be attributed solely to municipal efforts to eradicate it from the dunes. Daniel Welzer-Lang, *La planète échangiste: les sexualités collectives en France* (Paris: Payot, 2005), pp. 379–80.

[58]   AMA, document not yet catalogued, in the mayor's files, André Brunel to the mayor's office, September 14, 1994.

But here too Agde had a problem. By 1990, Cap d'Agde was the most heavily visited tourist center in all of France, with more than 300,000 residents in July and August. And Agde had only 90 police officers. For additional coverage during those months, the city relied every year on additional support from the CRS, the Compagnies Républicaines de Sécurité, who are perhaps best known as the riot police called in during political demonstrations in France. In 1990, the city received 32 CRS officers, only 20 of whom were "operational." Some of the CRS were CRS-MNS [Maîtres Nageurs de Sauvetage], who were posted at the beach as lifeguards in both the textile and *naturiste* areas of Cap d'Agde. But in the *quartier naturiste*, the CRS had the additional function of policing the beach and the dunes, ensuring that sexual activity was not taking place. The problem was manpower, and the city was quite lucid in its analysis of the situation.[59] Each year, the mayor called for greater assistance, and each year an overburdened CRS sent fewer officers than the municipality needed. In 1992 and 1993, the mayor specifically called for more help to control the situation in the dunes behind the beach, where CRS agents on horseback were posted to prevent public sex. In the late 1990s, the municipality closed the dunes to the public with an excuse that it was necessary for preservation of the environment.

Despite municipal concerns, little has changed since the 1990s. When swingers' publications issue their summer vacation guides, the Cap d'Agde has pride of place.[60] Non-residents may not enter the *quartier* after 8:00 pm, so outsiders coming only for the nightlife must arrive earlier. The dunes remain closed. According to long-time visitors, sex on the beach is less frequent in daytime hours, at least during the high season of July and August, when CRS agents supplement the municipal police.[61] An association of local *naturistes* is working in tandem with the police to reduce behavior when it is illegal, but the proprietors who profit from sex tourism to the *quartier* are hardly quiescent. The head of the *naturiste* association has received death threats,[62] and there are claims that a veritable mafia within the *quartier* is working against efforts to reform the situation.[63]

In theory, the municipality of course has long had an option for seriously reducing collective and public sexuality in the *quartier naturiste*, one that would chase away many of the very international tourists that made it possible. Legally,

---

59   AMA, document not yet catalogued, files of the mayor's office, Régis Passerieux, Mayor of Agde, to the Prefect of the Region of Languedoc-Roussillon, September 25, 1991.

60   "Cap d'Agde," *Magazine des loisirs et de l'amitié des années 2000: Spécial vacances*, no. 155 (July/August/September 2006): pp. 107–22.

61   Anonymous source, interview by the author, Agde, July 16, 2006.

62   Anonymous source, interview by the author, Agde, July 17, 2006.

63   Anonymous source, interview by the author, Agde, June 13, 2006.

the option would be quite simple. Agde could revoke municipal authorization of nudity. It would be a financial disaster, an option so unacceptable that it was not even part of Brunel's 1994 report laying out the municipality's legal alternatives. Once a small town dominated by the vineyards and a bit of fishing, Agde now has a well-developed and expensive tourist infrastructure that, apart from the *quartier naturiste*, is only near capacity in late July and early August. Without a nude beach, the now mostly antiquated and tiny apartments at the *quartier naturiste* would generate little revenue. In reality, the Oltra brothers' campground thrived precisely because it catered to international *naturistes*. Their success caused nude tourism to be written into the Racine Mission's state-sponsored development of Cap d'Agde. And the *quartier* grew quickly because it attracted foreign as well as French tourists. In a sense, the "naked city" has been a victim of its own rapid and wild success, adequately controlled neither by the municipality nor by the developers. And it has been a success due, in large part, to Europeans' demand for vacationing *au naturel*.

Chapter 4

From Alpine Tourism to the "Alpinization" of Tourism

Laurent Tissot

From the very first, the Alps were associated with the emergence of leisure travel. While the origin of the word "tourism" does not derive directly from the growing attraction of western Europe's highest mountains, visiting this region quickly became customary among European elites beginning in the early nineteenth century.[1] It is absolutely correct to speak about the emergence of an "alpine tourism" that, alongside spa, seaside, and urban tourism, varied regionally in intensity and form, yet which remained universally recognizable. Understanding the history of alpine tourism demands a consideration of myriad factors that converged during the eighteenth century to transform these mountains from being a "monde subi" to being a "monde aimé," from being an undesirable area to being a region adored by legions of visitors every year.[2] At the same time as the "désir du rivage" illustrated by Alain Corbin,[3] this "conquering sympathy" was fuelled by a subtle alchemy that explains its development, its perpetuity, and its success: scientific, technological, economic, political, social, physical, medical, geologic, symbolic, educational, and cultural dimensions joined and blended in the development of this new tourist model. It pulled its strength from human and material resources, often unfamiliar in the alpine environment, which modeled the new form of tourism according to plans and projects whose ultimate purpose was the domestication and exploitation of the mountain.

The tourist invention of the Alps did not remain strictly an alpine business. It quickly extended beyond the limits of a single mountain to reshape other

---

[1] On the creation of the word "tourism," see James Buzard, *The Beaten Track: European Tourism, Literature, and the Ways to Culture, 1800–1918* (Oxford: Oxford University Press, 1993).

[2] Paul Guichonnet, "L'homme devant les Alpes," in Paul Guichonnet (ed.), *Histoire et civilisations des Alpes* (Toulouse and Lausanne: Privat and Payot, 1980), pp. 169–248, p. 246.

[3] Alain Corbin, *Le territoire du vide, l'Occident et le désir du rivage 1750–1849* (Paris: Flammarion, 1988).

mountainous spaces. Alpine tourism carried with it the very seeds of its own distribution. Henceforth, alpine models circulated globally, providing plentiful representations and practices that were flexible enough to meet a number of needs. "Alpine" came to express a specific type of tourism that includes a range of activities suited to hilly environments; climbing clubs, mountaineering, and downhill skiing are all activities that can be practiced in mountainous regions, regardless of specific location. Such activities, along with the plants, animals, and rocks native to the high country, were now grouped together under a common heading and seen through a shared lens.

Alpine tourism is not simply a product of altitude. It would be reductive to explain the development of alpine tourism purely in terms of spatial, physical, or natural factors. Such a view would leave out a substantial part of the story. For example, we must consider the political and institutional parameters that made the alpine tourist model possible. Tourism was nationalized during the nineteenth century in both Europe and America. It was used as a cornerstone of a new conception of the nation and helped to shape identities and territorial representations.[4] From this perspective, the role of the Swiss Confederation must be emphasized. Art historians and literary critics alike have studied the role of the Confederation, showing its centrality in the assertion of the sensibilities and concepts that constitute the re-imagining of the Alps, not simply in Swiss areas but in the Savoy region if not in the whole of the western Alps as well.[5] Aesthetic sensibilities are rife with political and philosophical content, even if the substance is stripped down and streamlined to more easily convey the vision of authors or artists. Through seemingly apolitical vectors, alpine Switzerland grew, little by little, into a "civic myth." The Helvetic Republic emerged as a carrier of authentic and eternal values such as freedom,

---

[4]   Among a voluminous literature, see: Christopher Ely, *This Meager Nature: Landscape and National Identity in Imperial Russia* (De Kalb: Northern Illinois University Press, 2002); R.J.B. Bosworth, "The Touring Club Italiano and the Nationalization of the Italian Bourgeoisie," *European History Quarterly* 27/3 (1997): pp. 371–410; Orvar Löfgren, "Know Your Country: A Comparative Perspective on Tourism and Nation Building in Sweden," in Shelley Baranowski and Ellen Furlough (eds), *Being Elsewhere: Tourism, Consumer Culture and Identity in Modern Europe and North America* (Ann Arbor: University of Michigan Press, 2001), pp. 137–54; Alexander Vari, "From Friends of Nature to Tourist-Soldiers: Nation Building and Tourism in Hungary, 1873–1914," in Anne E. Gorush and Diane P. Koenker (eds), *Turizm: The Russian and East European Tourist under Capitalism and Socialism* (Ithaca: Cornell University Press, 2006), pp. 64–81; Marguerite Schaffer, *See America First: Tourism and National Identity, 1880–1940* (Washington, DC: Smithsonian Institution Press, 2001).

[5]   Claude Reichler, *La découverte des Alpes et la question du paysage* (Genève: Georg Editeur, 2002).

democracy, peace, harmony, happiness, and simplicity. The "helvetism" movement reinforced this intellectual trend. Consumption of the Alps through tourism further bolstered the political and social idea of alpine terrain as both the foundation for and unifying force behind the Confederation while at the same time legitimizing the region as a universal cradle of egalitarian virtues. Thus, the politicization of this alpine space contained the germs of a unique Swiss identity, a "*Sonderfall*" that could stand as a worthy example for the rest of the world.[6]

As the Swiss Alps were transformed into a symbol, they simultaneously began to generate an emotional response. Alpine space and Swiss territory grew increasingly linked.[7] The Swiss people self-identified with the Alps and, reciprocally, alpine tourism took on distinctive Swiss features.[8] Therefore, we must question why the alpine tourist model found in its Swiss referent, besides the political, symbolic, and aesthetic parameters that were already attached to it, the economic and technical anchorage points that explain, during the nineteenth century, its development and its widespread distribution.

Fully explaining the spread of a regional "playground"[9] to the wide world requires that attention be paid to the totality of the actors involved. We must not only study the "builders" (entrepreneurs, financiers, employees, innkeepers, guides, politicians) and the "inspirers" (artists, painters, writers, philosophers, authors, scientists, historians, journalists) but also those who utilized alpine space such as mountaineers, scientists, hikers, tourists, students, sportsmen, and patients. If alpine tourism led to an "alpinization" of tourism, it is important to examine the process broadly, including both distribution channels and modalities.

In this chapter, particular attention will be paid to three specific moments in this process. The first section examines the invention of the Alps as a tourist site, a period when summits and altitude were explicitly celebrated. The second section traces how the invention of the Alps as tourist site was so intimately tied to its Helvetic frame. The third, and final, section illustrates the mechanisms that allowed for the widespread dissemination of this model worldwide.

---

[6]   Oliver Zimmer, "In Search of Natural Identity: Alpine Landscape and the Reconstruction of the Swiss Nation," *Comparative Studies in Society and History* 40/4 (October 1998): pp. 637–65.

[7]   François Walter, "La montagne des Suisses. Invention et usage d'une représentation paysagère (XVIIIe–XXe siècles)," *Études rurales* 30/121–4 (1991): pp. 91–107.

[8]   Marc Boyer, "Les Alpes et le tourisme," *Histoire des Alpes* 9 (2004): pp. 24–7.

[9]   Leslie Stephen, *The Playground of Europe* (London: Fredonia Books, 1871, 2004).

The Tourist Invention of the Alps: Making Altitude Multifunctional

The emergence of an alpine tourist ideal largely rested on an almost obsessive search for new heights. This pursuit has little equivalent in human history, leading some to suggest that the conquest of the highest summit in the Alps by Horace-Bénédict de Saussure represented a new chapter in the evolution of society.[10] Already celebrated by scientists such as Johann-Jakob Scheuchzer[11] and Albert de Haller, and subsequently popularized by Jean-Jacques Rousseau, the Alps were recognized globally as a unified geographic space. More than this, they elevated those who climbed them, both literally and spiritually. The individual could find fulfillment in the mountains, where everything seemed to fall into perspective and man could discover all that really matters. Much more than a simple playground, although they were that too, the peaks helped make the sick well and they revitalized the spirit.[12]

Yet summit conquests also demonstrated the advantages of a meritocratic hierarchy, illustrating the benefits of effort and calculation. Nothing more clearly showed the success of such a civilization. From a nineteenth-century perspective, a successful climb symbolized man's ability to dominate nature, just as he did during the concurrent process of industrialization. Alpine ascents vindicated faith in progress and science, as well as a belief in the power of technology. Alpinists clearly demonstrated the strength of positive values and mountains offered a clear reference point with which to judge the success of human endeavor. To conquer new heights, one had to call upon all available resources, whether political, economic, financial, technological, social, or cultural, assuring that positive results reflected on civilization as a whole.

Alpine tourism represented a convergence of a set of needs, expectations, experiences, certainties, and hopes that together helped convert the Alps into a tourist product. This brand of tourism required that mountains could be dominated while also assigning them attributes that rendered them perfectly consumable. The result was a process whereby a certain number of appropriate economic supports and technical arrangements were introduced to realize

---

[10]   In particular, see: Philippe Joutard, *L'invention du Mont-Blanc* (Paris: Gallimard, Julliard, 1986) and Nicolas Giudici, *La philosophie du Mont Blanc: De l'alpinisme à l'économie immatérielle* (Paris: Grasset, 2000).

[11]   Simona Boscani-Leoni, "Johann Jakob Scheuchzer (1672–1733) et la découverte des Alpes: Les *itinera alpina*," in Christiane Demeulenaere (ed.), *Explorations et voyages scientifiques de l'antiquité à nos jours* (Paris: Comité des travaux historiques et scientifiques, 2008), pp. 81–100.

[12]   Jon Mathieu and Simona Boscani Leoni (eds), *Les Alpes!: Pour une histoire de la perception européenne depuis la Renaissance* (Bern: Peter Lang, 2005).

demand while also assuring future expansion. From the second half of the nineteenth century, a number of material changes were introduced to allow for just such development:

- the introduction of technological innovations such as mountain railroads, rack-trains, funicular railways, railway tunnels, cable cars, elevators, and so forth;
- the construction of luxury mountaintop hotels that were impressive both technologically and in terms of taste, comfort, and sophistication;
- the application of medical knowledge to the mountains through the development of high altitude sanatoriums featuring treatments such as aerotherapy and heliotherapy, both of which contributed to a growing cult of fresh air, as well as to much older remedies involving the use of water such as thermalism;
- the further introduction of mountain sports such as climbing, hiking, skiing, and sledding in order to further transform the Alps into a mountain playground filled with fun and excitement;
- the creation of landscapes designed to enhance the beauty of the mountain setting, such as panoramic viewpoints and carefully signed scenic vistas, by clearly telling visitors where to look for the most spectacular views.

Put another way, Alpine tourism is a system comprised of various constituent parts—a notion that has sparked numerous studies and commentaries.[13] To comprehend it, one must understand the composition of the system itself and a system cannot be reduced to a single object. Each part only makes sense in relation to its constituent parts. Even public acceptance demands that each component work together. It follows that the technological system of alpine tourism is inseparable from the social, administrative, human, organizational, political, and aesthetic devices that mold it. In this respect, Thomas Hughes speaks about socio-technical systems.[14] In a similar vein a system comprises many components that interact and evolve based on constraints related to devices, but also to actions, which can depend on choices and which give a style or a

---

13   With regard to the railway system, see; François Caron, "La naissance d'un système technique à grande échelle: Le chemin de fer en France (1832–1870)," *Annales: Histoire, Sciences Sociales* 53/4–5 (1998): pp. 859–85; and concerning the electrical system: Thomas Hughes, *Networks of Power: Electrification in Western Society, 1880–1930* (Baltimore: Johns Hopkins University Press, 1993).

14   Thomas Hughes, "L'histoire comme système en évolution," *Annales: Histoire, Sciences Sociales* 53/4–5 (1998): pp. 839–57.

profile to a particular system. In fact, this concept of system makes it possible to understand how these multiple components can hold together and give a direction to the disseminated product. In the case of the tourist system, one can characterize these constituents in the following way:

- technical constituents relating to the construction and operation of transportation networks (road, railway, maritime, air), to urban developments (esplanades, parks, walkways), to the organization of attractions (museums, ski lifts, casinos, theatres), to the establishment of the reception infrastructures (hotels, boarding houses, restaurants, etc);
- economic constituents relating to the creation and the organization of travel agencies and tour operators in the development of an integrated, coherent, and effective offering for tourist. They also relate to the sale of the tourist product and the financial consequences that it implies in terms of flows and liquidities;
- political constituents relating to the role of the communities (states, regions, municipalities) in the definition of a tourist policy and to the share left to private initiatives in the construction and the operation of activities;
- professional constituents relating to the creation of a formal, certified, recognized, and transmissible tourist expertise (installation of hotel schools or tourism schools, professionalization of the functions and trades);
- cultural constituents relating to information and promotion through the publication of travel guides, tourist folders, and the opening of tourist offices entitled to inform the public about the existence of the product, its quality, its price, its accessibility, and its availability;
- symbolic or psychological constituents relating to the development of an image or the representation of the product suitable to associate it with a certain form of tourism, with reaching certain consumer sensitivities or creating needs. This data is summarized beautifully by film director Daniel Schmid who associates tourism with "the invention of paradise" or with Mediterranean Club which promises the embodiment of "utopia."[15]

This list, although far from exhaustive, illustrates the extraordinary complexity of the development of a tourist region. Yet the story is even more complicated as a result of the expectations expressed by both users and consumers—a reality

---

[15] Peter Christian Bener and Daniel Schmid, *Die Erfindung von Paradies* (Zurich: Beobachter, 1983) and Gilbert Trigano, "Consommation de loisir et nouvelle convivialité," *Temps Libre* 1 (1980): p. 83.

that is difficult to measure or fully understand. The world of "desire" is linked to multiple considerations such as changes in taste, transformation of consumption patterns, and behavior modifications.[16] In the case of alpine tourism, these configurations can prove to be extremely variable, making the system highly unstable. From this perspective, it may be misleading to speak of a "tourist model" because doing so fails to acknowledge the particularities of individual cases. The attraction of the Alps as a tourist environment utilizes images that are forever evolving because they are altered by the ever-changing mountains themselves as well as by shifting ideas about space and man's emotional relationship to the landscape. If the development of tourist places is bound up with emotional, cultural, and social vectors, so too, such spots (to say nothing of areas trying to develop a tourist following) utilize a variety of instruments of dissemination that take into account their geographic and economic situation, their traditions, as well as the creativity of the publicity agents involved in marketing. This is to say that a tourist system is carrying on several models over the long term, not necessarily complementary, but not at all contradictory. Thus, futuristic or avant-garde ski areas, such as appeared after 1960 in the French Alps at Avoriaz and Morzine or in the Alpes Valaisannes at Thyon 2000, endeavor to domesticate the landscape and the consumer, while offering a tourism free of any constraint. In contrast, several other results offer a symbiosis between tourism and tradition, for example Zermatt or Lauterbrunnen. Such facilities endeavor to ally modernistic style with the construction of cable railways and residential mountain chalets, while at the same time preserving a pronounced village-like character, even if that means relying on imagined authenticity. From this point of view, the essence of alpine tourism—and tourism in general—is to create and recreate a specificity that allows the illusion of either traditional or modern attractions. Therefore, we cannot say that there was ever a single "invention of the Alps," but rather there is a continual process of invention and reinvention of various models within a vast playground. Within the alpine arc, imitation is but one process that allows the perpetuation of tourism, even as it is central to more widespread development. To a large degree, imitation kills the creativity or, in any case, reduces it.

Another characteristic is associated with the touristic operation of alpine playgrounds: "pluriactivity" or the capacity of a space to be adapted to changing situations through the above-mentioned transformations. Its plasticity strengthens its highly attractive potential. This capacity of adaptation and creativity can be seen in the alpine world in many ways. The renewal of ideas

---

[16] I have developed these points more fully elsewhere. See: "Storia del turismo e storia economica: considerazioni metodologiche ed epistemologiche," in Andrea Leonardi and Hans Heiss (eds), *Tourismus und Entwicklung im Alpenraum, 18–20. Jh.* (Innsbruck: Studien Verlag, 2003), pp. 23–41.

and the rebirth of initiatives are constant: the extension of the season, the diversification of destinations, the exploration of new tourist activities assures the rekindling of the process.[17]

It is true that the dramatic growth of tourist products over the long term, combined with the top-down effort of tourism developers, resulted in a homogenization and a standardization of tourism. "Fordist" mass tourism results in the unlimited reproduction of an accessible product to the largest possible clientele. However, at the same time, the tendency toward sameness is offset by an equally powerful move toward distinctiveness and individual site recognition. Amid homogenization is found not only the will of producers to attract legions of product-hungry tourists, but also the possibility of attracting new tourists through the introduction of new attractions. Thus, the appearance of "fun" sled-related sports re-energized many winter resorts, which, by the 1980s, had begun to suffer as a new generation grew less interested in their parents' "traditional" ski holiday. The tourist development cycle follows a logic that was already in place during the nineteenth century. It rests on the re-appropriation of distinctiveness by whole sectors of the industry. If "inventing the consumer" requires the tourist promoters' continuous effort, the challenge involved rests on the convergence of, on the one hand, the peculiarity of the consumer, and, on the other hand, the similarities between tourists. Tourism promoters must assume that tourists are unique while at the same time reproducing them on a mass scale—such is the essence of tourist development.

If tourism developers have flexibility for innovation and creativity, the tourist is not necessarily a passive being. Far from it. The image of a herd of bleating tourists marks virtually all of the tourism literature and continues to concern scholars. The stereotype of the "idiot tourist"[18] consuming tourist products in a virtual state of unconsciousness is usually contrasted with the "true" traveler who truly seeks to understand the ins and outs of the places she visits. The birth of the tourist industry in the nineteenth century simply amplified an already latent phenomenon in much older forms of travel. To a certain extent, this view is based on an infantilization of the consumer, yet many examples show that consumers are every bit as influential as are producers. Indeed, we might fairly suggest that the consumer is even more demanding, capricious, innovative, and unconstrained than are those responsible for creating tourist sites. Perhaps most notably, tourists are apt to be more sensitive to environmental impact or to the

---

[17]   Readers interested in exploring many more specific examples should consult: Laurent Tissot, *Naissance d'une industrie touristique: Les Anglais et la Suisse au XIXe siècle* (Lausanne: Editions Payot, 2000).

[18]   For more on this subject, see the work of the sociologist Jean-Didier Urbain, *L'idiot du voyage: Histoires de touristes* (Paris: Editions Payot, 1993).

impact of tourism on native cultures than are tourism developers. Many tourists are well aware of the often predatory and destructive nature of the tourist industry and they increasingly demand newer forms of leisure travel that leave behind a smaller footprint. "Ethical tourism" or "soft tourism," to limit ourselves to two recent examples, suggest a redefinition of the relationship between hosts and guests, a redefinition that imposes entirely new criteria on developers, on tourists, and on tourist practices.

Nationalization of the Alpine Model: Switzerland as a Privileged Space of High Grounds

The identification of the Swiss alpine space with the alpine tourist model took place in confused conditions, largely because the operation of mountain tourism was established outside of the Helvetic Confederation. France, Italy, Austria, Germany, and Slovenia all participated to a greater or lesser extent in the process of alpine tourist development. If alpine tourism was actually international from the start, how should we understand the emergence of a Swiss model, which subsequently pioneered alpine tourism across the tourist map? I have already outlined the generic basis on which alpine tourism was able to take off and develop itself. Pursuing this analysis further, Marc Boyer sees in Switzerland a space where the characteristics of the alpine were most pronounced. It was here that emotional attachments were the strongest, the attractions the liveliest, and experiences the most easily replicated. Boyer insists on four elements that played an essential role in Switzerland's election:

- the verticality criterion in its spatial dimension: in other words, "the higher or the deeper the place is, the more it is worth visiting." Guides published during the nineteenth century primarily focus on accurately indicating the height of summits, depths of gorges, heights of bell towers, etc.;
- the verticality criterion in its temporal dimension: the more ancient the site, the more "ecstasy" experienced by the tourist. The search for the origins of the world deeply marked the rediscovery of the Alps because the discovery of fossils and rock bands offered a window into the beginning of the world;
- the "Rousseauist" criterion involving a search for inner peace and the comfort of the "womb." Tourists search for happiness in the admiration of nature and its plenitude, finding both a source of pacification and serenity;

- the "anecdotal" criterion. The Swiss Alps abound in stories which tourists are fond of—most notably that of Guillaume Tell, hero of freedom, independence, and enfranchisement.[19]

By emphasizing the ideal type represented by the Helvetic alpine territory, Boyer draws attention to the spectacular, emotional elements likely to attract the tourist in her frantic search for mountains. In other words, in the greater history of tourism, Switzerland had the best assets. Still, nothing could be left to chance. Predisposition is not itself sufficient; simply having resources is not always enough. The development process, shaped by factors that extend beyond geographic and natural dimensions, is a determining factor as well. Let me describe several points that appear to be especially significant.

Welcome Structures

Tourists must find places to welcome them to a region, most notably hotels. In the case under discussion, the great luxury hotels of La Belle Époque played a particularly important role, standing as emblems of mass alpine tourism.[20] The construction of new establishments was first visible from the 1830s but expanded dramatically in the last third of the nineteenth century—so much so that by the eve of World War I, in certain regions at least, there was a relative over abundance of luxury accommodations, brought about by an impressive level of entrepreneurial investment.[21] These structures assumed a recognizable profile in both their monumentality and architectural style. Although grand hotels developed elsewhere, a product of larger transnational tourist trends, they nevertheless contributed significantly to the marketing of Swiss alpine territories. Such buildings profoundly alter the landscape on which they are established, bringing about completely new cityscapes and landscapes, while also redefining more isolated terrain such as mountainsides or alpine summits.

---

[19]   Boyer, "Les Alpes et le tourisme," p. 26 and also *Histoire de l'invention du tourisme, XVIe-XIXe siècles* (Tour d'Aigues: Editions de l'Aube, 2000), p. 135.

[20]   Roland Fluckiger-Seiler, *Hotel Traüme zwischen Gletschern und Palmen: Schweizer Tourismus und Hotelbau 1830-1930* (Baden: Hier + Jetzt, 2001) and also *Hotelpaläste: Zwischen Traum und Wirklichkeit: Schweizer Tourismus und Hotelbau, 1830-1920* (Baden: Hier + Jetzt, 2003).

[21]   Peter Püntener, "Der Beitrag des Fremdenverkehrs zur Entwicklung der Schweizer Wirtschaft (1850-1913)" in Andreas Ernst, Thomas Gerlach, Patrick Halbeisen, Bettina Heintz, and Margrit Müller (eds), *Kontinuität und Krise: Sozialer Wandel als Lernprozess* (Zürich: Chronos, 1994), pp. 51-60, p. 57.

Technological Aspects

The Swiss alpine model also features very high technological demands. Continuing with the example of the hotel business, from the start, luxury hotels needed to feature the latest inventions, competing to display ingenuity and boldness, in terms of both technology and design. Thus, luxury hotels were among the first to introduce electric lighting, hot water, improved sanitary facilities, elevators, and other such innovations. Incessant improvement testifies to the concern of innkeepers to be leaders in the process of modernization. Even the design of buildings and the design of interior spaces reflect an obsessive need to anticipate consumers' needs, creating a universe free of everyday constraints. Collectively, the effort is to assure control of time, places, and practices while also guaranteeing total safety with regard to a mountainous environment that might otherwise be perceived as threatening.

The construction of mountain roadways and tunnels, an endeavor so bold that it helped to advertise the accessibility of formally horrifying places, reflects the same concerns. Indeed, the tourist exploitation of the Swiss Alps resulted in technological knowledge that has influenced roadway construction since the 1880s. The drilling of the Saint-Gothard, Simplon, and Lötschberg tunnels contributed to the consolidation of this as a center of excellence in mastering and developing technologies adapted to mountainous regions.[22]

Politico-Institutional Aspects

In Switzerland, as in most places, tourism developed without any state intervention during the nineteenth century. Even if local development regulations sometimes harmonized well with private initiatives to improve tourism growth, public support for such development was minimal. No official organization actively considered the contribution of tourism to regional or national economies and there was little political support for more coordinated action on a development plan. Nevertheless, as more people recognized that tourism might actively contribute to economic growth, political attitudes gradually shifted beginning in the last quarter of the nineteenth century. In an effort to supplement agricultural earnings, tourist development was gradually promoted as an important element of general development policy. Although Swiss developments pale in comparison with efforts undertaken

---

[22] Laurent Tissot, "La philosophie du Saint-Gothard ou la naissance d'un profil touristique alpin" in *Bollettino storico della Svizzera Italiana*, forthcoming.

in the Tyrolean Alps, for example, the idea gradually took hold that tourism might slow rural depopulation.[23] In the absence of a classic industrial economy, tourism represents a new form of industry capable of creating jobs and raising revenue—a fact made more important as skill level requirements and salaries dropped steadily in urban areas.

Increased support for tourism development resulted in an increase in vocational training as illustrated by the creation of the Lausanne Hotel School in 1893.[24] In this area, professional associations, in particular the Swiss Society of Hotels, played a critical role. The professionalization and certification of tourism-related careers helped to strengthen development activities that were increasingly listed in economic studies as a separate sector with its own rules, its own market, its own dynamism, and its own constraints.

Symbolic Aspects

With tourist symbolism, we encounter the vector by which an image of the Swiss Alps was rapidly disseminated to the wider world through advertising campaigns and effective marketing. Tourism is intimately bound to the creation of dream worlds. The principle challenge, then, is to recognize and understand the development of the myths that founded a separate alpine identity. This symbolism had a broad reach and conveyed an image of both Switzerland and the Swiss to the wider world. That part of this image involved technological innovation, allowing for a melding of modernity and tradition, only added to the appeal, joining further substance to the idea of Swiss tourism.[25] Advertising campaigns combined to form a virtual "carousel" of images, both traditional and modern: bridges, tunnels, railroads, and electricity, were merged with lugers, skiers, fishermen, natives in traditional costume, twinkling lakes, customary homes, churches, and so on.[26] This telescoping might make one's head spin, but it is why Switzerland is so attractive to such diverse constituents. Together, those elements that make the mountain appealing combine to create a coherent system

---

23   Compare with Laurent Tissot, "Tourism in Austria and in Switzerland: Models of Development and Crises 1880–1960," in Timo Myllyntaus (ed.), *European Crises and Restructuring in History: Experiences of Small Countries* (St. Katharinen: Scripta Mercaturae Verlag 1998), pp. 285–302.

24   Philippe Gindraux, *L'art et la manière: L'école hôtelière de Lausanne: 100 ans d'existence* (Lausanne: Editions Payot, 1993).

25   *Rêves de voyages: Anton Reckziegel (1865–1935). Pionnier de la publicité touristique* (Lausanne: Musée historique de Lausanne, 1999).

26   Guy P. Marchal and Aram Mattioli (eds), *La Suisse imaginée: Bricolage d'une identité nationale* (Zurich: Chronos, 1991).

which places the mountain in the natural order of things from the second half of the nineteenth century: power, knowledge, hierarchy, strength, regeneration, and peace.

Diplomatic Aspects

The foundation of the Swiss Federal State in 1848 contributed to a large-scale movement that generated institutional, political, economic, and symbolic profits. By joining the chorus of nations, Switzerland not only attained greater international legitimacy, it was also thrown into sharper contrast with other places, appearing more unique and recognizable by comparison.[27] Beyond maintaining political independence or defending its national interests, Swiss diplomatic action was particularly focused on showcasing national distinctiveness during the second half of the nineteenth century.

Little by little, diplomatic initiatives defined the image of Switzerland as a distinct nation-state. The notion that Switzerland represented a "*Sonderfall*" supported the idea of the country as an excellent tourist destination. Promoting this difference represented a kind of warfare by other means, defining Swiss independence using different tools than were traditionally drawn upon during major power conflicts. If Europe still represented a "battlefield," the presence of a "playground" at the center assured that Swiss tourism provided a safe harbor away from international confrontations and sheltered from nationalist reflexes. In this context, the hotel business came to play a fundamental role as a meeting place, as a place of exchange, and as a diplomatic space.[28]

Universalization of the Alpine Tourist Model

Far from limited to its place of birth, Helvetic-style tourism quickly spread beyond Swiss borders. It is safe to say that from the middle of the nineteenth century there was an "alpinization" of tourism that made altitude a primary reference point. The universalization of this tourist model rested on several elements, which, for lack of substantial research on the subject, remain difficult to measure precisely. The German geographer Irmfried Siedentop has pointed

---

[27] Urs Altermatt, Catherine Bosshart-Pfluger and Albert Tanner, *Die Konstruktion einer Nation: Nation und Nationalisierung in der Schweiz, 18.-20. Jahrhundert* (Zürich: Chronos, 1998).

[28] Bertrand Muller, "Construire l'événement: hôtellerie de luxe et diplomatie: Le Beau-Rivage Palace et la Conférence de Lausanne de 1922–1923," in Nadja Maillard (ed.), *Beau-Rivage Palace* (Gollion: Infolio, 2008), pp. 116–28.

to 116 areas in the world with the "Swiss" label.[29] They are mainly situated in Germany. In this process, various modalities played a role. In an illuminating article, François Walter considers graphic arts and photography to be responsible for this "astonishing spreading."[30] But this diffusion of images goes together with a vaster movement that operates in the end of the eighteenth century and, to a greater extent, during the first three decades of the nineteenth century.

We can distinguish three of them, each of which enjoyed particular periods of intense reproduction. The first modality involved both the climbers and climbing; in essence, climbers and their sport made mountains seem both accessible and controllable, without necessarily making alpine areas seem corrupted. The second modality grew from the impact of tourist promoters—railroad companies, travel agencies, development officers, and editors of travel guides among others—who generated reams of advertising material and distributed it on a global scale. These efforts assured that the alpine model was relentlessly in the public eye and that it was therefore always topical. The third modality involved the spread of hotel practices where a focus on accommodation and reception was soon associated both with alpine hotel architecture and with the model of hotel management utilized in Swiss resorts.

This distinction may seem arbitrary insofar as, as I have just shown, it was the *combination* of numerous elements that was central to the successful construction and assertion of the alpine tourist model. Without any real hierarchies, it falls within the scope of the functioning of a socio-technical system to give additional roles to the various actors involved. This organizational overlap does not imply the idea of absolutes. The global system conditions the emergence of sub-systems because a particular tourist profile can emphasize certain activities instead of others, on certain grounds to the detriment of others, on certain consumers instead of others, on certain promoters to the detriment of others. In this respect, the construction of tourism is parallel to that of a tourist market where competitors are confronted, not only at the national level, but also at the regional as well as local levels. However, in every case, competition is based on the dissemination of a generic model that gains support by adapting to more localized contexts.

Although difficult to fully quantify its real impact, it is imperative to consider the major role of mountaineering in the spread of the alpine model. This

---

[29] Irmfried Siedentop, "Die Schweizen—eine fremdenverkehrsgeographie Dokumentation," *Zeitschrift für Wirtschaftsgeographie* 28 (1984): pp. 126–30. In a former article, he counted 90 places. Irmfried Siedentop, "Die geographische Verbreitung der Schweiz," *Geographica Helvetica* 1 (1977): pp. 33–43.

[30] François Walter, "La montagne alpine: Un dispositif esthétique et idéologique à l'échelle de l'Europe," *Revue d'histoire moderne et contemporaine* 51/2 (2005): pp. 64–87, at p. 73.

practice gained significant stature from the 1830s under the influence of British mountaineers who, by using the Alps as their privileged playground, established a true model of action that, gradually, inspired mountaineers in other countries. Mountaineering corresponded to the Victorian mentality of "self help" which bourgeois elites emphasized as a means of furthering the industrial revolution and which stressed work, perseverance, self-abnegation, and precision.[31] In fact, even if inspired by these ideas, the sport remained in British hands for only a few years. That alpine clubs were quickly established in most European countries illustrates an infatuation that spread beyond national borders and which soon exploited, little by little, all that the Alps could offer in terms of ascents. In England, the Alpine Club was created in 1857. It was followed by the Austrian Alpine Club (1862), the Swiss Alpine Club (April 1863), the Italian Alpine Club (October 1863), the German Alpine Club (1869), the French Alpine Club (1874), and the list then extended to new European countries, as well as to places outside of Europe.[32] Even so, it would still be too early to speak about a globalization of mountaineering because the sport functioned primarily to express strong nationalist feeling, a fact made clear by the need to display national flags on alpine summits or by the importance assigned by national leaders to being "first" atop mountain peaks. Yet, at the same time, the fact that the sport was so quickly made an important means of national expression illustrates the widespread and important role of mountaineering.

Despite being so associated with nationalism, the institutionalization of the sport in European life assured that it was soon disseminated to a larger and larger public. The first years in which mountaineering formed into a coherent sport, between 1830 and 1860, are central to the recognition of the Alps as a generic tourism model. Generally speaking, the mountaineers' expectations became confused with those of mountain-seeking tourists. A multimedia stage show developed by Albert Smith in 1852 and 1853 on his successful ascent of Mont Blanc is exemplary in this respect. The show enjoyed enormous success. Two hundred thousand people attended the production, which became one of London's most popular attractions.[33] Travel guides, which appeared everywhere

---

[31]   Olivier Hoibian (ed.), *L'invention de l'alpinisme: La montagne et l'affirmation de la bourgeoisie cultivée (1786–1914)* (Paris: Belin, 2008), and Claudio Ambrosi, Michael Wedeking (eds), *L'invenzione di un cosmo borghese: Valori soziali e simboli culturali dell'alpinismo nei scoli XIXe et XXe* (Trento: Museo Storico, 2000).

[32]   Dominique Lejeune, *Les 'Alpinistes' en France (1875–1919)* (Paris: Éditions du Comité des travaux historiques et scientifiques, 1988), p. 22.

[33]   Peter H. Hansen, "Albert Smith, the Alpine Club, and the Invention of Mountaineering in mid-Victorian Britain," *Journal of British Studies* 34 (July 1995): pp. 300–324.

in Europe during the period, also fueled "alpine mania." The proliferation of this literature stimulated curiosity, increased the desire to see specific sites/sights, and helped make alpine tourism a mass phenomenon.[34] Gradually, the desire to see the Alps infected a broader and broader population.

The dramatic spread of mountaineering did not stop the creation of additional behavioral models, each related both to specific actors but also to the larger practice of climbing. As ordinary tourists increasingly sought to consume alpine spaces, mountaineers, still confined to exclusive and elitist circles, continued to exercise a considerable influence on the public mind. By successive adaptation, alpinists spread a vision of a territory to be cherished, to be wandered, and to be explored through various other means and other forms. The repercussions of this process are very perceptible, even as the original mountaineering model merged into a formless mass in which mountains more or less became an ordinary consumer good.

One can easily understand why mountaineering underwent an important evolution during the last third of the nineteenth century. Bored with their old alpine playground, now overrun with an increasing number of tourists who diminished the apparent challenge of the Alps, many mountaineers sought more challenging, higher, and more technical summits. Expeditions traveled to the Pyrenees, to the Caucasus, to the Himalaya, and to the mountains of the Americas.[35] Yet these new destinations were explored using the same models and approaches developed in the Alps. In other words, mountaineers carried a model with them that was created in a space with which they no longer associated themselves. By utilizing other mountainous regions, these climbers felt that they could save the purity of the alpine model.

The extension of mountaineering beyond the Alps was not simply a product of climbers seeking new challenges but also reflected a growing mountaineering literature published in both mass media outlets such as newspapers and magazines as well as in more specialized alpine guidebooks and climb narratives. All of these works celebrated a very active and very cosmopolitan worldview while, at the same time, constantly referring back to the alpine matrix as a way of establishing new trends and developments. With the proliferation of climbing clubs, the development of a climbing literature perpetually reiterated recognition of the Alps as original space. In 1892, the New Zealand Alpine Club was created, modeled on the English Alpine Club. Enthusiasts created the Canadian Alpine Club in 1906. Other clubs followed around the world.

---

[34] Tissot, *Naissance d'une industrie touristique*, p. 28 et sq.

[35] Compare with Peter Hansen, "Confetti of Empire: The Conquest of Everest in Nepal, India, Britain and New Zealand," *Comparative Studies in Society and History* 42/3 (2000): pp. 307–32.

Along these lines, professional mountain guides played one of the most important roles in disseminating the alpine model. Guides (especially those from Switzerland and Austria) were significant in several mountainous regions, clearly showing the strength of the alpine matrix in the sensibilities of mountaineers. While the history of these guides is relatively well known, grey areas remain in the study of their influence on the internationalization of the Alps.[36] The extension of mountaineering territories was largely made with the cooperation of alpine mountain guides. Great mountain guides such as Peter Taugwalder worked in other regions and provided developers in these areas with expertise. Canada, especially the Rocky Mountains and the Selkirks, is an excellent example. The opening of the Canadian Pacific Railway in 1885 first drew attention to these mountains and generated the first significant tourist promotion of the area. Very quickly, tourism developers published advertising leaflets and other travel guidebooks that were nearly identical to those written about the Alps.[37] To further promote the Rockies and the Selkirks, the Canadian Pacific Railway Company invited two mountain guides from Interlaken in Switzerland. The guides were a hit, strolling around in traditional costumes and posing for photographers. John Marsh estimates that they played an invaluable role in creating a "desire for the mountain" in Canada.[38] Over the next 30 years, the arrival of additional Swiss guides continued to strengthen the influence of the alpine model on the conquest of the Rockies—a trend further solidified by the continuing professionalization of the tour guiding profession in Switzerland. The arrival of Swiss guides, even if only for short periods, assured that a whole "alpine science" was imposed on areas that might otherwise have developed their own approach to the utilization of mountain resources and tourism development. A similar process is apparent in the Rocky Mountains of the United States.[39]

Further systematic research of the role played by mountain guides in the global spread of alpine tourism would be fruitful. However, the alpinization of tourism cannot solely be explained by the efforts of far-traveling Swiss guides, the process took place at other levels as well.

---

[36] Among a few titles, Thomas Antonietti, *Bauern, Bergführer, Hoteliers: Fremdenverkehr und Bauernkultur: Zermatt und Aletsch 1850–1950* (Baden: Hier + Jetzt, 2002) and Bellwald Werner, *Ins Feld und Firn: Bergführer und Bergsteiger in Geschichte und Gegenwart* (Kippel: Lötschentaler Museum, 1994).

[37] E.J. Hart, *The Selling of Canada: The CPR and the Beginning of Canadian Tourism* (Banff: Altitude Publications, 1983).

[38] John Marsh, "The Rocky and Selkirk Mountains and the Swiss Connection 1885–1914," *Annals of Tourism Research* 12/4 (1985): pp. 417–33.

[39] "Mountain Vacations in North America West," *Expedia.com*. Available online at: http://www.expedia.com/daily/vacations/mountain/west.asp [accessed September 13, 2009].

Tourism promoters, in the broad sense of the term, also facilitated the spread of the Swiss model. In commercial terms, the Swiss model was imitated in an effort by mountain areas to better compete with one another. A careful study of the introduction of winter tourism in France at the end of the nineteenth century shows that tourism developers made constant reference to Swiss efforts in terms of transport, hospitality, lodging, and leisure activities.[40] In the Pyrenees, Jean-Raoul Paul, the director of the Compagnie du Midi, which handled the development of winter sports, declared the need to "Swissify" the Pyrenees.[41] Efforts in Chile follow a similar path. During the 1920s, the Chilean National Railways undertook a promotional program that celebrated the "Chilean Alps."[42] In Argentina, the process was the same.[43]

The "alpinization" of tourism is also perceptible in terms of architecture. Ever since the National Exhibition held in Geneva in 1896, at which visitors were filled with admiration for the "Swiss Village" which was the high point of the event, the chalet has represented an important symbolic element of the Swiss identity.[44] The Swiss chalet had a long history before it became a ubiquitous Helvetic trademark. This type of structure took hold during the nineteenth century and continues to be built in mountain centers around the world; some entrepreneurs even advocated chalet construction as an aesthetically pleasing addition to any garden. Ultimately, the worldwide proliferation of

---

[40]   Bertrand Larique, "L'économie du tourisme en France des années 1890 à la veille de la Seconde Guerre mondiale. Organisation et développement d'un secteur socio-économique" (Ph.D. diss., Université de Bordeaux, 2006), p. 208 et sq.

[41]   Christophe Bouneau, "La construction et les mutations de l'économie touristique pyrénéenne du milieu du 19ème siècle au second conflit mondial," in Laurent Tissot (ed.), *Development of a Tourist Industry in the 19th and 20th Centuries: International Perspectives* (Neuchâtel: Editions Alphil, 2003), pp. 127–44, p. 140 and "La politique touristique de la Compagnie du Midi entre 1852 et 1937," *Midi. Revue de sciences humaines et de littérature de la France du Sud* 3 (June 1987): pp. 77–87.

[42]   I would like to thank Rodrigo Booth for forwarding his not-yet-published article to me: "Turismo y representación del paisaje. Una mirada a la invención del sur de Chile en la *Guía del Veraneante* (1932–1962)."

[43]   Some aspects of the development of "Argentina's Little Switzerland" are developed in the work of Anahí Ballent and Adrián Gorelik, "País urbano o país rural: La modernización territorial y su crisis," in Alejandro Cattaruzza (ed.), *Crisis económica, avance del Estado e incertidumbre política (1930–1943)*, Tomo VII de la Nueva Historia Argentina (Buenos Aires: Sudamericana, 2001), pp. 143–200.

[44]   Bernard Crettaz, *Ah Dieu! Que la Suisse est jolie!* (Lausanne: École Polytechnique Fédérale de Lausanne, Département d'Architecture, Commission d'Information, 1997) and Jacques Gubler, "Le chalet à bâtons rompus: Conversation avec Serge Desarnaulds, poète," in Jacques Gubler, *Motions, émotions: Thèmes d'histoire et d'architecture* (Gollion: Infolio, 2003), pp. 130–48.

chalets represents a global marketing of Switzerland at home, a place of refuge for everyone.[45] To resume discussion of the Canadian Pacific Railway, the company constructed its flagship hotel, the Glacier House Hotel, in 1887, in an architectural style featuring design elements associated with Swiss chalets.[46] The company went even further to "Swissify" the Canadian mountains by recreating a Swiss village called Edelweiss in every detail. Built to welcome the Swiss mountain guides, the village consisted of six houses and was ready to receive occupants in 1911.[47] A similar effort to "Swissify" territory is found in Latvia where a whole tourist dynamic known as "Livonian Switzerland" was developed at the end of the nineteenth century in the current province of Vidzeme, formerly the south part of Livonia.[48] Although the space does little to remind one of the harshness of the Alps, travel guidebooks to the region celebrate the area's beautiful hills and valleys, suggesting that a difference in altitude, however small, still indicates alpine influence. The construction of several Swiss chalets adds to this identification.

To a great extent, the alpine seizure of this type of tourism originates in the spread of hotel management models. One can undoubtedly assert that the advent of hotel science largely originated from experiences realized within the framework of the alpine model. Great hotel chains such as Seiler, Badrupp, and Ritz quickly imposed themselves as model hotels, providing patrons with a higher quality gastronomic, but also architectural experience. With the institutionalization of education, the experience gained in these hotels found its way into textbooks that were, in turn, translated into several languages. Certain educators and popularizers of tourism, men such as Albert Junod and Jules Klopfenstein, helped to establish an approach to hotel training that was soon widespread. The École Hôtelière de Lausanne, established in 1893, was the first of its kind and it rests at the heart of this system. The school truly demonstrates international recognition of a "Swiss school" of hotel management.

---

[45] Compare with Michel Vernes, "Le chalet infidèle ou les dérives d'une architecture vertueuse et de son paysage de rêve," *Revue d'histoire du XIXe siècle* 32 (2006): pp. 111–36. This article is available online at: http://rh19.revues.org/index1099.html [accessed September 13, 2009].

[46] John Marsh, *A History of Glacier House and Nakimu Caves: Glacier National Park British Columbia* (Peterborough: Canadian Recreation Services, 1979).

[47] Roxroy West, "Swiss Guides and the Village of Edelweiss," *The Beaver* 310/1 (Summer 1979): pp. 50–53.

[48] C. Schulz, *Livlandische Schweiz* (ca. 1880).

Conclusion

With the invention of the Alps at the end of the eighteenth century, tourism was able to become a truly large-scale phenomenon that in turn prompted unexpected results. Although rooted in a specific geographic region and political territory, various actors and developments transformed alpine tourism into a globally recognized model that permeated activities using altitude as a development principle. The alpine model was easily applied in other places and could readily be used to promote successful economic and technical exploitation of mountainous areas. It simultaneously associates a mental construction gathering together political, philosophic, as well as cultural elements whose convergence amplifies the scope of alpine tourism. If the enjoyment of spectacular scenery remains the foundation of tourism in alpine areas, further study will better demonstrate how the various factors described in this article combined to create the Swiss character of mountain tourism. The simple outline provided here already offers a variety of avenues for future study. Although tourism is generally understood in terms of national identities and identification with specifically promoted places, the alpine model contributed dramatically to an internationalization and universal character of tourist forms. By becoming commonplace through access to a greater segment of the population, by showcasing technical expertise, by assuring the perpetual invention of new practices, by creating new jobs and professions, Swiss-style alpine tourism took hold far from its place of origin. Understanding the grammar of alpine tourism demands consideration of overlapping factors and uses that are, in turn, linked together by sometimes-contradictory logic.

Chapter 5

"Come to the Fair": Transgressing Boundaries in World's Fairs Tourism

Angela Schwarz

A Mental Journey into the World of World's Fairs

From the Great Exhibition of the Works of Industry of all Nations in 1851 onwards promoters hailed world's fairs as "meeting-places of nations,"[1] as "jubilé[s] des peoples,"[2] as "Welt- und Völkerfeste"[3] of a truly international character, or as great events showing "como todos se reunen."[4] Though doubts about the economic benefit of the exhibitions always sat uneasily alongside eulogies of the events' effect on human progress and world peace, the fairs' impact on developments in many other areas is firmly established. Some of the these developments impinge directly on the way they transformed tourism and the tourist industry.

First of all, fairs brought people, goods, technologies, ideas, and values together, and in so doing reflected an obsession with all-encompassing knowledge and a panoramic view of the world prevailing long into the twentieth century. In showcasing objects as well as people with their national, ethnic, social, and cultural identities, world's fairs initiated competition on a scale and with a public recognition hitherto unknown. Trying to come up with a proper term to describe the phenomenon, contemporaries could only fall back on the highest

---

[1]   William Elliot Griffis, "The Paris Exposition: Historical Aspects," *The Outlook* (November 10, 1900), p. 662.

[2]   François Ducuing, "Chronique," in François Ducuing (ed.), *L'Exposition Universelle de 1867 illustrée*, 31st installment, vol. 2 (August 19, 1867): p. 15. See as well François Ducuing, "Chronique," in François Ducuing (ed.), *L'Exposition Universelle de 1867 illustrée*, 4th installment, vol. 1 (1867), p. 63.

[3]   Anon., "Von der wiener Weltausstellung: Die feierliche Eröffnung der Weltausstellung," *Illustrirte Zeitung* 1560 (May 24, 1873), p. 387.

[4]   José Castro y Serrano, quoted in Jean-Louis Guereña, "España en Paris: Les Espagnols à l'Exposition Universelle de 1867," *Études Hispaniques* (University de Tours) 4 (1982): pp. 77–117, p. 79.

form of rivalry: war between nations. The international exhibitions, though, were perceived not as destructive wars, but as wars "of love, concord and affection."[5]

Secondly, to the world of the mid-nineteenth century, a world that was only just opening up travel and particularly foreign travel to a greater number of people, the universal expositions offered a unique experience: a visit to "the world" with a journey to just one place, just one city. In a way not surpassed until the second half of the twentieth century, fairs brought people face to face with a whole spectrum of national "types" and their idiosyncrasies, in many cases for the first time in their lives. At least right up to World War II, many people continued to see this journey as a special treat, full of new sights, sounds, and experiences, something to remember for a long time, if not for life. As the guide to the Exposition in Paris in 1867 put it: "One does not hesitate to cross all of Europe to come to a universal exposition. A complete family goes there. This journey is the treat of their lifetime."[6]

Thirdly, to an enterprising class of businessmen the international exhibitions ushered in the age of tourism as an industry.[7] It was the Great Exhibition in 1851 that enabled Thomas Cook to expand his operations to the national scale and to inaugurate the beginnings of the package holiday. It was the International Exhibitions in Paris in 1855 and 1867 that induced him to venture into foreign travel.[8] Cook was only the tip of the iceberg; individual railway and steamboat companies in Britain and on the continent rushed to advertise their special offers of the fastest or most comfortable journey to the exhibitions and to send forth their agents to ensnare would-be travelers.[9] But not only logistics suggested

---

[5] "Why Should Working Men Visit the Exhibition," in *Thomas Cook's Exhibition Herald and Excursion Advertiser* 1 (May 31, 1851), p. 2, quoted in Susan Barton, *Working-Class Organizations and Popular Tourism, 1840–1970* (Manchester: Manchester University Press, 2005), p. 50.

[6] "On n'hésite pas à traverser l'Europe pour venir à une Exposition universelle. Une famille entière se déplace. Ce voyage fera époque dans sa vie." *L'Exposition Universelle de 1867. Guide de l'exposant et du visiteur avec les documents officiels, un plan et une vue de l'Exposition* (Paris: Librairie Hachette et Cie, 1866), p. 13.

[7] Susan Barton has made out the origins of the package holiday in the arrangements for travels to the Great Exhibition, "a key development in popular tourism." See Barton, *Working-Class Organizations*, p. 41f.

[8] Compare with F.M.L. Thompson, *The Rise of Respectable Society: A Social History of Victorian Britain, 1830–1900* (London: Harvard University Press, 1988), p. 261f.

[9] A German visitor to the first exhibition in London began his description of this visit with a reference to this: "Schon in Aachen, noch mehr aber auf den Belgischen Stationsplätzen, tritt dem Reisenden die große Weltausstellung in allen möglichen Angeboten und Einladungen vor Augen. Riesige Plakate der verschiedenen Eisenbahn- und Dampfschiffahrtsgesellschaften, wovon eine mehr als die andere den kürzesten und billigsten

itself as profitable business. Accommodation, catering, and entertainment on the fair grounds and beyond were boosted when a city became host of such an event. The transformations these industries underwent in the process were closely connected either to arrangements at a previous fair or to local, regional or national forms of accommodation, catering, and entertainment.

It is undeniable that the universal exhibitions of the nineteenth and early twentieth century had a deep impact on the development of tourism. No other single event so effectively promoted mass tourism than international exhibitions. No other contributed so markedly to a specific tourist experience that went far beyond the typical national framework. No other contributed so much to the emergence of a European consumer culture, tourism being one of its main elements.[10] This chapter brings together the approaches and research of the history of world's fairs, nationalism, tourism, and consumerism, more often than not studied separately. As will be argued, despite the reality that the fairs involved considerable competition between either nations or host cities (at least until Chicago 1933 or arguably until New York 1939/40) to generate the most impressive and memorable event, the international exhibitions promoted a rapprochement and finally a synthesis of national styles on various levels of culture and consumerism.[11]

Going to the Fair: The Visitors

Although doubtful that the revenue from entrance fees would cover costs, the organizers of the first international exhibition quickly received a pleasant surprise. During the first three days after the opening, when tickets still cost as much as three pounds,[12] some 58,000 visitors strolled through the Crystal Palace

---

Weg verspricht, bedecken die Mauern, und viele Agenten drängen sich wetteifernd herbei, in jeder Cultursprache versuchend, sich Kunden zu erwerben." Consult Hermann Scherer, *Londoner Briefe über die Weltausstellung* (Leipzig: Schultze, 1851), p. 1. In addition to these commercial enterprises, a growing number of non-profit organizations such as workers' travel clubs and associations contributed to the steady increase of journeys to world's fairs. Consult Barton, *Working-Class Organizations*, p. 53f.

[10]   One might even argue that this type of event paved the way for a common or to a certain extent standardized experience in the Western world.

[11]   For how that synthesis of national styles could evolve in the field of a local or regional folk culture at international exhibitions see Angela Schwarz, "The Regional and the Global: Folk Culture at World's Fairs and the Reinvention of the Nation," in Timothy Baycroft (ed.), *Folklore and Nationalism in Europe during the Long Nineteenth Century* (Leiden and Boston: Brill, 2011, forthcoming).

[12]   Consult Scherer, *Londoner Briefe über die Weltausstellung*, p. 51.

and through the exhibits. When organizers reduced the price of day tickets to one shilling, weekly admittance numbers rose to more than 200,000 per day, a figure not surpassed until the closing of the Great Exhibition in October.[13] A total of more than six million people came to the fair.

Subsequent worlds' fairs strove to exceed the impressive numbers achieved in London. Up until World War II, most of them succeeded in doing so. With the exception of the first exposition in Paris in 1855, the second in London in 1862, and the one in Vienna in 1873 visitor statistics of the major exhibitions in Europe never fell below the ten million mark. The Paris Exposition Universelle et Internationale in 1900 represented the high water mark, welcoming more than 50 million visitors. Up until then nearly 150 million people had been present at one or more of these "potlatches" in Europe.[14]

Though critics reiterated their complaint of a surfeit of monumental festivals of progress and peace, the expositions continued to draw large crowds.[15] Just before the Great War, more than 22.5 million visitors saw the fairs in Brussels 1910 and Gent 1913; after the war, 31 million attended the Paris World's Fair in 1937. These astonishing figures were again surpassed when, only two years later, 45 million people saw the New York World's Fair.[16]

Judging from the number of autonomous countries sending exhibits, a figure varying between 20 and 50, attendance at the expositions truly was international. Considering the fact that visitors came from many more countries, they were rightly called festivals of peoples or "meeting-places of nations." However, it is not easy to place each contingent within the total of visitors or to give exact numbers for those fairgoers from a particular country; at the early exhibitions, no data was collected to answer this question.[17]

Drawing on hotel registrations in Paris in 1867, published in the report by the Commission Impériale in 1869, it is reasonable to assume that some 200,000

[13] Consult Winfried Kretschmer, *Geschichte der Weltausstellungen* (Frankfurt am Main and New York: Campus Verlag, 1999), p. 34.

[14] Consult Burton Benedict, *The Anthropology of World's Fairs: San Francisco's Panama Pacific* (London and Berkeley: Scholar Books, 1983), p. 7.

[15] The tone had been set when, in her opening speech, Queen Victoria proclaimed the Great Exhibition a "peace festival"—quoted in Kenneth W. Luckhurst, *The Story of Exhibitions* (London and New York: Studio Publications, 1951), p. 112—and *The Times* welcomed the event as the dawn of a new day in the history of mankind.

[16] Consult Kretschmer, *Geschichte der Weltausstellungen*, pp. 297–300.

[17] It is estimated that no more than 42,000 out of six million visitors to the Crystal Palace in 1851 came from abroad. Consult *Amtlicher Bericht über die Industrie-Ausstellung aller Völker zu London im Jahre 1851*, by the Report Committee of the governments of the German Zollverein, vol. 3 (Berlin: Verlag der Deckerschen Geheimen Ober-Hofbuchdruckerei, 1853), pp. 689, 743.

foreigners who stayed in area hotels went to see the exposition grounds. The majority of these were British, followed by Germans and Austrians, Belgians, Central and South Americans, Italians, Swiss, Spanish, Dutch, and Russians, as well as Swedes and Norwegians.[18] With 11 to 15 million visitors to the 1867 event, which initiated so many features that became staple fare of the universal exhibitions, foreign attendance must have been far more numerous and more varied in terms of national origin than even these figures show.

In addition, figures can only give an idea of the statistics of foreign attendance, since not all foreigners counted at an exhibition were tourists. Some fairgoers of foreign birth lived permanently in the country or city of the event, some took it as a welcome change from a business journey, and some were motivated by something other than a trip to the exposition. Even if they came as tourists, attendees might have come primarily for a visit to the host city, the exposition being only an added attraction. Paris, in the nineteenth century called the "capital of Europe,"[19] is a case in point.

Who of the people traveling to the universal exhibition is to be counted as a visitor or a tourist? World's fairs attracted a great variety of attendees:

- officials, deputed by governments, local boards, to set up a country's presentation, to report on its success with the public, and on the presentations of other countries;
- workers from foreign countries erecting/constructing the buildings and booths;
- officials elected as members of the various juries awarding medals, prizes and other honors;
- members of the companies exhibiting their products;
- journalists and writers;
- participants of congresses being held as part of the exposition;
- staff of the ethnographic presentations;
- staff of the restaurants, cafés, beer-halls, and so on;
- members of clubs and societies deputed by their institutions (for example, workers sent by their political party, trade union, or mechanics' institute);

---

[18]   Consult Commission Impériale, *Rapport sur l'Exposition universelle de 1867 à Paris* (Paris: Imprimerie Impériale, 1869), p. 488; Table no. 42, quoted in Guereña, "España en Paris," pp. 82f.

[19]   Ducuing, "Chronique," in Ducuing (ed.), *L'Exposition Universelle de 1867*, 31st installment, vol. 2 (August 19, 1867), p. 15. Compare with *The Times*, May 24, 1867: "Whatever other city may lay claim to the title of the metropolis of the world, no can certainly dispute with Paris the vaunt of being the capital of Europe."

- and the most numerous group, the private travelers who came primarily for pleasure, often with the expectation of being educated, or entertained, or both.

All of them, persons with an official role included, could be and very often were at one time or another tourists or fairgoers looking for a good time.

At the Fair: Catering for the Wants and Needs of the Solvent Masses

Projected to demonstrate Britain's success as the first industrial nation and to educate the masses—the British middle classes in terms of style and taste, the British working classes in terms of craftsmanship, diligence, and social harmony—the Great Exhibition did not ignore the fact that people wanted to be entertained as well as instructed and educated.[20] In fact, with an ample supply of distraction and refreshments, the Crystal Palace acted as the prototype of universal exhibitions in the field of popular amusement just as it did in that of showcasing technology and industrial prowess. In short, it helped establish the modern leisure industry.[21] London taught those emulating the event a valuable lesson, making fun, humor, and pleasure essential to incite and boost the "excursion habit"[22] and thus to make the costly undertaking work and pay off.

Consequently, after 1851 it did not take long for clever businessmen to conceive of more profitable sources of income than the ones devised by the hosts of the Great Exhibition. Even in 1851, there were many objects of desire available. Visitors could purchase maps of the grounds, brochures, guidebooks,[23] handkerchiefs, boxes, sheets of writing paper, and other portable items with the

---

[20]   As a guidebook to the exposition in 1867 put it: "Une Exposition doit être un enseignement pour le travailleur, une étude pour l'industriel et le savant; toutefois, il ne faut pas oublier que d'après son nom meme, c'est avant tout un attrayant spectacle." *L'Exposition Universelle de 1867. Guide de l'exposant et du visiteur avec les documents officiels, un plan et une vue de l'Exposition* (Paris: Librairie Hachette, 1866), p. 13. It was a lesson learnt in Paris where organizers of the exposition of 1878 tried to give the education element ascendance over amusement. In 1889, as in 1867, the agreeable was again "abundantly" mixed with the useful: "... elle melera abondamment l'agréable à l'utile." A. Morillon, "L'Exposition universelle de 1889," *Le Correspondant* 154 (1889): p. 1030.

[21]   Consult Richard D. Altick, *The Shows of London* (Cambridge, MA and London: Belknap Press, 1978).

[22]   Consult Luckhurst, *The Story of Exhibitions*, p. 116.

[23]   The prolific guidebook literature became part and parcel of advertising an exposition. Papers and books abounded in information for the curious traveler. For a guidebook recommendation for the English tourist to Vienna in 1873 see, for example, *Illustrated*

image of the Crystal Palace on them as souvenirs. In addition, merchants sold everyday things marked as special to the exhibition such as hats, cigars, matches, puddings, and all the refreshments the firm of Schweppe and Company could provide.[24] At least one visitor was struck by the commercial effort to turn the exhibition frenzy into money.[25]

"Revanche pour Londres" ["Revenge for London"] was a phrase coined by French exhibitors at the Crystal Palace, but *"revanche"* for the previous exposition might be taken as the motto of all the organizers and firms involved in every world's fair. When Paris hosted its first exposition in 1855, Napoleon III did not only expect a lavish display of goods and technologies but an impressive staging of a specific image of the French nation as well. What is more, by attracting millions, the British fair was to be outdone by its French successor. Businessmen took up the challenge and adopted the idea of "everything under one roof,"[26] transferring the concept of the first department store, opened that same year in Paris, to the exhibition grounds. Exhibiting became systematically intertwined with marketing goods and entertainment. In combination with the constant expansion of categories and the number of exhibits, the industrial exhibition evolved into a universal one.

Paris expositions, particularly the ones of 1867 and 1878, fundamentally changed the character of fun and spectacle at world's fairs. With an ever-increasing number of objects to exhibit, organizers of the 1867 event found the space of the central building too confining and decided to open up the area around it for a *"parc étranger,"* ["foreigners' park"] where room was given to official and commercial exhibitors craving the opportunity to present their businesses in a more individual fashion. This strategy attracted the attention of contemporaries more and more weary of the repeated praises of wondrous, unheard-of, and awe-inspiring presentations.[27] Thus, the exhibition grounds, at least in part, transformed into a shop, with goods being bought and sold as commodities and as symbolic objects, as keepsakes from the fair.

London News (July 26, 1873), p. 86, for a map of the grounds *Illustrated London News* (August 16, 1873), p. 160.

[24]   Consult Lothar Bucher, *Kulturhistorische Skizzen aus der Industrie-Ausstellung aller Völker* (Frankfurt am Main: Lizius, 1851), p. 19.

[25]   Consult *Amtlicher Bericht*, vol. 3, p. 729.

[26]   This concept of assembling the whole range of products in one building was copied in subsequent world's fairs. Consult Russell Lewis, "Everything under One Roof: World's Fairs and Department Stores in Paris and Chicago," *Chicago History* 12 (1983): pp. 28–47.

[27]   Commentators like the German journalist Adolf Ebeling expected it to become that part of the exposition which visitors would find the most interesting. Adolf Ebeling, *Die Wunder der Pariser Weltausstellung 1867* (Köln: Bachem, 1867), p. 113.

Furthermore, Frédéric Le Play, the man responsible for the French presence at the 1862 London fair, invited participants to erect their own structures at the subsequent Paris exposition. These buildings were to express people's customs and culture. Le Play even developed a separate category for working-class cottages that was designed to juxtapose national approaches to such buildings in order to identify the most economical and exemplary.[28] Since some countries were slow to take to the idea and some, with a predominantly rural population, erected peasant dwellings instead of workmen's houses, this section of the *parc étranger* took on a different thrust than intended. Still, the concept made participants design buildings supposedly characteristic not only of a region or social class, but of the whole country and its people. Visitors from abroad actually interpreted the building or buildings as representative of the essence of a given nation. For instance, the seven farmhouses transplanted from all over the Habsburg Empire to Paris in 1867 to form an "Austrian village" were regarded as "the summary of the whole Austrian monarchy."[29] This idea was the start of a notable and long-lasting identification, a phenomenon played upon by many nations from fair to fair and beyond.

The introduction of this ethnographic element spilled over from the official presentation of a nation into the area of amusement and refreshments. In fact, both were combined to provide a new form of catering, marketed as the epitome of a national culture and lifestyle, and thus like a recognizable brand. As the official part of the world's fair more and more transformed into the display of nationally identifiable objects, these ethnographic cafés, restaurants, winehouses, and beerhalls promised an additional and far more relaxing excursion to a foreign country. Many visitors accepted them as such, though they undoubtedly saw them first and foremost as places of rest and recreation. From 1867 onwards, these booths, pavilions, and ensembles, complemented by various other attractions, remained a popular element of world's fairs as well as of industrial, regional or country fairs on a smaller scale.[30] The most lavish provisions at nineteenth-century fairs could be found at the world's fair in Chicago in 1893, where some 27.5 million visitors were lured to the Midway Plaisance, an "extravaganza of

---

28 Consult "Die Nationenpavillons auf dem Pariser Marsfeld," *Illustrirte Zeitung* 1244 (May 4, 1867): p. 312.

29 It was supposedly "le résumé de toute la monarchie autrichienne." François Ducuing, "L'Empereur au Champ du Mars et l'ouverture de l'exposition. IV A Propos au village autrichien," in François Ducuing (ed.), *L'Exposition Universelle de 1867 illustrée*, 2nd installment, vol. 1 (1867), p. 23.

30 Consult John Allwood, *The Great Exhibitions* (London: Studio Vista, 1977), p. 42, Martin Wörner, *Vergnügung und Belehrung. Volkskultur auf den Weltausstellungen 1851–1900* (Münster, New York, Munich and Berlin: Waxmann, 1999), p. 50.

Figure 5.1   Advertisement for the German Village, Chicago 1893, the most
               popular of these "villages" in the amusement zone[32]

entertainment"[31] and the forerunner of today's fun or theme parks. It contained
a Ferris Wheel—introduced at the Chicago exhibition and copied in European
expositions thereafter—all the common paraphernalia of a fun fair, and Austrian,
German, Irish, and other "villages," offering typical beverages and dishes.[33] As
insinuated in the ad (see Figure 5.1), these features guaranteed to offer more

---

[31]   Robert Muccigrosso, *Celebrating the New World: Chicago's Columbian Exposition of
1893* (Chicago: Ivan R. Dee, 1993), p. 154.

[32]   Wörner, *Vergnügung und Belehrung*, p. 121.

[33]   For a systematic overview of transnational and transatlantic transfers between the
world's fairs, see Angela Schwarz, "Transfer transatlantici tra le esposizioni universali, 1851–

Figure 5.2   Indian wigwam and the Styrian winehouse "in the neighbourhood"

than the simple satisfaction of bodily needs. Each of these displays of commerce and a certain image of national culture promised a day off in Austria, Germany, Ireland, as well as "refreshment, pleasure and study."

While the owners or licensees of the cafés and restaurants unfailingly stressed the authentic character of their establishments, down to the last napkin or glass as truly Austrian, German, Irish, or whatever, many of their guests willingly immersed themselves in these illusions without giving much thought to how genuine these presentations really were. How authentic, for example, were the African-Americans, the "strapping negro lads,"[34] waiting on them in a wigwam showcased as a typical dwelling of Native Americans? By 1867, and even more so 1873, visitors to the world's fairs came to appreciate the chance to move from

1940," in Alexander C.T. Geppert and Massimo Baioni (eds), *Esposizioni in Europa tra Otto e Novecento: Spazi, organizzazione, rappresentazioni* (Milan: FrancoAngeli, 2004), pp. 61–93.

[34]   The paper drew attention to "prächtige[] Negerburschen." *Neues Wiener Tagblatt* (May 4, 1873), quoted in Martin Wörner, *Die Welt an einem Ort. Illustrierte Geschichte der Weltausstellungen* (Berlin: Reimer, 2000), p. 225.

one "country" to the next by simply strolling from the Turkish café to the Styrian Winehouse or the "Indian" Wigwam (Figure 5.2).[35]

In 1878, again while staying in Paris, people had even more intriguing opportunities to transgress boundaries, when a "Rue des Nations," a "Rue du Caire," and people as living and breathing specimens of so called primitive cultures first made their appearance at world's fairs. It was then and there that universal expositions began truly to acquire the quality of a walkable tableau of the world, a *tableau vivant*, conveying an even stronger feeling of a tour of the world than previous exhibitions had done when displaying mainly inanimate objects.

Georges Berger, Director of the Foreign Sections, came up with the idea to condense the concept of buildings symbolizing a country's most striking features into a single street on the exhibition grounds instead of spreading them throughout a park. This Rue des Nations in the inner courtyard of the industrial palace resulted from the suggestion to decorate each entrance to a national section with an architecture characteristic of that nation.[36] Architecture became an exhibit in itself and a means to create an image of cultural individuality and national identity.[37] Forms and size of the contributions varied as did the sources of inspiration countries used to create an image of something so abstract as "the nation" or national identity: some emulated rural architecture, others urban styles, some turned back in history to a specific era, others mingled styles of different centuries into one, some were small, others so large that they dominated the whole Rue. The order of façades did not follow any geographical or logical pattern, which could have an irritating effect. Still, the fact that the following fairs in Chicago in 1893 and Paris in 1900 again included these streets speaks for itself.[38]

In the most popular of all European universal exhibitions, the one held in Paris in 1900, the experience of this street was even more intensified by a new technical attraction.[39] Instead of setting the objects in motion, as the new medium film did, and in order to convey the feeling of a mobilization of vision, people themselves were moved. On a *Trottoir roulant* [moving walkway], carrying fairgoers along at two different speeds—with a third and static lane

---

[35]   *Illustrated London News* (September 13, 1873).

[36]   Consult Louis Rousselet, "Les palais des nations étrangères," in Louis Rousselet (ed.), *L'Exposition universelle de 1900* (Paris: Librairie Hachette et Cic, 1901), pp. 56–108.

[37]   Consult Wörner, *Vergnügung und Belehrung*, p. 28.

[38]   See, for photographs of the Quai des Nations, Ludovic Baschet (ed.), *Le Panorama 1900: Exposition Universelle* (Paris: Librairie d'Art, 1900), pp. 43, 70.

[39]   A moving sidewalk, a much smaller version of the *Trottoir roulant* and less well integrated into the fairgrounds, had been introduced in Chicago seven years before to take fairgoers from the quays to the entrance of the Columbian Exposition.

serving to freeze the image[40]—visitors no longer had to exert themselves walking past one foreign palace, and thus one nation after the other, in the Rue des Nations. They could stay put while the world, at least that part of it the Western World cherished most, passed by. This concept turned the tourist experience of traveling and crossing borders before entering a new territory upside down. Now fairgoers could enjoy the illusion of moving between countries without any effort or discomfort, while "countries," or rather their stereotypical image pressed into architectural form, flew by in quick succession. In a certain sense, this display anticipated the experience of touring by car and rendered that feeling accessible to millions who could not afford a car ride, let alone traveling abroad by automobile. In another way, the view from the *Trottoir* structured the experience of the universal exhibition, gave it direction, and made the visitor feel less like a "cork tossed around on the ocean."[41]

Whereas contemporaries may have felt distanced from their neighbors in Europe, whom they encountered as visitors and exhibitors at the world's fairs, they began closing ranks when confronted with geographically and culturally more distant nations. To Europeans—in fact to all Westerners—the display of non-Western peoples, particularly in the expositions up to the Great War, allowed for transgressions in more senses than the literal one of crossing a state border. In 1878 people could stroll along a Rue du Caire for the first time, a diluted and stereotypic version of the outlook and atmosphere of an oriental city. Richly adorned buildings, cafés, restaurants, conjurers and other entertainers, camel rides, harems, and other sights advertised as commonly hidden from the curious Western eye, sprawled out for everyone to gaze at and to enjoy. An instant success in a Europe that was intrigued by the Orient, the presentations exploited a concept of distance that was to give onlookers the thrill of the exotic. Buildings with "authentic" interiors, inhabited during opening hours by "natives" in "authentic" costumes, reflected an image of oriental societies that was widespread in the West at the time, one of societies stagnating in history.[42]

---

[40]   See, for a photograph, Baschet, *Le Panorama 1900*, p. 100. The moving visitor and the moving image were combined in the films showing the "journey" on the *Trottoir roulant*. See, for footage showing the "travelers," "Paris in 1900, Exposition universelle (Rare Footage)": http://www.youtube.com/watch?v=n-4R72jTb74 (4:25–5:30), for a view from the *Trottoir*, "Panorama from the Moving Broadway, 9 August 1900, Thomas A. Edison": http://www.youtube.com/watch?v=BjpCVQgKZsc [accessed November 15, 2010].

[41]   "... wie ein Stückchen Kork im Weltmeer". Alfred Julius Meyer-Graefe, "Einleitung," in Alfred Julius Meier-Graefe (ed.), *Die Weltausstellung in Paris 1900. Mit zahlreichen photographischen Aufnahmen, farbigen Kunstbeilagen und Plänen* (Paris and Leipzig: Krüger, 1900), p. 1.

[42]   Johannes Fabian, *Time and the Other: How Anthropology Makes Its Object* (New York: Columbia University Press, 1983), p. 67.

Similarly, the showcasing of indigenous peoples from Africa, Asia, or Southern America welded the otherwise separated European onlookers together, united in a specific view of the non-white "other" as strange, inferior, and backward.[43] The Paris exposition of 1878 was the first to have some 400 Africans and South East Asians transplanted to the fairgrounds in the French capital along with their tools, their weapons, their huts, and even their complete villages. After the earlier displays of inanimate objects and dummies had lost their appeal and novelty, fairs needed this new "live" approach to again attract and entertain large crowds. By the time of the Paris Exposition of 1889 the number of different cultures present in the "capital of Europe" soared. Europeans, moving on from the halls displaying the most recent advances in technology like the telephone or the phonograph to these "natives," were invited to appreciate the distance between themselves and "the others" and to interpret it as evidence for the progressive nature of their own culture and society. To ensure this, organizers integrated these *tableaux vivants* into the anthropological and supposedly scientifically verified sections in the official part of the world's fair as well as into the continually expanding amusement zones, where "exotic mannequins"[44] were to assist white males and females in passing (at least mentally) the threshold into strange and distant lands (see Figure 5.3).

Up to the Great War and even into the 1920s this overall structure of catering for the wants and needs of the masses barely changed. With an eye on organizing a profitable world's fair, the variety and number of ways in which to spend an enjoyable and entertaining day at the exposition continued to increase.[45] Contractors at a particular event competed with each other, as did the cities or nations staging an exhibition. What had proven profitable at one event, be it on a local, a regional, or an international level, was emulated at another. Sometimes the organizers only transferred the basic concept and adjusted it to their own needs, and sometimes they took the whole element lock, stock, and barrel—as happened, for instance, with the Rue du Caire.[46] This process of superseding

---

[43] "Mixing entertainment with education, these spectacles painted the world at large in microcosm, with an emphasis on the 'strangeness' of the unfamiliar." Zeynep Çelik, *Displaying the Orient: Architecture of Islam at Nineteenth Century World's Fairs* (Berkeley, Los Angeles, and Oxford: University of California Press, 1992), p. 18.

[44] Consult Thomas Schriefers, *Für den Abriss gebaut? Anmerkungen zur Geschichte der Weltausstellungen* (Hagen: Ardenku Verlag, 1999), p. 20f.

[45] Little wonder then that visitors to the last world's fair before World War II in New York could choose from the greatest number of amusements. Consult Peter Greenhalgh, *Ephemeral Vistas: A History of the Expositions Universelles, Great Exhibitions and World's Fairs, 1851–1939* (Manchester: Manchester University Press, 1988), p. 43f.

[46] This quickly provoked complaints such as the one that the "oriental riffraff" ("das orientalische Gesindel") had moved on from Chicago to infest the exhibition in

Figure 5.3   Rencontre insolite (Congolese woman, European man), Paris in
               1889[47]

nationally specific traditions was the basis of a rapprochement between European
societies in the field of leisure culture, the beginnings of a Europeanization of the
tourist experience that came into its own in the late twentieth century.

At the Fair: Tourists and the Transgression of Boundaries

Providers alone did not decide what would become a success story in leisure travel
and leisure culture more generally. It was the visitors who, with their attendance,

---

Antwerp. Consult F. Neubaur, "Von der Ausstellung in Antwerpen," *Die Gartenlaube* 94
(1894): p. 622.

[47]   Reproduced in Caroline Mathieu (ed.), *1889 La Tour Eiffel et l'Exposition Universelle*
(Paris: Réunion des Musées Nationaux, 1989), p. 117.

decided which of the so-called "attractions" actually deserved the name. Many included a tour around the host city in their journey to the world's fair; such a tour completed and intensified their trip. For those who had never been abroad or had hardly ever left their hometown or village, the journey itself and then the arrival in the big city already brought with it excitement and amazement.

Alfred Ziegler, a 16-year-old Austrian from a middle-class family, visited the Great Exhibition in Vienna in 1873 with his father. The boy was too excited to fall asleep on the train journey, feeling "a mixture of joy for traveling, agitation of the body all out of sorts and a vague expectation of the things to come."[48] Furnished with a set of rules explained by his father on how to behave on the streets of the metropolis, with a card giving the address where to return to if he got lost, and an illustrated map of the exhibition grounds, young Alfred was supposed to be ready for his adventure.[49]

Very often a tour of the city was included in the itinerary. An American commentator thought Paris, as *the* magnet for sojourners, the reason why Parisian expositions differed from all the other international fairs. He called it "the vortex of life," "the whirlpool of human existence,"[50] a quality which intensified the impression of the exposition.[51] In turn, the sojourners staying in the city for a visit to the world's fair heightened the cosmopolitan flair of the city streets.[52] And they gave them an even more crowded look—making some wish themselves back to peace and solitude.[53] Heinrich Kissing, an entrepreneur from a small town in Westphalia, counted his steps while crossing the grounds of the Paris exposition of 1867 in both width and length. He concluded, quite stunned, that his whole hometown would find room enough in its expanse. Until World War I

---

[48] "Wenn einem das Reisen nicht zur Gewohnheit wurde, befällt den Reisenden oft das sogenannte Reisefieber, *eine Mischung von Freude über die Reise, Aufregung des aus der Ordnung gekommenen Körpers und ungewisse Erwartung der Dinge, die da kommen sollen.*" Alfred Ziegler, "Übersichtliche Beschreibung meiner Reise zur Wiener Weltausstellung und mein Verweilen daselbst," unpublished manuscript, December 1873 (transcription, p. 2), with kind permission of the Ziegler-Family.

[49] Ibid., p. 3.

[50] Edward Insley, "Paris in 1900 and the Exposition," *Harper's Monthly Magazine* 101 (1900): p. 485.

[51] Ibid., p. 486.

[52] Consult Dietmar Simon, "Eine Reise nach Paris. Ein Mendener Unternehmer besucht die Weltausstellung von 1867," *Der Märker* 49 (2000): pp. 71–8, p. 75. Heinrich Kissing, whose account has only been retrieved in parts, spent several days on the fair grounds. In addition, he also took ample time during his three-weeks sojourn to Paris in order to tour the French capital and sights nearby such as the palace of Versailles.

[53] Max Eyth, *Im Strom unserer Zeit (Erster und Zweiter Teil). Wanderbuch eines Ingenieurs* (Heidelberg: Winter, 1905), p. 534.

Paris remained exceptional in this respect, though to visitors from the provincial towns or countryside, cities like Vienna, Brussels, or Barcelona had the touch of the exotic just as well. Even a visitor to Vienna from Paris could acknowledge the qualities of the heart of the Empire as *une grande capitale.*[54] Alfred Ziegler is one example of this. Like so many others before and after him, he included a tour of the city in his itinerary. The palace and grounds of Schönbrunn, the zoo, large crowds, an ocean of houses, a tram-ride through the bustling city: all this emanated the essence of metropolitan life.

Young Alfred repeatedly pointed out that there was a lot to see and to learn in the capital itself, even before getting to the exhibition.[55] He pointed this out since he wrote the report for his father to whom he dedicated it "in deepest gratitude." But he was not the only one.[56] In fact, many members of the educated middle classes emphasized this aspect of education in their reports and letters, extending from the official presentations of the exhibition to the sights of the urban environment. After the turn into the twentieth century, especially after the Great War, the need for fairgoers to stress the educational benefit of their trip receded a little, since the fun aspect achieved greater acceptance generally and particularly in the middle and upper classes. However, it never really disappeared, even less so, since the fairs were always marketed as sites of knowledge and technologies on the verge of changing the present and the future. They were designed first and foremost to enlighten the public.

In approaching a universal exhibition, fairgoers could choose from a great variety of ways to organize their individual tour. They could visit the grounds on their own, thus becoming more free to decide on which parts they wanted to focus and how much time they would spend on them. Alternatively, they could be joined by family and/or friends, which gave the experience a different hue. Visitors' choices often impinged upon the tour and on the way things were perceived. With a whole range of guiding aids, touring the ever-increasing exhibition palace or palaces and the grounds need not be done completely on one's own account. There were maps of the exhibition area, brochures, guidebooks by individual authors or issued by major publishing houses, such as the *Guide bleu du Figaro*, special sections in some exposition guidebooks, for instance a

---

54   Victor Fournel, "De Paris à l'Exposition de Vienne. Journal d'un Chroniqueur en Voyage," *Le Correspondant* 93 (1873): p. 134.

55   Consult Ziegler, "Übersichtliche Beschreibung meiner Reise zur Wiener Weltausstellung und mein Verweilen daselbst," p. 4f.

56   To name but one further example: Eike Wolgast, "Ein Mecklenburger auf der Londoner Weltausstellung 1862," *Mecklenburgische Jahrbücher* 108 (1991): pp. 119–27, p. 119.

section on the Exposition of 1889 in the Baedeker for Paris,[57] and voluminous catalogues detailing the exhibits and providing general information—which made one visitor in 1900 wonder when the "encyclopædias roulants"[58] would be introduced, a kind of "library on wheels" allowing the fairgoer to answer every question on his or her way through the exhibition halls. And, of course, visitors could choose one of the more or less professional tour guides to show them around. As fairgoers quickly learned, opting either for the book or for the personal guide each had its respective merits:

> For those who will try to see everything in a week, and buy education "at bargain sales," the "personally conducted" is eminently the best. It has the merit of method, to which few who go their own way pay sufficient attention. And it prevents the tourist from making funny mistakes.[59]

As the number of exhibits and the territory encompassed by the fairs increased, fairgoers came to crave a means by which to do the tour in a less exhausting fashion than on foot. To cater for this need and to offer additional attractions, organizers added carriages, steam trains, elevated trains, a "sky ride" (Chicago 1933), moving sidewalks, and even *fauteuils roulants* to assist fairgoers in seeing it all. At the same time the different means of transportation made sure that the visitors could not only see, but be seen, the latter being as important to many as a good view of the exhibits. In the words of a sojourner in the Rue de Paris at the Exposition in 1900:

> ... it is funny and pleasurable to promenade in this street—at least in the evening. A mostly very elegant crowd is shuffling through the alley—ladies in evening dress have themselves carried along in "fauteuils roulants," and at the tables in front of the three or four restaurants in the Rue de Paris the leisurely are sitting, eyeing, criticizing, and greeting the *flâneurs*. There is a very cheery atmosphere and one can see that most of the people have dined well and have come determined to have fun.[60]

---

57   Consult Bernhardine Schulze-Smidt, *Bleistiftskizzen. Erinnerungen an die Pariser Weltausstellung von 1889* (Bremen: Kühtmann's Buchhandlung, 1890), p. 4, Reference to the *Guide bleu* in hand while on the way to the exposition, Ibid., p. 24.

58   Insley, "Paris in 1900 and the Exposition," p. 497.

59   Ibid., p. 496.

60   "Aber es ist doch lustig und vergnüglich, in dieser Strasse zu promenieren—wenigstens am Abend. ... Eine meist sehr elegante Menge schiebt sich durch die Allee—Damen in Dinertoilette lassen sich in 'Fauteuils roulants' über den Kies rollen, und an den Tischen vor den drei oder vier Restaurants der Rue de Paris ... sitzen die Bequemen

Whatever the means of transport, whatever the motive, up until World War II, fairgoers would agree without a moment's hesitation that their tour around the exhibition grounds resembled or even equaled a tour around the world. This view, of course, could be held of the more recent exhibitions with a stronger claim to correctness than of the pioneer events in the mid-nineteenth century. Visitors unremittingly came back to the idea that the tour of the world's fair was indeed a tour around the world: "*un voyage autour du monde*," "*Rundreise durch die Welt*."[61] In fact, many believed that the fair offered a better way to complete such a tour, claiming: "The expositions have simplified the tour around the world in a unique way. On the Champ de Mars, it hardly needs half a day to get around the inhabited world."[62] To societies on the verge of or in the age of modernity, more and more aware of time and its scarcity, the promise of as much instruction or fun as could be had in a short period of time seemed unsurpassable. "In a flash around the world!—And how comfortable and inexpensive. This truly is the ideal way to travel."[63]

An awareness of the entire event required a specific perception of its individual parts. A typical example is the following description by a German visitor to Paris in 1867:

> The Grande Avenue formed the border between France and England, and with a single leap we could get from England to Mexico or into a log cabin of the North American hinterland. "I promised to meet with a friend in Morocco, could you be so kind as to show me the way?" "Gladly. You start here from North America via Italy, pass between Tunisia and Egypt, leave Syria on your right, at the Temple of Edfou turn in the direction of China, ... and turn, when you see the tower of Romania on your right, into the street, which leads straight on. Morocco lies before you. In half an hour, you can be back in Russia." I have to admit that such a route seems fantastic enough, though I crossed the globe in even stranger leaps

---

und betrachten, bekritteln und begrüssen die Promenierenden. Und es herrscht eine sehr vergnügte Stimmung und man merkt, die meisten haben gut diniert und sind mit dem festen Entschlusse gekommen, sich zu amüsieren." "Im Innern der fremden Paläste," in Meyer-Graefe, *Die Weltausstellung in Paris 1900*, p. 60.

   61   Kissing, quoted in Simon, "Eine Reise nach Paris," p. 79.

   62   "Les expositions universelles ont singulièrement simplifié les voyages autour du monde. Au Champ de Mars, il faut à peine une demi-journée pour parcourir le monde habité." Henry Houssaye, "Voyage autour du monde à l'exposition universelle," *Revue des Deux Mondes* 28 (1878): p. 365. This idea was voiced as early as 1851. Consult Scherer, *Londoner Briefe über die Weltausstellung*, p. 73.

   63   "Im Fluge durch die Welt!—Und wie bequem und billig. Wahrlich das ist das Idealreisen. 'Le Tour du Monde,'" in Georg Malkowsky (ed.), *Die Pariser Weltausstellung in Wort und Bild* (Berlin: Kirchhoff, 1900), p. 59.

later on, irrespective of language, conventions, and customs of the peoples, whom I wanted to visit in their own house, or whose territory I had to cross.[64]

To talk about starting from North America, passing Tunisia and Egypt, to have "Syria on your right," or to go on to Spain, to enter Russia, or to wander through countries,[65] was a common way of linguistically expressing the experience. Yet to the tourists at universal exhibitions, at least up to World War II, it was a lot more than that. Such phrases gave expression to the feeling that one was actually transgressing national boundaries, actually meeting with foreign countries and their culture as epitomized—however correctly or stereotypically—in the objects government officials had decided to set up in a certain fashion.

Reactions to the Rue des Nations confirm this. Some commentators repeatedly criticized their mixture of styles as, for instance, "an architect's Walpurgis Night,"[66] and the confusion of geography. Edmond Villetard, writing in *Le Correspondant*, described the Rue des Nations as a menu made up of dishes from different parts of the world: a plum-pudding, caviar, and hotpot all on one plate.[67] However, even critics like Villetard had to admit that these façades were a great success among fairgoers and the Rue one of their favorite spots to take a

---

[64] "Die Grande Avenue bildete die Grenze zwischen Frankreich und England, und ein einziger Sprung konnte uns aus England wieder nach Mexiko oder in die nordamerikanischen Hinterwälder in ein Farmerhaus versetzen. 'Ich habe versprochen, mich mit einem Freunde in Marokko zu treffen, können Sie mir gefälligst den Weg angeben, den ich zu nehmen habe?' 'Gern. Hier gehen Sie von Nordamerika aus über Italien, zwischen Tunis und Aegypten durch, lassen Syrien rechts, am Tempel von Edfu nehmen Sie dann genau die Richtung nach China zu, gehen aber hart an der Grenze hin und schlagen, wenn Sie links die Thürme von Rumänien sehen, die Straße ein, welche gradaus führt. Marokko liegt vor ihnen. In einer halben Stunde können Sie wieder in Rußland sein.' Man muß gestehen, daß eine solche Reiseroute phantastisch genug klingt, trotzdem habe ich später die Erde in noch viel merkwürdigeren Sprüngen durchmessen, ohne Rücksicht auf Sprache, Sitten und Gebräuche der Völker, denen ich einen Besuch im eignen Hause abstatten wollte, oder durch deren Gebiet ich ziehen mußte." Oswald M. Mohl, *Die Wunder der Weltausstellung zu Paris: Schilderungen der Erlebnisse in einer Weltstadt im Jahre 1867* (Leipzig: Otto Spamer, 1868), p. 70.

[65] "Nun ging es nach Spanien ... Rußland, welches man jetzt betrat ... von all den Ländern, die man bereits durchwandert hatte." Kissing, quoted in Simon, "Eine Reise nach Paris," p. 78.

[66] "Paris in 1900—Review of Paris. By Augustus J.C. Hare. 2 vols. London: Allen, 1900," *Edinburgh Review* 192/393 (July 1900): p. 135.

[67] "On nous servait sur une seule assiette une bouchée de plum-pudding entre un petit tas de caviar et une cuillerée de potage au nid d'hirondelle." Edmond Villetard, "Promenade à travers l'Exposition universelle," *Le Correspondant* 111 (May 25, 1878): p. 668.

deep breath and to rest.[68] Many took the stroll along the Rue, in 1900 enlarged to a "Quai des Nations," as an experience, both amusing and instructive:

> For you see here not only more or less brilliant works of art, more or less beautiful exhibits—but something very different. One simply sees the spirit of the nations itself. ... Only be attentive enough and you will always—or nearly always—find something like an elucidation on the true character of the nation.[69]

The need for clear-cut categories, the possibility to identify certain architectural styles, art forms, products, or technologies with nations was boosted as a marketing strategy and very often accepted as a means to structure and order the otherwise unmanageable amount of impressions assailing a fairgoer even after a short time. People were not only willing to find their national stereotypes corroborated, but very often expected it. This reality applied specifically to the amusement zones, to the restaurants, bars, and cafés which claimed to showcase an authentic image of a national culture.[70] Here guests were even less likely to second-guess what they were presented as a national characteristic as long as they thought it entertaining and cogent.

The reception of the "Indian Wigwam" in Vienna in 1873 is just one example in a long line. At the time of the Vienna exposition it was already common to complain about an excessive amount of entertainment facilities.[71] Some visitors were disappointed that the wigwam, which housed a café, did not live up to the ethnographic presentations in the official exhibition. A great many others curiously eyed the strangely constructed tent with its scary paintings and were curious to venture into its interior.[72] They welcomed the opportunity to spend time in what a lot of them took for a tamed version of the American West. In many other cases, tourists acclaimed the strangeness of the whole layout and the singularities of the different nations.[73] Most of all they cherished the illusion of stepping into another

---

68   Ibid.

69   "Denn man sieht hier nicht nur mehr oder weniger glänzende Kunstwerke, mehr oder weniger schöne Ausstellungsobjekte—man sieht etwas ganz anderes, man sieht ganz einfach den Geist der Nationen selber. ... Man schaue nur aufmerksam hin und man wird immer, oder doch fast immer, etwas wie eine Aufklärung über den wirklichen Nationalcharakter finden." "Im Innern der fremden Paläste," in Meyer-Graefe, *Die Weltausstellung in Paris 1900*, p. 41.

70   Consult Mohl, *Die Wunder der Weltausstellung zu Paris*, p. 84; Neubaur, "Von der Ausstellung in Antwerpen," p. 622.

71   Consult Fournel, "De Paris à l'exposition Vienne," p. 137.

72   Consult "Von der wiener Weltausstellung: Das Indianerzelt," *Illustrirte Zeitung* 1564 (June 21, 1873): p. 480.

73   Consult "Die Restaurants auf der Pariser Weltausstellung," in Malkowsky, *Die Pariser Weltausstellung in Wort und Bild*, p. 188.

place or culture and another time; this journey into the past was a fantasy attached to the presentations of oriental cultures in particular.[74]

Returning Home: A Short Summary

Over 200 million people traveled to the world's fairs in Europe between 1851 and 1937. To many theirs was a journey of exploration, of discovering the other and the self, be it at an individual level, or at that of the nation or of European culture more broadly. It worked that way because the Great Exhibition emphasized the importance of national prowess and introduced the element of competition between the participating nations. "The nations are, so to speak, transported in person to the Champ de Mars, with their conventions, customs, monuments and their means of production."[75] It was they or rather their members that brought the fairgrounds alive as a huge forum for meeting and exchange.

Despite the fact that the visitors from different countries usually perceived each other as representatives of another nation, coming to the fair constituted a specific tourist encounter in which national categories no longer applied. The fairs helped develop a range of new transnational experiences. Visitors felt the advantages and disadvantages of traveling to a major event. They faced being one in a large crowd, tossed around on "the waves of a cosmopolitan stream of people."[76] Fairgoers allowed themselves to be the source of income to an ever-increasing number of businessmen and constantly courted, if not harassed. And visitors witnessed the extraordinary alignment of services inherent in these massive gatherings. All this was part of the fair experience. These and other features were not unique to universal exhibitions, but were introduced or fueled by the convocation of the world in one place for a short period of time.

Moreover, the tourist experience of a world's fair did not only align with that of a subsequent fair. For changes on this level trickled down on activities on the national, regional, or local level. The tourists took home their impressions and perceptions, and so did those who had catered for their wants and needs. Viennese cafés, Russian restaurants, American bar rooms, Turkish baths, and

---

[74] Consult "Von der wiener Weltausstellung: Das Indianerzelt," p. 481.

[75] "Les nations se sont, pour ainsi dire, transportées en personne au Champs de Mars, avec leurs mœurs, leurs habitudes, leurs monuments et leurs moyens de travail..." François Ducuing, "L'Empereur au Champ du Mars et l'ouverture de L'exposition. VI La fête du 1 avril," in François Ducuing (ed.), *L'Exposition Universelle de 1867 illustrée*, 2nd installment, vol. 1 (1867), p. 31.

[76] "die Wogen des kosmopolitischen Menschenstromes," Schulze-Smidt, *Bleistiftskizzen*, p. 28.

other popular attractions of the great exhibitions could be transplanted from the fair grounds into the capitals or big cities all over Europe, slowly at first, with more speed after the wars. Long before the advent of mass consumerism from the 1950s onwards, the Europeanization of tourism and the tourist experience was well on its way. In fact, it had returned home from the world of world's fairs.

PART II
Selling the National
in a Transnational Context

Chapter 6

From "Paris of the East" to "Queen of the Danube": International Models in the Promotion of Budapest Tourism, 1885–1940[1]

Alexander Vari

City marketing represented a specific niche within overall efforts of European modernization and economic development during the second half of the nineteenth century. After Paris of the Second French Empire (1851–70) emerged as one of the most important urban tourism destinations on the continent, several other capital cities elaborated marketing strategies of their own, building both on local resources and attempts to copy the Parisian and other Western models.[2] These developments were not limited to Europe. Cities in North and South America, Africa, and Asia followed in the same footsteps turning city marketing into an inter-regional and global practice. The creation of an early urban tourism industry between the period marked by the re-building of Paris during the 1850s–1860s and World War II (WWII) was thus a local, regional, national, and at the same time, transnational enterprise.

Although contemporary city marketing has an extensive literature, less has been written on its development before WWII.[3] In the case of those

---

[1] The author would like to thank Shelley Baranowski, Robert Nemes, Eric Beckett Weaver, Nathan Wood, and Eric Zuelow for their useful suggestions and feedback.

[2] On the rise of urban tourism in Paris and its connections to consumerism, spectacle, and leisure, see Dean MacCannell, *The Tourist: A New Theory of the Leisure Class*, 3rd ed. (Berkeley: University of California Press, 1999), pp. 57–76, and David Harvey, *Paris, Capital of Modernity* (New York and London: Routledge, 2003), pp. 209–24.

[3] See, among others: Dennis R. Judd and Susan S. Fainstein, *The Tourist City*, 3rd ed. (New Haven: Yale University Press, 1999); Dennis R. Judd, *The Infrastructure of Play: Building the Tourist City* (Armonk: M.E. Sharpe, 2003); Miriam Greenberg, *Branding New York: How a City in Crisis was Sold to the World* (New York: Routledge, 2008); Leo van den Berg, Erik Braun, and Alexander H.J. Otgaar, *Sports and City Marketing in European Cities* (Aldershot: Ashgate, 2002); Alberto Vanolo, "The Image of the Creative City: Some

works that have looked at pre-WWII city marketing the focus has been on the North American and Western European context[4] with very little research on non-Western cities.[5] Looking at other contexts than the Western one, however, is important to better understand processes of interaction between cities at a European and global level. From the perspective of East-Central Europe, Budapest provides a relevant case for the study of these processes. The Hungarian case also allows us to explore the antithetical views of urban tourism promotion as city marketers and nation builders imagined Budapest differently: either as a cosmopolitan regional capital (modeled after Western cities) whose sphere of attraction (as a result of offering enticing and diverse attractions) transcended ethnic and state borders or as a national capital offering a model for the celebration of national culture and traditions for provincial cities.

Keeping this broader context in mind, this chapter looks at the implementation of international models in Budapest's urban tourism promotion in order both to highlight the frequency of such borrowings as well as to explain the specific reasons behind their local incorporation or rejection, a conflict-laden duality that defined the city's marketing strategies from 1885 to 1940. In the process we will look at the role late-nineteenth-century world's fairs and other transnational spectacles had played in creating a local mass leisure industry and at how the outbreak of World War I (WWI), the dissolution of Austria-Hungary, and the conservative and nationalist mold

Reflections on Urban Branding in Turin," *Cities* 25/6 (2008): pp. 370–82; and Tim Coles, "Urban Tourism, Place Promotion and Economic Restructuring: The Case of Post-Socialist Leipzig," *Tourism Geographies* 5/2 (2003): pp. 190–219.

[4]   Stephen V. Ward, *Selling Places: The Marketing and Promotion of Towns and Cities, 1850–2000* (London: E & FN Spon, 1998); J. V. Beckett, *City Status in the British Isles, 1830–2002* (Aldershot: Ashgate, 2005); Catherine Cocks, *Doing the Town: The Rise of Urban Tourism in the United States, 1850–1915* (Berkeley: University of California Press, 2001); Victoria E. Dye, *All Aboard for Santa Fe: Railway Promotion of the Southwest, 1890s to 1930s* (Albuquerque: University of New Mexico Press, 2005); Jonathan Mark Souther, *New Orleans on Parade: Tourism and the Transformation of the Crescent City* (Baton Rouge: Louisiana State University Press, 2006); and Anthony J. Stanonis, *Creating the Big Easy: New Orleans and the Emergence of Modern Tourism, 1918–1945* (Athens: University of Georgia Press, 2006).

[5]   For a few exceptions, see: Thomas Biskup and Marc Schalenberg (eds), *Selling Berlin: Imagebildung und Stadtmarketing von der preussischer Residenz bis zur Bundeshauptstadt* (Stuttgart: Franz Steiner Verlag, 2008); Timothy Pursell, "Stadt der Natur oder Stadt der Avantgarde? —Tourismusförderung und Identitätsentwicklung in Hagen im 20 Jahrhundert," *Informationen zur Modernen Stadtgeschichte* 1 (2005): pp. 11–17; and Jill Steward, "Gruss aus Wien: Urban Tourism in Austria-Hungary before the First World War," in Malcolm Gee, Tim Kirk, and Jill Steward (eds), *The City in Central Europe: Culture and Society from 1800 to the Present* (Aldershot: Ashgate, 1999), pp. 123–44.

of public life in interwar Hungary reshaped former city marketing strategies, developments well reflected in a switch from Budapest's pre-war branding as the "Paris of the East" to that of "Queen of the Danube" after WWI.

Promoting Budapest Tourism through Fairs, 1885–96

During the last three decades of the nineteenth century, Budapest grew from an urban center made up of three separate settlements with a combined population of 260,000 people to a unified metropolis of almost 800,000 inhabitants.[6] The capital shed its provincial outlook and acquired the features of a modern world-city [*világváros*] with broad boulevards, monumental buildings, and a pulsing street-life.[7] Budapest came to resemble Vienna and Berlin and to a certain extent Paris, whose urban redevelopment, by Georges-Eugène Haussmann during the Second French Empire, was considered by many contemporaries to have been its main inspirational model.[8]

In this spirit, from the late 1880s some local boosters advertised Budapest as a "Paris of the East," a promotional slogan that emphasized the scale and pace of its urban development and took pride in its newly acquired Western features.[9] Besides emphasizing similarities with Paris and other Western metropolises (especially regarding the city's newly opened wide boulevards) what promoters of Budapest (made up of big merchants and industrialists) wanted to achieve was its inclusion in the circuit of international fairgoers.[10] The world's fairs held in London in 1851 and 1862, and especially the ones organized by Paris in 1855, 1867, and 1878, and Vienna in 1873, were keenly discussed in the local press, attended by thousands of Hungarians, and singled out by Hungarian industrialists as events worth emulating. They were interested in promoting Budapest on the international stage through a display of artifacts showing the progress of national industry while, at the same time, making room for foreign pavilions as was done at previous world's fairs. These objectives figured

---

[6]   The towns of Buda, Pest, and Óbuda were brought under a common administration in 1873, giving rise to modern Budapest.

[7]   John Lukacs, *Budapest 1900: A Historical Portrait of a City and Its Culture* (New York: Weidenfeld and Nicholson, 1988).

[8]   See László Siklóssy, *Hogyan épült Budapest, 1870–1930* (Budapest: Közmunkák Tanácsa, 1931), p. 76.

[9]   See Berthold Weiss, *Budapest és a keleti vasutak* (Budapest: Pesti Könyvnyomda, 1887).

[10]   On the role of international fairs (and later Olympics) in promoting city status and urban tourism, see John R. Gold and Margaret M. Gold, *Cities of Culture: Staging International Festivals and the Urban Agenda, 1851–2000* (Aldershot: Ashgate, 2000).

prominently on the agenda of the Countrywide Exhibition [Országos Kiállítás] organized by Budapest in 1885. In addition to serving as a display window for the products of the national industry another goal of the fair's organizers was to attract numerous foreigners to Budapest in order to have them appreciate the progress that the city had made since 1867.[11] As a clear attempt at marketing the city abroad, during the course of the fair, several groups of journalists from Paris, Vienna, and Lemberg (L'viv) were invited to come to Budapest to witness the changes. Also from 1885, and as another proof of Budapest's growing importance as a destination, the Ticket Office of MÁV (the Hungarian State Railways) officially recorded the number of foreigners who came to the city.

Out of the groups of foreign journalists invited to Budapest, most of the municipality and the local press's attention were devoted to the visit of a large French delegation made up of writers, artists, and journalists. In August 1885 the French were taken to the fair, and then shown the city's main architectural attractions, before finally being taken on an exhilarating journey across the country.[12] French reactions, however, were less enthusiastic of the progress made by the city than expected by their hosts. In their depictions of Budapest and the country, the French visitors' attention was captured by exotic aspects (such as Gypsy music, the medieval costumes of the Hungarian aristocracy, the latter's lavish spending and hard drinking habits), which ultimately led to their visit being catalogued as a fiasco by the Hungarian press.[13] Therefore, when a few years later promoters of Budapest led by Count Jenő Zichy (the President of the 1885 Countrywide Exhibition) argued that the Millennial celebrations scheduled for 1896 should be held as part of a huge world's fair that would attract droves of tourists to the Hungarian capital,[14] they found themselves in a minority position *vis-à-vis* a vocal nationalist press (which came to be supported by the Hungarian government as well). Contrary to Zichy, nationalists rejected plans for a world's fair for the sake of a national-minded event that instead of embracing the cosmopolitanism and commercialism of recent fairs such as the

---

[11]   As a result of the dualist pact between Austria and Hungary, from 1867 Budapest housed an independent Hungarian government. The decision of the Andrássy government (1867–71) to set up a Board of Public Works in 1870 and to borrow money from foreign lenders for urban development projects played an important role in the growth and embellishment of the city during the 1870s and 1880s.

[12]   István Lelkes, *A francia-magyar barátság aranykora, 1879–1889. Fejezet a magyar liberalizmus történetéből* (Budapest: Sárkány-nyomda, 1932), pp. 208–60.

[13]   Mario Proth, *Le voyage de la délégation française en Hongrie* (Budapest: Pallas, 1886) and Louis Ulbach, *La czardas* (Paris: Levy, 1888).

[14]   Jenő Zichy, *Országos vagy világkiállítás kell-e nemzetünk ezer éves ünnepére?* (Budapest: Lampel, 1891).

ones held in Paris in 1889 and Chicago in 1893 was to be devoted to the more "noble tasks" of displaying only the products of the national industry and that of celebrating the national past.

The inauguration of the Millennium Exhibition in May 1896 showed the increasing strength of Magyar nationalists against the camp of urban promoters who were influenced by Western models.[15] In spite of this new ratio of forces the nationalists' goal of rejecting all Western influence was hard to attain. The turn that the world's fairs experienced, from the didacticism of the Exhibition of All Nations held in the Crystal Palace in London in 1851 to the commercial character and emphasis on entertainment that the latest ones came to be known for, was replicated at the Millennium Exhibition held in Budapest in 1896 as well. In addition to replicas of historic buildings glorifying the Hungarian past and the products celebrating the achievements of the national industry, the exhibition sported such popular attractions as Ős Budavára [Ancient Buda Fortress] and Konstantinápoly Budapesten [Constantinople in Budapest].[16] The first was a fairground recreation of Buda during Ottoman times (1541–1686) within the grounds of the official exhibition itself, while the other sold the illusion of visiting contemporary Constantinople in a large theme park located on the right bank of the Danube. The inspiration for the latter was clearly the Rue de Cairo featured at the 1889 Paris World's Fair and the Algerian Street, which delighted visitors of the Columbian Exhibition held in Chicago in 1893.

Borrowing from foreign models, however, turned into a source of both strength and weakness for the fair organizers. The turn toward mass entertainment as a driving engine of the world's fairs (and implicitly a powerful tool for urban promotion) was almost simultaneous to its emergence in a Western setting. The attractions that Budapest exhibited in 1896 turned the city into a more appealing tourist destination. However, municipal authorities deemed the number of Western visitors who made it to the fair insufficient, while in turn the nationalist hysteria surrounding the Millennium celebrations discouraged non-Magyars and tourists from Serbia and Romania from attending the event. Promoting Budapest tourism through fairs, thus, only led to modest financial returns. Recognition of this fact encouraged a turn towards different city marketing strategies by the dawn of the new century.

---

[15]   For a detailed contemporary presentation of the Millennium Exhibition and related festivities see László Köváry, *A millenium lefolyásának története és a millenáris emlékalkotások* (Budapest: Athenaeum, 1897).

[16]   See *A milleniumi kiállítás csodái: Ős-Budavár és Konstantinápoly Budapesten* (Budapest: Laurencic Gyula, 1896).

Other International Models in the Promotion of Turn-of-the-Century Budapest Tourism

What made this shift possible was the professionalization of urban tourism promotion in Hungary. The creation of a Tourism and Travel Company (TTC) in 1902 represented a new beginning in the history of city marketing in that country. The next decade was a period when Budapest was promoted abroad by borrowing heavily from marketing strategies implemented by other cities. By 1900 city marketing turned into a type of economic activity that was shaped and dominated by many players. Several new entrants into the unfolding inter-city race now challenged more established capitals such as Paris and London, giving a new global dimension to the old competition between them. Recognition of this fact was made even in the self-proclaimed Capital of the World: Paris, where a publication entitled *Les capitales du monde*, labeling no less than 20 other cities with this epithet, was published in several editions during the 1890s.[17] Chicago and New York were two among the new metropolises that most prominently challenged—especially as a result of the quickening spread of Americanization from the New to the Old World—the leading role played up to then by Paris. Travel between all these metropolises was fostered by travel agencies such as Cook's, American Express and the Compagnie Internationale des Wagon Lits et des Grands Express Européens. The International Hoteliers Association founded in 1869 in Koblenz also played an important role in fostering awareness of the need for the modernization of hosting infrastructure in the tourist-receiving metropolises.[18] Thus, urban tourism turned into a specific segment of a global network of travel with many regional centers that were connected to each other by land and sea, their representation and promotion being cared for by several national and transnational organizations.

The Tourism and Travel Company came into being in the very year when Budapest hosted a congress of the International Hoteliers Association. Interaction between managers of this agency and the Hungarian company as well as their study of city marketing strategies implemented by other cities soon led to the formulation of an ambitious tourism promotion program for Budapest. The first step in this direction was the creation of a Tourist Information Center. Given the appeal that the Casino operating in

---

[17] See *Les capitales du monde* (Paris: Hachette, 1892), 2nd ed. (1896).

[18] For more on this association see Leemam Cromwell White, *International Non-Governmental Organizations: Their Purposes, Methods and Accomplishments* (New Brunswick: Rutgers University Press, 1951), p. 50 and *60 Jahre internationaler Hotelbesitzer-Verein, 1869–1929. Jubiläums-Ausgabe. Die Geschichte des Internationalen Hotelbesitzer-Vereins* (Köln: Dumont Schauberg, 1929).

Monte Carlo had on international tourists, there were also talks in 1902 about opening a similar establishment on the Margaret Island (a project that ultimately failed). However, in the spring of 1903 and 1904, the TTC in cooperation with the Hungarian Automobile Club was able to organize flower-decorated automobile pageants in Budapest. The company's attempts to boost urban life through the insertion of artificial events such as these were clearly inspired by similar pageants organized during this time period in Nice and Monaco.[19] Furthermore, to increase the appeal of the Danube Festival (a regatta on the Danube held in the spring of 1903), the TTC used fireworks and electric spotlights to illuminate the city's new monumental buildings (the building of the Parliament, the Fishermen's Bastion, and the Elizabeth bridge) and thus implemented a set of urban tourism promotion techniques that had initially been tested in Paris.[20] Spanish bullfights represented another form of tourist entertainment that had been tested elsewhere and which the company transplanted to Budapest. Before the corrida came to Budapest in June 1904, Paris, Brussels and several other northern French cities also hosted bullfights. Finally, the air shows that became so popular everywhere were also embraced by Budapest in 1909 when the TTC organized Louis Blériot's trip to the city.

Some of these city marketing efforts, however, triggered a xenophobic response from nationalists in Budapest. Turning the corrida into a permanent entertainment—as was initially intended by the TTC—failed only a few weeks after its opening. Fearing popular unrest and heeding the lobbying of nationalist journalists and opposition politicians the government finally forbade the continuation of bullfights in July 1904. In spite of the corrida's failure to become a permanent touristic attraction in Budapest[21] and the need for concessions made to the nationalist camp (which was more interested in fostering domestic rather than international tourism to Budapest), the company was successful in promoting the city abroad through various other means. For instance, during the years preceding WWI, Budapest turned into a city hosting many international conferences. Conference tourism emerged first in the major Western metropolises which hosted world's fairs. Budapest promoters recognized early on that hosting international conferences could add considerably to the number of visitors that the city received

---

[19]   See József Klaudy, "Az európai legelső Nemzeti Utazási Iroda története. A MÁV hivatalos Menetjegyirodájának negyven éve," *A magyar idegenforgalom évkönyve* (1943): pp. 199–318. See especially p. 236.

[20]   Ákos Kovács, *Játek a tűzzel. Fejezetek a magyarországi tűzijátékok és díszkivilágítások XV–XX. századi történetéből* (Budapest: Helikon, 2001), pp. 64–73.

[21]   For more on these developments see my "Bullfights in Budapest: City Marketing, Moral Panics and Nationalism in Turn-of-the-century Hungary" *Austrian History Yearbook* 41 (2010): pp. 143–69.

each year. 1896 was not only witness to a peak of nationalism in Hungary but also the year when Budapest hosted an International Pacifist Congress in the shadow of the shrill Millennium celebrations.[22] The number of international congresses hosted by the Hungarian capital then increased from year to year. Conference tourism was an important booster not only for the local economy but also for Budapest's inclusion into this specific niche of the emerging global tourism sector. As a sign of its importance it is worth mentioning that in 1909 over 5,000 doctors attending the 16th International Medical Congress visited Budapest.[23]

Older theme parks such as Ancient Buda Fortress and Constantinople in Budapest, and the international spectacles and attractions that the TTC organized and transplanted to Budapest during the first decade of the twentieth century, together with the flourishing of nighttime establishments (which will be discussed later in this chapter) played an important role in the creation of a transnational mass leisure industry in the city. Nationalists criticized their commercial and foreign character throughout this period. In spite of such criticism and resistance, however, during the decades preceding WWI marketing professionals continued to present the Hungarian capital as a city open to the world by borrowing ideas and practices implemented elsewhere.

The Interwar Period: Rejections and Borrowings

The influence of transnational trends that shaped to a great extent Budapest's marketing strategies at the turn of the century, however, was tempered after WWI. Historical events such as the dissolution of Austria-Hungary, the creation of a territorially reduced Hungary on the ruins of that empire, the replacement of the first Hungarian bourgeois-liberal government that took over the reins of the country in October 1918 with a communist government led by Béla Kun in the spring of 1919, followed by an Allied intervention which led to the replacement of the latter by a coalition of conservative, right-wing political forces, changed the dynamic and content of Budapest's marketing strategies for the remainder of the interwar period.

It is important to note though that new foundations for Budapest's marketing were laid down even before the end of WWI. A Budapest Tourism Office [BTO;

---

[22]   See *Bulletin officiel du VII congrès universel de la paix tenue à Budapest, 17–22 septembre 1896* (Berne: Bureau International de la Paix, 1896). For more on the history of this and other peace congresses held before WWI in Europe see Sandi E. Cooper, *Patriotic Pacifism: Waging War on War in Europe, 1814–1914* (Oxford: Oxford University Press, 1991).

[23]   Gábor Veress, "Budapest szerepe a magyar idegenforgalomban," in *A hetvenéves Budapest* (Budapest: Globus, 1943), pp. 157–66, p. 160.

Budapest Székesfővárosi Idegenforgalmi Hivatal] was created as a branch of the Municipality in 1916. The reason for its creation was the fact that citizens and wounded soldiers of the Central Powers—landlocked as they were by the fighting taking place on the Western, Eastern, and Southern fronts, including refugees from the newly opened front between the Austro-Hungarian and Romanian armies in the Carpathians—came in greater and greater numbers to Budapest. They looked in the Hungarian capital for recovery and entertainment, whose provision was soon taken up by the new office. It is worth pointing out that refugees and wounded soldiers represented an unorthodox group of tourists. Through their circumstances, they greatly differed from the pleasure tourists who visited Budapest before WWI. It is ironic, too, that it was fighting on the fronts and not the world's fair that Budapest planned to organize in 1917 (and whose convocation was cancelled because of the outbreak of WWI) which provided a new institutional departure for the organization of Budapest tourism.

The people in charge of the BTO survived the war and the regime changes that the country experienced in 1918–19 and led it, almost uninterruptedly, throughout the interwar period.[24] By the 1930s, however, they were not the only agency involved in city marketing. A host of other official institutions and booster associations emerged in the intervening period so that the BTO became part of a larger institutional structure interested in turning tourism into a source of economic revenue for Hungary. Institutions such as the National Tourism Office [Országos Idegenforgalmi Iroda], the Federation of the Hungarian Tourism Agencies [Magyarországi Idegenforgalmi Érdekeltségek Szövetsége], the Baross Federation [Baross Szövetség], an informal alliance of supporters of the development of tourism in Hungary, and the Economic Division [Közgazdasági Osztály] responsible, among others, for the development of tourism in the Ministry of Foreign Affairs, were all active in elaborating plans and voicing opinions regarding the countrywide management of tourism, including urban tourism. The recognition of the economic importance of tourism by the Hungarian state, the Budapest municipality and key political actors of the interwar period led, at the same time, to the strong politicization of tourist propaganda. Rejections and borrowings from international practices came thus to depend on their fit with an increasingly conservative, Christian, anti-Semitic, and nationalist agenda that shaped Hungarian politics from 1919 to 1945.[25] Therefore practices and city marketing methods that were seen as too

---

[24] Dr Béla Markos, *Jelentés Budapest Székesfőváros Idegenforgalmi Hivatalának huszonötesztendős munkásságáról, 1916–1941* (Budapest: Budapest Székesfőváros Idegenforgalmi Hivatala, 1941), pp. 11–86.

[25] For more on this see Paul A. Hanebrink, *In Defense of Christian Hungary: Religion, Nationalism and Anti-Semitism, 1890–1944* (Ithaca: Cornell University Press, 2006).

cosmopolitan or transnational in character were rejected for the sake of local color and ethnic specificity mirrored by *völkisch* costumes, artifacts, and (often newly invented) traditions that in the opinion of nationalist leaders stood for Magyar national values. At the same time, however, as discussed later in the chapter, those interested in promoting Budapest and attracting visitors to Hungary could not fully ignore transnational trends and developments in an industry whose flourishing was based on constant interaction between members of different nations. Therefore the city marketing strategies that were implemented in Hungary during this time period were shaped by constant ideology-fed rejections of projects that appeared too cosmopolitan, not to say "anti-national," with such rebuffs being moderated by borrowings that were deemed necessary in order to keep the business of city marketing up to international standards.

The Queen of the Danube: Geography, Nationalism, and Religion

One of the first reflections of a more conservative ideological stance in the field of city marketing during the interwar period was the BTO's abandonment of the old slogan which tried to sell Budapest abroad as the "Paris of the East," for the sake of a new one which promoted the city as the "Queen of the Danube." Budapest was seen by its new nationalist promoters as being defined not by the pre-war attempts local promoters made to present it as a world city competing with Paris but by its location on the banks of the Danube.[26] The new emphasis on geography can be interpreted as an attempt to root Budapest in the Hungarian soil. This was all the more important, since after 1919 both conservatives and nationalists looked at the capital as being different from the rest of Hungary. While the country and the Magyar-speaking peasantry were depicted as the authentic source of Magyar nationality, the capital was seen as a foreign environment shaped by Western and Jewish influences.[27] The support that many inhabitants of Budapest (belonging mostly to the urban intelligentsia, the Jewish middle-class, and the internationalist-minded working class) gave to the two revolutionary governments that took charge of the capital in the fall of 1918 and in the spring of 1919 was turned into political capital by the nationalists (supported at the time by members of the conservative

---

[26]　Béla Mátéka, "Budapest mint idegenforgalmi célpont," BFL (Budapest City Archives), XIII. 7 Mátéka család iratai.

[27]　Such representations existed before the war as well, but they were turned into mainstream ones only after 1919. For a discussion of nationalist representations of Budapest before and during WWI see Péter Bihari, *Lövészárkok a hátországban: középosztály, zsidókérdés, antiszemitizmus az első világháboru Magyarországán* (Budapest: Napvilág Kiadó, 2008), especially pp. 57–63.

Hungarian gentry and small town petty bourgeoisie) who depicted Budapest as a "Guilty City" that needed to expiate the sins it committed against the Magyar nation. At the same time, derogatory comments such as those made in his speeches by Vienna's turn-of-the-century mayor, Karl Lueger, who—because of the large number of Hungarian Jews living in the city—often referred to Budapest as "Juda-Pest," gained a new relevance in the atmosphere of anti-Semitic agitation that turned into an everyday reality in Hungary and especially in Budapest during the interwar period.[28]

The process of transitioning from the old to the new marketing slogan was not smooth. From 1919 to 1926, the BTO and the conservative, right wing, anti-Semitic, and nationalist lobbies that constantly tried to influence its activity were not yet able to override more liberal manifestations of city marketing. In fact, the slogan of presenting Budapest to its visitors as a "Paris of the East" hardly disappeared. It was used by press organs geared to foreign visitors in the immediate aftermath of the war as well as during the mid-1920s.[29] Many local promoters still saw the Hungarian capital as better defined by its marketing as a "World City" comparable to Paris and other world metropolises than a city defined by the surrounding natural environment.[30] The turn towards geography as a referent for Budapest gained prominence in the tourist propaganda brochures that the BTO published from 1926 on. The new slogan employed by the agency, which presented it in several languages to foreigners as the "Queen of the Danube," highlighted the aesthetic features of Budapest's panorama as seen from the top of the Gellért Hill, changing in the process the very terms of reference that urban promoters had employed before. If up to then Budapest was foremost compared to Paris on grounds of architectural similarities, its cosmopolitan life, and civilizational achievements, once the emphasis fell on the beauty of Budapest's panorama the city came to be favorably compared not to the French capital but rather to Naples and Rio de Janeiro.

Capitalizing on the city's insertion in an aestheticized landscape that was seen as a representative summation of Hungary's natural features was only one of the devices that city marketers used to nationalize Budapest's promotion abroad. Another interwar development was the nationalization of the touristic season in Budapest by organizing promotional events that were tied to ideologically-charged commemorations of national heroes. From 1926 on the "Queen of the Danube" brochures that the BTO published in French, English, German,

---

[28]   See János Gyurgyák, *Ezzé lett magyar hazátok. A magyar nemzeteszme és nacionalizmus története* (Budapest: Osiris, 2007).

[29]   See, for instance, the 1919 issues of *Budapesti Látogatók Lapja* and the 1925 issues of *Budapest Világváros.*

[30]   Op-ed in *Budapest Világváros* I/1 (November 1925).

Italian, Spanish, and Esperanto (and which were sent in several million copies abroad) presented St. Stephen's week as the high point of the touristic season in Hungary.[31] During the interwar period, St. Stephen, the first Christian king of medieval Hungary, turned into a potent political symbol as Christian values were embraced and equally promoted by conservatives and right-wing nationalists. Celebrated every year on August 20, St. Stephen's worship as the patron saint of interwar Hungary evolved from a rather marginal event before WWI into a national holiday, and from 1926 on, into a week-long festival that included pageants, sports games, outdoor spectacles, and the re-enactments of popular traditions.[32] At the core of the festival, however, was the religious procession that took the mummified right hand of St. Stephen, a medieval relic returned to Budapest by Habsburg Empress Maria Theresa in 1771, on a tour of the Castle Hill.[33] Concomitant to encouraging the rise of national sentiment among Magyars from Hungary and those living in territories lost in 1920, the festival also attempted to attract foreigners through the greater pomp that it acquired from year to year.[34] As part of a similar endeavor, 1930 was singled out by tourist officials as the year of St. Imre (St. Stephen's early-deceased pious son), while 1938 was the year when St. Stephen's celebration acquired a special meaning as the Hungarian government commemorated with it the passing of 900 years since the king's death.

With this last event, however, the meaning of previous nationalist commemorations of St. Stephen as the founder of Hungary was broadened through its insertion in the calendar of the supranational religious celebrations organized by the Roman Catholic Church.[35] Thus, in addition to being declared the year of St. Stephen, 1938 was also the year when Budapest hosted the 34th International Congress of the Eucharist. During the last week of May of that

---

[31] In 1930 alone the Budapest Tourism Office sent abroad no less than 215,669 "Queen of the Danube" brochures published in these languages. The overall figure for the entire period was in the range of millions. See BFL (Budapest City Archives), Budapesti Idegenforgalmi Hivatal Vegyes Iratok IV 1501 f, vol. 17: Propaganda iratok (1930).

[32] See András Sípos, "'Megmaradt országunknak csodás kincse ...' Törekvések Budapest nemzetközi szerepkörének kiépítésére Trianon előtt és után," *Limes* 3 (2004): pp. 65–79, esp. 75 ff.

[33] For more on the history of the early celebrations of St. Stephen's Day see Béláné Csitáry, *Szent István ünnepe hajdan és ma* (Budapest: Szent István-Társulat, 1918), 2nd ed. (1938) and Gyula Gábor, *A Szent-István napi ünnep története* (Budapest: Franklin, 1928).

[34] Sípos, "Megmaradt országunknak csodás kincse ...," pp. 75–6.

[35] For a discussion of the evolution in this direction see Chapter 8 "Der Stephanskult zwischen Katholizismus, Revisionismus und Antifaschizmus (1919–1944)" in Árpád von Klimó, *Nation, Konfession, Geschichte: Zur nationalen Geschichtskultur Ungarns im europäischen Kontext, 1860–1948* (Munich: R. Oldenbourg Verlag, 2003), pp. 244–88.

year Budapest was visited by the special emissary of the Pope, Bishop Eugenio Pacelli (the future Pope Pius XII) and turned into a pilgrimage center for devout Catholics from Hungary as well as abroad. All tourist operators recognized the importance of the event in marketing Budapest abroad. The Celebration of the Eucharist in Budapest was turned into a spectacular event in which fireworks, a huge electric cross located on top of the Gellért Hill, spire-like electric spotlights illuminating the night sky, lit bridges, and a festively decorated regatta of small boats on the Danube powerfully endorsed Budapest's promotional claim of being the "Queen of the Danube."[36]

In a gesture of religious internationalism, the Eucharist celebrations connected the city to an illustrious lineage of 33 other cities across the world that had hosted international congresses of the Eucharist before.[37] The Hungarian capital thus joined many other cities in Europe, Asia, Africa, Australia, and the two Americas—which following in the footsteps of nineteenth-century Lourdes and Marpingen—tried to boost their economy and international appeal by turning into venues of pilgrimage tourism.[38]

The Village in the City: *Völkisch* Costumes and Dances, and the Magyar Soul

In spite of its strong draw among peasants who flocked in droves to the capital,[39] the 1938 Celebration of the Eucharist was an event that was enjoyed mostly by moderate nationalists and members of the conservative and Catholic Hungarian aristocracy.[40] More extremist Magyar nationalists were less excited about making the city appealing to Catholics from all over the world. For ethnic populists

---

[36]   See Károly Huszár, *Az Eucharisztikus Kongresszus csodálatos éjszakája* (Budapest: Stephaneum, 1941).

[37]   The first international Eucharist Congress was organized in Lille, France in 1881, followed by congresses held in Avignon, Paris, Jerusalem, Reims, Rome, Montréal, Chicago, Sydney, Carthage, Buenos Aires, Manila, etc. For a full list of the cities that hosted Eucharistic congresses between 1881 and 1937 see Jenő Gergely, *Eucharisztikus világkongresszus Budapesten, 1938* (Budapest: Kossuth, 1988), pp. 22–3.

[38]   See Suzanne Kauffmann, *Consuming Visions: Mass Culture and the Lourdes Shrine* (Ithaca: Cornell University Press, 2005), and David Blackbourn, *Marpingen: Apparitions of the Virgin Mary in Bismarckian Germany* (Oxford: Clarendon Press, 1993).

[39]   Erika Vass, "Kitárult világ: az 1938-ban rendezett eucharisztikus világkongresszus a turizmus szemszögéből," in Zoltán Fejős and Zsolt Szijjártó (eds), *Helye(in)k, tárgya(in)k, Émleke(in)k: A turizmus társadalomtudományos magyarázata*, Tabula könyvek 5 (Budapest: Néprajzi Múzeum, 2005), pp. 97–107.

[40]   See the enthusiastic description of this event in Prince Sándor Erba-Odescalchi, *Testamentum: Életem regénye* (Budapest: Dovin, 1991), vol. 2, p. 304.

Budapest represented "a crucial battlefield, where the Magyar struggle for life will be decided." They saw the capital—as it was often in the grip of international fashions—as being "sick and foreign." They described Budapest's buildings as a collection of "Austro-German kitsch, with some ghetto architecture, and a sprinkling of failed Magyar efforts" to give more substance to this eclectic amalgam. Extremist nationalists wanted to turn Budapest more into a Magyar city than it was and a window display of the "Magyar soul." They planned to do this by bringing, instead of foreigners from outside Hungary's borders, the world of the Magyar village to Budapest.[41]

To achieve this goal they wanted to use the inhabitants of the Magyar villages who were already living in the capital as pawns in a process of social engineering that would lead to the creation of institutions representative of the Magyar soul. As one of them put it in 1935, "In Budapest one needs to create popular gardens filled with peasant homes. In these homes there should be a library, a conference room, peasant arts and crafts workshops, a stage, dance floors, and a peasant pub."[42] One such village was to be located in the City Park on the Pest side of the city, while another would take up the open space behind the Castle Hill, known as the Vérmező in Buda.

Although the implantation of these villages in the urban texture was never seriously considered or endorsed by governmental and municipal authorities, a focus on peasant themes had infused the work of Budapest tourism officials since at least the early 1920s.[43] Initially, however, their focus on the countryside was meant to add to the appeal of Budapest, and nationalistic overtones were expressed only at higher levels. For instance, referring to the strong interest that the Magyar peasant costumes provoked among a group of Vassar College students and faculty that he took in 1922 to Mezőkövesd (a village with a strong folk tradition about 130 kilometers east of Budapest), Béla Mátéka, an employee of the Budapest Tourism Office, urged his superiors in several reports to include displays of peasant artifacts and ads about rural excursions in Budapest's foreign tourism propaganda materials. By 1923 larger groups of French, American, British, Dutch, and Spanish tourists were recruited in person by Mátéka from various Budapest hotels and taken in a chartered Pullman car on day trips by

---

[41]   See "A Falu Budapest" in Dezső Szabó, *Az egész látóhatár*, vol. 1 (Budapest: Magyar Élet, 1939), pp. 294–9.

[42]   Ibid., p. 295.

[43]   One should also point out that similar ideas were voiced by turn-of-the-century left-wing Magyar populists as well. What connected Szabó and Károly Kós's vision (the turn-of-the-century architect of the Wekerle Telep in Budapest) were their common Transylvanian roots and fascination with the architecture, ethnic costumes, and peasant artifacts of the Magyar villages in the vicinity of Cluj/Kolozsvár.

railway to Mezőkövesd. On their return to Budapest some of them were even introduced to Miklós Horthy, the Governor of Hungary who—in a direct reference to the government advocated non-national character of Budapest— praised the Mezőkövesd peasants by emphasizing that "under their Magyar costumes also pulses a Magyar heart."[44]

Other promoters also urged the inclusion of peasant-themed attractions such as "folk costumes, songs, music and national dances" in Budapest's tourist propaganda.[45] In fact, associations such as the Turanic Society [Turáni Társaság] organized peasant fairs and Turanic song contests in the city that were included in Budapest's seasonal offerings.[46] But the most important breakthrough— from the point of view of nationalist critics of Budapest's pre-war marketing strategies—was the creation of a professional dance team, the Gyöngyös Bokréta [the Pearly Bouquet] that from 1932 on was singled out as one of the important highlights of the annual St. Stephen's festivities held in the city.[47] Led by choreographer Béla Paulini, the Pearly Bouquet interpreted Magyar dances and plays throughout the 1930s and was highly recommended in the "Budapest Queen of the Danube" brochures as an attraction not to be missed by foreign tourists who visited Budapest during that time period.[48]

Budapest Spa-City: A Brief Case Study

While the interwar turn to geographic, nationalist, religious, and *völkisch* motives in Budapest's tourism propaganda was highly ideological in character, there was another attempt made during these years to promote it, on ideologically more neutral grounds, as a Spa-City [*Fürdőváros*]. The origins of promoting Budapest as a "Mecca for rheumatics" go back to the last decade

---

[44] See Béla Mátéka, Untitled report (August 1922) and "Hogyan jött létre az első Mezőkövesdi nagyobb társaskirándulás," BFL (Budapest City Archives), XIII. 7. Mátéka család iratai.

[45] Mihály Gellér, *Ujabb idegenforgalmi feladataink* (Budapest: Magyar Idegenforgalmi Érdekeltségek Szövetsége, 1929), p. 8.

[46] "Turáni Társaság által rendezett turáni dal s népünnepély tervezete" (June 1928), BFL (Budapest City Archives), IV 1501 f, Budapesti Idegenforgalmi Hivatal: Vegyes iratok, box 2.

[47] See Arpád Halász, *Budapest húsz éve: 1920–1939. Fejlődéstörténeti tanulmány* (Budapest: Wolff Károly Emlékbizottság, 1939), p. 211. For some precedents see "Az első Magyar táncbemutató létrejövetele Szent István hetén" (1927), BFL (Budapest City Archives), XIII. 7. Mátéka család iratai.

[48] See program for "Hungarian Plays, under the direction of Béla Paulini, May 21, 1938," BFL (Budapest City Archives), XIII. 7. Mátéka család iratai.

of the nineteenth century.[49] Shortly afterwards, a Balneology Committee [Fürdőügyi Bizottság], formed in Budapest in 1901, pressured the government to support the development of a few already existing spas, including the Turkish and mineral baths within the perimeter of the capital.[50] Although the demolition of the Tabán, a Buda slum, and the pre-WWI effort to create a spa district there failed because of financial backing, the opening of new baths such as the Széchenyi (1912) and the Hotel Gellért spa complex (1918) created a modern services and accommodation-providing infrastructure. The Budapest Spa-City Association [Budapest Fürdőváros Egylet], founded in 1926, and the Budapest Wellness and Spa Central Committee [Budapesti Központi Gyógy- és Üdülőhelyi Bizottság], created in 1934, were all too eager to exploit these resources for city marketing purposes.[51] The 1926 opening of the first artificial wave pool in Europe on the premises of the Gellért Hotel represented an important addition to Budapest's interwar touristic offerings. Led by Grand Prince József Ferenc, a prominent member of the Habsburg family who chose to settle in Hungary after WWI, the Budapest Spa-City Association promoted the organization of an international balneology congress in the city in 1929. In October 1937, in an effort to add to the international prominence of the Hungarian capital, the same association organized the visit of 350 foreign delegates representing 30 nations who decided to create an International Spa Association with its headquarters located in Budapest.[52]

As the headquartering of this association in Budapest suggests, the context within which we should locate the emergence of the Budapest Spa City idea was one that was truly international. The first petition made by local promoters to make better use of Budapest's mineral springs and baths was inspired by the economic success and international appeal of nineteenth-century health resorts such as Bath, Brighton, Spa, Ostende, Baden-Baden, Karlsbad (today Karlovy Vary), Marienbad (Márianské Lázně), Nice, and Monte Carlo. By the interwar period this context was broadened to include comparisons between Budapest and North American leisure places such as Atlantic City, Saratoga Springs,

---

[49]   Endre Liber, *Budapest-fürdőváros kialakulása különös tekintettel a székesfőváros községi fürdőpolitikájára* (Budapest: Székesfővárosi házinyomda, 1932), p. 6.

[50]   "A fürdőügy a képviselőházban," *Balneologiai Értesítő* (1901): pp. 27–9 and appendix, pp. 1–24.

[51]   See *Jelentés a Budapesti Központi Gyógy- és Üdülőhelyi Bizottság 1935–1938, 1940–1947 évi müködéséről.* (Budapest: Egyesült Nyomda, 1936–48).

[52]   "30 nemzet 350 képviselője Budapesten megalakította a Nemzetközi Fürdőszövetséget," *Fővárosi Hírlap,* October 13, 1937, p. 6.

Hot Springs, and French Lick.[53] Comparing Budapest to these resorts allowed promoters to make a significant step in the direction of city branding.

The juxtaposition of two different contexts, that of spa cities and the European metropolises that Budapest competed against, was an important moment in the history of Budapest's marketing. As a student of Budapest's place in the business of international tourism argued in 1932:

> Paris is famous because of the multitude of its artistic riches, its sphere of cultural influence, and the number and variety of its entertainments. London attracts [visitors] through its size, stunning traffic and the emphasis on its traditions. Rome appeals through its ancient and medieval buildings, and as the seat of the Papacy. Naples is defined by its wonderful panorama, while Venice [owes its fame] to its lagoon. Berlin stands out through the American rhythm and rich economic life.[54]

What could make the Hungarian capital different from all these cities was the fact that—as he and other tourism promoters emphasized—in Budapest one could find both the pleasures provided by a world city and the relaxation and health benefits that one would find only in a health resort.

Budapest by Night: Incorporating Private Initiatives in Budapest's Tourist Propaganda

If watching historical pageants and religious processions and going to the baths could well fill the day of Budapest visitors during the touristic season, what about their nighttime activities? While up to the mid-nineteenth century bourgeois tourists were happy to go to bed after a copious meal in the restaurant of the hotel that they stayed in, by the turn of the century the demand for nighttime entertainment turned into a mainstay of the urban tourist's schedule in almost every city in the world. The emergence of Montmartre as Paris' main nighttime entertainment district during the 1880s and the 1890s (a district receiving worldwide attention through the appeal of establishments such as the Chat Noir, Moulin Rouge, and Folies-Bérgères, among others) turned into a model that many Western metropolises imitated. The names of the Montmartre cabarets became synonymous with the very concept of urban nightlife.[55]

---

53   Sándor Károlyi, *A magyar idegenforgalom jövője* (Budapest: Athenaeum, 1937), p. 11.

54   János Benyó, *Budapest fürdőváros és az idegenforgalom* (Budapest, 1932), p. 38

55   For a comparative look at the development of nightlife in the major European metropolises of the time, see Joachim Schlör, *Nights in the Big City: Paris, Berlin, London, 1830–1940* (London: Reaktion Books, 1998).

Following the trend, cabarets with names like Kék Macska [Blue Cat], Vörös Macska [Red Cat], Tarka Macska [Spotted Cat], and Folies Caprice were also opened in Budapest during the last quarter of the nineteenth century.[56] As another instance of Montmartre's distant echo, the French restaurant located on the precincts of Ancient Buda Fortress (the theme park erected on the grounds of the Millennium Exhibition in 1896) entertained visitors with frequent performances of French cancan.[57] But the range of international influences was not just French. Vienna's popular entertainments and Berlin's early-twentieth-century cabarets also played a prominent role in shaping turn-of-the-century Budapest's nightlife. For instance, the Berlin tingel-tangel, rebaptized *tinglitangli* in Hungarian, turned into another mainstay of the city's nightlife offerings, second only to the French-inspired *kabaré*.[58]

In spite of strong German competition, the influence of Montmartre's nocturnal establishments survived and even strengthened after WWI. A cabaret with the name of Fekete Macska [Black Cat] opened in Budapest as late as 1920. Establishments such as the Parisien Grill, Jardin de Paris, Tabarin, Alhambra, and Moulin Rouge turned into mandatory stops for foreign visitors responding to the appeal of the Budapest night during the 1920s and 1930s. A new development, however, which eclipsed previous ones, was the opening in 1932 by Sándor Rozsnyai, a Hungarian Jewish entrepreneur, of a new nightspot that he named Arizona Bar. The establishment earned fame almost overnight. The owner's wife turned into a celebrated local cabaret star, often favorably compared to Mistinguett, the French singer who enchanted foreign audiences in Paris. Rozsnyai was also interested in technical innovations; the rising and rotating dance floor that he built (later copied and popularized in the Hollywood films of the era) turned the Arizona Bar into a continental sensation that attracted rich and select travelers— the Prince of Wales, Count Ciano, and Eda Mussolini (Benito Mussolini's wife) being just a few among the many.[59] According to its owner who was not shy to market his establishment, Arizona was a staple not to be missed in Budapest's nightlife, the "most beautiful and gayest city of the world."[60]

----

[56]   It should be noted though that the Kék Macska (a.k.a. the Blaue Katze) was not named after the Chat Noir but rather the name of its owner, a certain Katzer.

[57]   "Tarka krónika: Mikor a kegyelmes úr kankant táncol," *Pesti Napló*, July 9, 1904, p. 13, and "Tarka krónika: A budapesti cancan," *Pesti Napló*, July 19, 1904, p. 16.

[58]   See Pál Péter Molnár, *A pesti mulatók* (Budapest: Helikon, 2001), pp. 5–7.

[59]   See Ella Megyery, *Budapesti notesz* (Budapest: Dante, 1937); Vilmos Tarján, *Pesti éjszaka* (Budapest: Általános nyomda, könyv és lapkiadó Rt, 1940); and Róbert Rátonyi, *Mulató a Nagymező utcában* (Budapest: IPV, 1987).

[60]   See Sándor Rozsnyai, "Gypsy Music—Barack—Arizona," *Pesti esték* I/1 (1936): pp. 8–9.

The name chosen by Rozsnyai for his locale was also symptomatic of the spread of a fascination with jazz and American popular culture that after reaching a high point in Paris and Berlin during the 1920s reached Eastern Europe as well by the late interwar period.[61] Local city marketing agencies such as the BTO could not ignore such developments. Although tourism officials recommended that nighttime spots include more Hungarian music and dances in their offerings, the spread of jazz and other foreign trends proved impossible to stop.[62] Therefore, as a pragmatic gesture bowing to reality, in the propaganda material that the office sent abroad, the Arizona Bar came also to occupy a place. For instance, the materials that a subsidiary office of this agency, located in Cairo, distributed in 1936 to rich Middle Easterners, Indian maharajahs and cosmopolitan Westerners, included ample textual and visual references to this establishment.[63]

As the official promotion of this nighttime establishment shows, the cosmopolitan pleasure-oriented and commercial character of European urban tourism was by the 1930s a given which, in spite of the increasing nationalist and anti-Semitic orientation of Hungarian politics, the Budapest Tourism Office and other touristic agencies in Hungary had to take into account if they wanted to increase the amount of money foreign tourists brought to the capital. Indeed, the sensuous offerings of the Budapest night turned into serious pull engines of the local urban tourism business, playing an important role in boosting the number of foreign visitors to the higher levels which they reached between 1932 and 1938.[64]

Learning from America: Local Tourism Propaganda and the American Way

Budapest's transformation into an exciting destination increasingly sought by German, Austrian, British, American, and French tourists was ultimately proof of the professionalization of the tourism business in Hungary. By the

---

[61]   For more on this see Victoria de Grazia, *Irresistible Empire: America's Advance through Twentieth-Century Europe* (Cambridge, MA: Belknap Press, 2005), esp. pp. 284–335.

[62]   "Mátéka Béla javaslata a Royal Orfeum, Parisien Grill, Papagály, Jardin de Paris és Tabarin igazgatóságának a Bp. Székesfővárosi idegenforgalmi hivatala nevében" (April 9, 1931), BFL (Budapest City Archives), XIII. 7 Mátéka család iratai.

[63]   See "A kairoi iroda jelentése" (1936), BFL (Budapest City Archives), IV 1501 f, Budapesti Idegenforgalmi Hivatal: Vegyes iratok, box 6.

[64]   In 1937, the peak year of Budapest tourism, for instance, the city was visited by 183,000 foreign tourists. For detailed statistics see Halász, *Budapest húsz éve*, pp. 212–16, while for a study analyzing these numbers from a *longue durée* comparative perspective (with a strong emphasis on the inter-regional competition between Budapest and Vienna) see the chapter on "Comparative Tourism Growth: Austria and Hungary, 1870–1988," in József Böröcz, *Leisure Migration: A Sociological Study of Tourism* (London: Pergamon, 1996), pp. 53–81.

late interwar years tourist officials in Hungary learned to pay more attention to global developments, and in spite of the constant nationalist rhetoric and promotion of rural values that infused the domestic tourist discourse, to allow for foreign borrowings if they carried a strong economic rationale.

North America increasingly drew the attention of tourism officials. An internal document brought to the attention of the BTO as early as 1922, for instance, emphasized the importance of implementing American propaganda methods to boost local tourism. The urgency of doing so was all the more necessary because it was only through the use of such methods, as the author of the document put it, that American tourists—who represented a "golden flow" of visitors across the Atlantic after WWI—could be convinced to make it to Budapest.[65] To achieve this goal, Hungarian tourism officials had to start an aggressive press campaign, targeting especially English and American newspapers, so as to enable "foreign audiences to hear about Hungary and Budapest" as often as possible.[66]

The necessity of advertising Budapest abroad was recognized by many other tourism professionals as well in the aftermath of the war. To give more traction to their opinion some contrasted the city's status in post-war Hungary with that of pre-war Austria-Hungary. One of their arguments was that pre-war Budapest received many foreign visitors due both to its proximity to Vienna and to the mere fact that it was part of a European great power. In contrast, after the war, as the capital city of a small country that allied with the losing side during the recent bloody conflict, Budapest now had to spend large amounts of money in order to advertise itself abroad.[67]

During the mid-1920s over one million pengős were spent annually on updating the Budapest tourist brochures, publishing them in several foreign languages, shipping them to over 500 luxury hotels in Europe, and on maintaining active correspondence with such major foreign tourism agencies as the Wagon Lits, Cook's, American Express, Mittel-europäisches Reisebüro and Chiari Sommariva. Brief ads praising the beauties of Budapest were also inserted in the radio broadcast of the Hungarian State Railways.[68] In order to attract more foreign visitors, and especially American tourists, in

---

65   On the massification of transatlantic tourism see Lorraine Coons and Alexander Varias, *Tourist Third Cabin: Steamship Travel in the Interwar Years* (New York: Palgrave Macmillan, 2003).

66   "Az amerikai propaganda szükségéssége," BFL (Budapest City Archives), XIII. 7. Mátéka család iratai.

67   Halász, *Budapest húsz éve*, pp. 207–8.

68   Béla Mátéka, "Budapest mint idegenforgalmi célpont," BFL (Budapest City Archives), XIII. 7 Mátéka család iratai.

1927 the Budapest Tourism Office sponsored a large delegation of American journalists to attend St. Stephen's festivities organized in August of that year. Tourism officials singled out the cultivation of the American connection as a very important task for the future of Budapest tourism.[69] Hungarians living in the United States contributed to the effort by sending their own private recommendations regarding diverse marketing strategies to the BTO.[70] For instance, Mihály Gellér, the manager of the St. Regis Hotel in New York, wrote a pamphlet urging tourism officials to rely on his expertise in order to turn Budapest into a fashionable destination.[71] In the same vein, local journalists urged public authorities and tourism officials to contact American businessmen in order to have them build modern hotels on the banks of the Danube.[72]

Some of this advice and especially the money that the BTO invested in American style propaganda bore fruit by the late 1920s. Although tourists from neighboring Austria were still leading the list of Budapest's foreign visitors, the number of Americans who made it to the Hungarian capital grew from 3,766 in 1925 to over 5,000 in 1927. It was also the Americans who spent a longer time in the city than tourists of other nations.[73] Overall, by 1929 foreign visitors spent 12 times more money in the city than the amount that was invested in touristic propaganda for Budapest that year.[74] Once the business of tourism started to flourish during the 1930s, however, references to former borrowings from foreign marketing models were discarded for the sake of a self-celebratory discourse that emphasized the unique merits of the Budapest Tourism Office in boosting urban tourism.[75]

---

[69]   BFL (Budapest City Archives), IV 1501 f, Budapesti Idegenforgalmi Hivatal: Vegyes iratok, box 6.

[70]   See "Milyen legyen az amerikai propaganda (egy philadelphiai magyar írása)" and "Borsodi Vilmos ügynök ajánlása amerikai propaganda kiterjesztéséről" (December 18, 1927), BFL (Budapest City Archives), IV 1501 f, Budapesti Idegenforgalmi Hivatal: Vegyes iratok, box 7.

[71]   Gellér, *Ujabb idegenforgalmi feladataink*, p. 7.

[72]   Sándor Nádas, "Budapest," *Pesti Futár* 15 (1929): pp. 3–4.

[73]   BFL (Budapest City Archives), IV 1501 f, Budapesti Idegenforgalmi Hivatal: Vegyes iratok, box 7.

[74]   Halász, *Budapest húsz éve*, p. 208.

[75]   See Ferenc Ripka, *Budapest a közép-Duna idegenforgalmának központja* (Budapest, 1933) and Markos, *Jelentés Budapest Székesfőváros Idegenforgalmi Hivatalának huszonötesztendős munkásságáról.*

Conclusion

The adoption of foreign models in Budapest's urban tourism promotion was like a litmus test reflecting strong local reactions. Promotion strategies adopted around the turn of the century led to Budapest's progressive integration into a transnational network of cities competing for new economic resources (with mass tourism turning fast into a major source of revenue). At the same time, TTC's adoption of a strong business orientation and turn toward sensationalist propaganda supported by tourism agencies elsewhere led to a nationalist counter-reaction in Hungary. The TTC's 1902 plan to boost Budapest tourism by building a casino on Margaret Island, and two years later the attempt to attract foreigners to the Hungarian capital through the organization of bullfights were seen by Hungarian nationalists as the aggressive infusion of a consumerist spirit into an urban society that, because of its rapid modernization, was already escaping their ideological control. Instead of business-mindedness and the adoption of transnational forms of urban entertainment, nationalists wanted historical pageants and a tourism promotion strategy focused on the Magyar past.

Although formulating tourism policies for Budapest was an activity that attracted a lot of governmental attention before WWI when Hungary, as the junior partner in the dual structure of Austria-Hungary, could not elaborate a foreign policy of its own, state and municipal interventions during the pre-war period were weak and the initiative stayed in the hands of the non-governmental Tourism and Travel Company. During the interwar period, however, this situation changed in favor of strong municipal and state intervention in the field of city marketing. As a result, the interwar institutions which were in charge of selling Budapest abroad were not fully able to replicate the freedom of initiative of tourism agencies and individual promoters in North American and Western European cities, and were instead charged with the task of coming up with marketing strategies that reflected the political concerns and dominant ideologies of the day. After 1919, transnational influences and models were carefully examined through the lens of a dominant nationalist ideology and adopted only if their spectacular character—such as in the cases of fireworks, lit crosses, festive illuminations, and boat parades—was relatively neutral and as such could not endanger the nation-building project. Although important exceptions, such as in the case of nighttime establishments and interaction between Hungary and the US, were also made, their economic pragmatism was subordinated to the broader concerns of the Christian-national political course that shaped interwar Hungary. The only agencies that could more or less escape the tight ideological grip of the state and nationalist lobbies and follow foreign precedents with more ease were the balneology associations which promoted Budapest abroad as a

Spa-City. As these developments suggest, the transition from Budapest's pre-war marketing as a "Paris of the East" to its representation as "Queen of the Danube" illustrated both the strong ideological character of urban tourism promotion in interwar Hungary and the nationalist ideology's inability to encompass and control every manifestation of it in an age when tourism was increasingly turning into an important transnational phenomenon. Overall, however, the marketing of Hungary's capital as the "Queen of the Danube" had lasting effects. As the travel books that one can pick up today before visiting Hungary prove, Budapest is still presented to visitors (with the brand's nationalist connotations now either ignored or forgotten) as a "Queen of the Danube."[76]

---

[76] See Péter Korniss and Miklós György Száraz, *Budapest: The Queen of the Blue Danube* (Budapest: Officina Nova, 1998), and Stephen Fallon, *Budapest: The Diva of the Danube*, 2nd ed. (Melbourne: Lonely Planet, 2003), p. 9.

Chapter 7

A Place Like Any Other?:
Publicity, Hotels and the Search
for a French Path to Tourism

Patrick Young

That organizers of the first national convening in 1913 of representatives from the various groups, offices, and enterprises working to develop tourism in France should officially designate it an "Estates General of Tourism" might seem at first glance a rather silly bit of self-inflation. In terms of historical significance, the meeting has certainly not posed any grave threat to its namesake, and even with the decline in the Revolution's fortunes within French history, does not look to do so anytime soon. Whether or not it was merited though, the choice of title did effectively convey an important shift in the way that tourism was being thought about in France, as well as in other European nations at the time. For the meeting's organizers were not at all mistaken in believing that tourism was coming to be newly harnessed to the French national interest. After all, Raymond Poincaré himself presided over the meeting, fresh off having been the first President of the Republic to undertake an official tourist voyage in the country. The Ministers of Public Works, Commerce, Agriculture, and Labor were also in attendance, as were nearly half the members of the Chamber of Deputies and Senate.[1] Just three years earlier, the French government had opened its first office dedicated expressly to the question of national tourist development, the Office National du Tourisme (ONT), under the auspices of the Ministry of the Interior. The argument that tourism was a matter of national import had clearly made significant headway in France.

Addressing the delegates, the Minister of Public Works indeed heralded the Estates General as welcome evidence of "a government taking into account the touristic organization of France, sketching out a program destined to carry it out, and moving this program from the realm of speculation to that of fact." It

---

[1]   Archives Nationales, Paris [hereafter AN], Estates-General of Tourism [hereafter EGT], 53AS/165, 1913.

showed, he added, that tourism was "not a pastime of the rich, nor a sport, still less an industry or form of commerce; it (is), literally, the entirety of France fully developed in its economic interests, encouraged in its regional life, conserved in its traditions, extended in its hospitality, beautified by its sites, increased ten-fold in all of its material, moral, intellectual and artistic riches."[2] This ambition to mine the nation-building potential of a formerly elite leisure activity was one that now more directly propelled tourist development efforts in France, as too in other European countries in the early twentieth century. From the establishment across Europe of touring associations, governmental offices and budgetary allotments dedicated to national tourist development, to the state-organized leisure initiatives of the 1930s in liberal and non-liberal regimes alike, it is clear that the nation was now far more present in tourism than it had been previously.[3]

Yet tourism also became *inter*national in new ways in this period. The premise of this volume invites greater attention to how the main forms and practices of modern tourism have emerged within an international, and more specifically trans-European, context. It is a question of particular salience for the first half of the twentieth century, when the national and international dimensions of tourism came into a far more complex relationship in Europe. "Crossing borders" in considering this key period, I want to suggest, means taking account of the new national ambitions driving tourist development, though also of how these coexisted—at times uneasily—with the realities of an increasingly diverse, international, and commercialized tourist circulation across the continent. As the first wave of tourist "planners" emerged across Europe in the early twentieth century, they undertook to build more modern and national tourist infrastructure in their respective countries,

---

2   AN, EGT, 53AS/165, Speech of M. Thierry, Minister of Public Works, 1913.

3   Recent perspectives on the new national investment in European tourism in this period include Orvar Löfgren, "Know Your Country: A Comparative Perspective on Tourism and Nation-Building in Sweden," in Ellen Furlough and Shelly Baranowski (eds), *Being Elsewhere: Tourism, Consumer Culture and Identity in Modern Europe* (Ann Arbor: University of Michigan Press, 2001), pp. 137–54. On fascist leisure and tourism initiatives, see Shelly Baranowski, *Strength through Joy: Consumerism and Mass Tourism in the Third Reich* (London: Cambridge University Press, 2007); Kristen Semmens, *Seeing Hitler's Germany: Tourism in the Third Reich* (New York: Macmillan, 2006); Victoria DeGrazia, *The Culture of Consent: Mass Organization of Leisure in Fascist Italy* (Cambridge: Cambridge University Press, 2002). On the leisure reforms of the French Popular Front, see Julian Jackson, "'Le Temps des Loisirs': Popular Tourism and Mass Leisure in the Vision of the Front Populaire," in Martin S. Alexander and Helen Graham (eds), *The French and Spanish Popular Fronts: Comparative Perspectives* (Cambridge: Cambridge University Press, 1989), pp. 226–39. Sasha D. Pack focuses mainly on the postwar Franco years, but also outlines the beginnings of a pre-1945 state investment in Spain in *Tourism and Dictatorship: Europe's Peaceful Invasion of Spain* (New York: Macmillan, 2006), esp. pp. 24–38.

and to realize specific national objectives in developing tourism; but they did so within a changing and increasingly competitive European and international climate for leisure travel, one that posed distinct organizational challenges. Appealing to and accommodating the dramatically expanded domestic and international clientele for tourism necessitated a rethinking of the central institutions and practices of modern tourism, and an often-uneasy adaptation to emerging international norms.

This chapter represents a limited attempt at analyzing the role of trans-European interchange and competition in the forging of ostensibly "national" tourist industries, which scholars have tended to treat too much in isolation. Using the French case as a point of entry, it will focus on campaigns around tourist publicity and the French hotel, two of the main early preoccupations of French tourist organizers as they undertook to develop the country more fully for both national and international tourist commerce. As two of the most important media of tourist interface, publicity and the hotel were pivotal in representing "France" to itself and to the world. The perceived imperative of modernizing them in the early twentieth century led French tourist organizers to enter into greater trans-European and trans-Atlantic awareness and dialogue, and to try to adapt to emerging international tourist standards and practices; yet it also pushed them into new ways of asserting and preserving what they felt to be an essential French distinctiveness. This was indeed a not uncommon dynamic across Europe in this period, as tourism became a means through which nations both integrated into and distinguished themselves within a changing European order.

The French Tourist "Industry" and the Question of Publicity

Over the roughly two decades preceding the 1913 meeting, a new coterie of actors endeavored to redefine the forms and meanings of French tourism, and to build a more modern tourist infrastructure and commerce across the country. Chief among these, and the group most instrumental in winning acceptance for the idea of tourism as a vital national interest, was the Touring Club de France, a voluntary and largely middle-class association founded in 1890. With the *syndicats d'initiative* (local and regional civic development groupings), the Alpine and Automobile Clubs, and the major rail and shipping lines, the Touring Club was vital in establishing the foundations of a modern French "tourist industry" in the early twentieth century.[4] While the French

---

4   The Touring Club first generalized usage of the term "industry" to describe the various associational, commercial, and governmental actors working to develop tourism in France in the first decade of the twentieth century. On the role of the Touring Club in the development of modern tourism in France, see Catherine Bertho-Lavenir, *La roue et le stylo: Comment nous*

Touring Club was the most sizable touring association in Europe during this period, Germany, Austria, England, Italy, Belgium, Holland, Denmark, Sweden, Switzerland, and Luxembourg, also by 1906, each possessed at least one national voluntary association dedicated to the promotion of tourism and tourist development.

What connected these varied groupings across Europe was a common ambition to ground travel in larger concerns—newly awakened nationalist commitments principally, but also kindred convictions related to the modern social need for movement, activity, and hygienic renewal, and the great economic and moral benefits of tourism. Though almost exclusively bourgeois in composition, European touring associations of this period played a pivotal (and still underappreciated) role in the long-term transition from elite to popular tourism, partly through engendering a new trans-European discourse on tourism that asserted its potential for advancing national and even international progress.[5] Tourism had long been a main forging ground for European elites, unfolding along itineraries and at specific sites that were often more international than national in character. The early modern tradition of the Grand Tour and its variants took travelers (predominantly young Englishmen) along largely fixed continental itineraries to commune with traces of a classical European cultural inheritance, and was largely brokered by transnational aristocratic linkages.[6] The continental spa and beach resorts that came to the fore of European tourism after 1815 in the wake of the Grand Tour's decline were often themselves highly

---

sommes devenus touristes (Paris: Odile Jacob, 1999); see also Patrick Young, "The Consumer as National Subject: Bourgeois Tourism in the French Third Republic, 1880–1914" (Ph.D. diss., Columbia University, 2000).

[5] The Ligue Internationale des Associations Touristes, established in 1898 in Luxembourg, brought together for the first time these national groupings, most of which had been founded in the 1890s. AN 53AS/163, "Origins of Touring Club." On the Touring Club Italiano, see R.J.B. Bosworth, "The *Touring Club Italiano* and the Nationalization of the Italian Bourgeoisie," *European History Quarterly* 27/3 (July 1997): pp. 371–410. On the promotion of tourism by nationalist associations in the Habsburg Empire, see Pieter Judson, "'Every German Visitor has a *Völkisch* Obligation he Must Fulfill': Nationalist Tourism in the Austrian Empire, 1880–1918," in Rudy Koshar (ed.), *Histories of Leisure* (Oxford: Berg, 2002), pp. 147–68.

[6] Jeremy Black has most extensively considered the Grand Tour tradition, focusing in particular upon the experiences of young Englishmen on the continent; see *The British Abroad: The Grand Tour in the Eighteenth Century* (London: The History Press, 2003); Black also has more specialized volumes relating to British travel in Italy and in France along the Grand Tour circuit; on women travelers along the Grand Tour, see Brian Dolan, *Ladies of the Grand Tour: British Women in Pursuit of Enlightenment and Adventure in Eighteenth Century Europe* (New York: Harper-Collins, 2001).

international locations, where bourgeois and aristocrats of diverse national origin mixed and assimilated international norms of taste and distinction.[7] With the rise of touring associations across Europe at the turn of the century, the nation, its territory, and its citizenry now became the subject of tourism as never before. Additionally and more practically, at a time when most European states still involved themselves only minimally in the encouragement and organization of tourist commerce, it was associations such as these that advocated most effectively for tourism; and even themselves often undertook the initiatives of tourist development that would over time help to build a more integrated modern tourist infrastructure both within individual nations and across the continent as a whole.

As they undertook to build a more modern and national tourism in France, Touring Club leaders had to reflect more deliberately upon France's position within international tourism, and take stock of French assets and disadvantages *vis-à-vis* its peer nations in Europe. There was for them little question of France's uncommon natural, cultural, and historical richness, though they also identified specific impediments to France's development of tourism as a vital national sector. Where the French tended toward being more *casanier* or "home-bound," ran one common refrain, the English and Germans in particular had fully developed a modern taste for movement and activity in the open air.[8] Likewise, states such as Switzerland and Austria-Hungary had already by the turn of the century begun to embrace a more rational and systematic approach to tourist development, and to mobilize resources and actors behind it as a worthy national project; an ingrained *égoisme* and inclination toward bureaucratic inertia meanwhile hindered similar progress in France.[9] For leaders of the Touring Club and the emerging French tourist industry, forging a more modern tourism in France meant better assimilating these new practices and habits of mind—often

---

[7]   On the Grand Tour tradition's long-term decline and transformation in the nineteenth century, see Lynne Withey, *Grand Tour and Cooks Tours: A History of Leisure Travel, 1750–1915* (London: Aurum, 1998); and James Buzard's excellent *The Beaten Track: European Tourism, Literature and the Ways to Culture, 1800–1918* (Oxford: Oxford University Press, 1993). On French beach and spa tourism, see Gabriel Desert, *La vie quotidienne sur les plages Normandes du Second Empire aux années folles* (Paris: Hachette, 1983); and Douglas Mackaman, *Leisure Settings: Bourgeois Culture, Medicine and the Spa in Modern France* (Chicago: University of Chicago Press, 1998).

[8]   This view was particularly prevalent in the pages of the Touring Club's monthly revue; see for example *Revue mensuelle du Touring Club de France*, February, 1899, p. 51. George Casella advances similar comparisons in *Le sport et l'avenir* (Paris: A.Z. Mathot, 1910).

[9]   Again a common refrain, but for an encapsulation of these concerns see in particular the medical doctor and Touring Club leader E.P. Léon-Petit's *Dix ans de Touring Club* (Paris: Touring Club de France, 1904).

more readily embraced by the country's European rivals—though doing so in a fashion that preserved what were felt to be distinctive French cultural traditions and hierarchies of value. If tourism carried rich promise for France's national development, in the view of many French elites, it also brought the risk of too readily commodifying or even standardizing the country and turning it into a place like any other.

Publicity Dilemmas in the "Age of Tourism"

These opposing concerns came into particular focus as tourist advocates grappled with the question of how best to organize and generate resources for an effective publicity or *propagande* (as they would more commonly refer to it into the 1930s) on behalf of France and individual sites in the country. The dawning "age of tourism" new leaders of the French tourist industry heralded in the early twentieth century raised dilemmas over promotion that had not been nearly as salient in earlier regimes of elite travel in the country and in Europe as a whole. The attractions of the Grand Tour were after all largely canonical ones fixed by convention and "available" only to a narrow elite, while the spa and beach resorts at the center of French and European tourism in the nineteenth century appealed to their clientele chiefly on the basis of an established social reputation or medical need. As tourism came to comprise a growing array of sites within the national territory, and to involve a more expansive French and international clientele at the turn of the century, so too did the need for more explicit publicity appeals announce itself. The issue of tourist publicity raised pointed questions of cultural value: could a formerly elite undertaking like leisure travel be popularized and more frankly commercialized without imperiling the hierarchies of taste upon which such value seemed in France to rest? Or to put it differently, was it possible to address tourists more directly as potential *consumers* without somehow diminishing the "product" on offer?

These kinds of questions had broader currency within elite circles in France at the turn of the century, as a range of prominent public figures debated the social, cultural, and political impact of a developing consumer culture in France.[10] The issue of publicity attracted particular attention, as early advertising professionals, business figures, and others weighed the merits of adopting more

---

[10]   On the turn-of-the-century debate in France over consumer culture, see Rosalind Williams, *Dream Worlds: Mass Consumption in Late Nineteenth Century France* (Berkeley: University of California Press, 1982); and Lisa Tiersten, *Marianne in the Market: Envisioning Consumer Society in Fin-de-Siècle France* (Berkeley: University of California Press, 2001).

scientific, aggressive (and often foreign) techniques in advertising.[11] Plaints about what seemed a peculiarly French aversion to risk-taking and modernity in matters of publicity became more commonplace at the turn of the century, especially among avatars of modern French advertising writing in publications such as the trade journal *Publicité*. In this view, French business measured poorly on the whole against its British and American competitors in particular with regard to the resources it dedicated to publicity, and its comparatively passive disposition toward markets.[12] Debate over the most appropriate form and organization for publicity continued into the interwar period, as business, advertising, and artistic elites sought to devise distinctively French ways of making mass appeals that would contain the presumed threats to cultural value posed by conditions of mass democracy and a spreading commercialism and American cultural influence.[13]

Such concerns entered commonly as well into the crafting of actual tourist publicity appeals. In addition to the main French transport companies and larger spas and beaches, it was the local and regional *syndicats d'initiative* that were the principal agents of tourist publicity in the years before and even after 1914, producing posters, brochures, guidebooks, and other materials for regions, cities, and individual resorts. The *syndicats* drew funds from voluntary donations and subscriptions by local businesses, organizations, and individuals who saw a benefit in increased tourist traffic in their area, and the civic groupings often dedicated the greater share of their budgets to efforts of publicity. The Touring Club from early on enthusiastically supported the *syndicats* in that role, seeing them as an effective means of fostering collaboration in publicity efforts and of maximizing still-limited advertising budgets. As against a more patently commercial publicity generated by the owners of individual sites, hotels, or restaurants, the *syndicats* promoted an entire town, region, or department; their efforts therefore stood to benefit all of the businesses in that area, in a practical

---

[11]   On the debate within French publicity circles in this period, and the influence of the American model of professional advertising, see Marie Emmanuel Chessel, *La publicité: Naissance d'une profession, 1900–1940* (Paris: CNRS, 1998); and Daniel Pope, "French Advertising Men and the American Promised Land," *Historical Reflections* 5/1 (Summer 1978): pp. 117–39. For a longer-term historical consideration of the evolution of French publicity, see Marc Martin, *Trois siècles de publicité en France* (Paris: Odile Jacob, 1992).

[12]   Such complaints were nearly continuous in *La Publicité*, but examples from 1906 include *La Publicité*, no. 34, May 1906, pp. 7–8, 15; no. 35, June 1906, p. 8; no. 39, October 1906, p. 18; one of the more influential French book-length treatments of modern advertising to advance this perspective is Jean Arren, *Sa majesté la publicité* (Tours: Mame, 1914).

[13]   Marjorie Beale, *The Modernist Enterprise: French Elites and the Threat of Modernity* (Palo Alto: Stanford University Press, 2000), esp. Chapter 1, "Advertising as Modernism," pp. 11–47.

illustration of the public-spirited initiative that the Club believed needed to guide French tourist development overall. Where a tourism—or tourist publicity—organized more in line with state planning or private commercial interest carried the risk of standardization, in this view, the *syndicats* stood better to safeguard the local particularity and initiative that were vital to upholding the singular value of France's touristic patrimony.[14]

Whether publicity generated chiefly by the *syndicats* was sufficient in a fast-changing international market for tourism, however, became a hotly contested issue within French tourist circles throughout this period. One of the earlier and more succinct articulations of this concern was the one presented by Louis Vergné, general secretary of the French Chambre Syndicale de la Publicité at the fifth national congress of *syndicats d'initiative* in 1906. As one of the most prominent prewar advocates of a more modern disposition in French uses of publicity, Vergné regularly impugned the tendency among French business interests as a whole to view publicity in narrow terms as a means of advertising a particular product or sale, instead of as an ongoing appeal to and even relationship with a more expansive, socially and internationally varied, and often unfamiliar clientele. While France's competitors in international tourist commerce were coming to appreciate the returns to be had from investing more liberally in advertising, Vergné lamented, French localities and business concerns remained wedded to more conservative and outdated conceptions for reaching markets. France measured badly not only against the "seductive and persuasive methods" of American advertisers and the imaginative thematic approaches of English publicity, but also against the comparative willingness of France's continental European neighbors to dedicate public funds to the promotion of tourism to foreigners. The *syndicats'* reliance upon voluntary contributions provided them with too meager and uncertain a funding base to undertake the kinds of sustained advertising campaigns now needed, while municipalities in Switzerland, Italy, and Germany were able to write publicity sums into their budgets and advertise themselves effectively to foreign tourists. Other countries were moving more concretely as well toward effective overall coordination of their tourist publicity efforts, whereas French efforts continued to founder in their "anarchic state."[15]

---

[14]   Among the many publications from this period outlining the intended role of the *syndicats* is Touring Club President Edmond Chaix' *Le syndicat d'initiative: Son but, ses moyens, son programme* (Paris: ONT, 1914).

[15]   M.L. Vergne, *Conférence faite à Nancy à l'occasion du cinquième Congrès des Syndicats d'Initiative de France* (G. de Malherbe, 1907); "La publicité: Nécessité de son enseignement, conférence faite le 17 Décembre à l'association des Hauts Etudes Commerciales."

In the view of Vergné and other advocates of new publicity techniques, French tourist materials in the prewar period suffered too in many instances from an adherence to standards of quality, authority, and permanence that compromised their potential reach. The pronounced affinity within French tourist circles prior to 1914 for more expensive and "artistic" media such as large format *affiches* [posters], illustrated albums, and literary guidebooks tended to represent attractions in a fashion that was expensive, unwieldy, and increasingly ill-suited to the direction in which tourism was heading. The case of tourist posters was indeed especially illustrative on this score, as the main French transport companies, and many of the larger resorts and *syndicats* continued to dedicate a sizable share of their advertising outlays to the production of large format posters into the interwar period, even as lower cost American publicity efforts began to make significant inroads across Europe and engender a "crisis of the poster" as an advertising medium.[16] French advocates of modernization in tourist publicity began prior to the war to argue for the adoption of smaller and cheaper formats (illustrated brochures in particular), ones deemed more appropriate to an increasingly mobile and broadly middle-class clientele and more realistic for the still-limited funds available for advertising efforts. But the notion that publicity needed still itself to embody the value of the attractions it represented remained a powerful countervailing one in France, and with it endured certain older conventions of elite tourist address.[17] The Touring Club's own guidebook series for the country for example, the 33-volume Sites and Monuments collection, resolutely avoided any "taint" of commercial or promotional motivation in presenting the attractions of the country in the authoritative and patrimonial style of a geography or illustrated album series.[18]

Even a highly successful private company like Michelin had to balance these competing concerns as it became a leading agent of tourist development and tourist publicity in twentieth-century France. In his history of Michelin, Stephen Harp has shown how aggressive pursuit of market share and a well-funded

---

[16] Victoria de Grazia, "The Arts of Purchase: How American Publicity Subverted the European Poster, 1920–1940," in Barbara Kruger and Phil Mariani (eds), *Remaking History* (Seattle: Bay Press, 1989), pp. 221–57.

[17] Each of these tendencies is on display in the wide-ranging collection of agendas and brochures of the PLM railway line and *syndicats d'initiative* at the Bibliothèque Fornay in Paris.

[18] On the Sites and Monuments campaign, see my article "A Tasteful Patrimony? Landscape Preservation and Tourism in the 'Sites and Monuments' Campaign, 1900–1935," *French Historical Studies* 32/3 (2009): pp. 447–77; on Germany's comparable effort to constitute a monumental patrimony in the *Heimatschutz* movement, see Rudy Koshar, *Germany's Transient Pasts: Preservation and National Memory in the Twentieth Century* (Chapel Hill: University of North Carolina Press, 1998); and Joshua Hagen, *Preservation, Tourism, and Nationalism: The Jewel of the German Past* (London: Ashgate, 2006).

publicity apparatus was essential to the company's business strategy within an increasingly competitive international economic climate, particularly in the decades after World War I. What won Michelin the praise of French advertising experts, however, was its capacity for combining commercial promotion with service of the larger national good, in varied projects such as its guidebook series, its transport infrastructure improvements, or its work on behalf of battlefield tourism in the wake of World War I. Indeed as Harp demonstrates, Michelin— not least through its ever-evolving trademark figure, Bibendum—was successful owing partly to its ability to "fuse its own image with that of France," using the modern media of consumer culture to propagate a compelling vision of France and "Frenchness" to domestic and foreign audiences.[19] Making France more available in tourism for Michelin as for other leading tourist concerns seemed to require precisely this delicate balancing of commercial and national imperatives.

Promoting France Abroad in the 1920s

World War I and its aftermath significantly changed the context for French publicity appeals. Arguments French tourist leaders had been advancing in favor of tourism as a vital national interest took on added ballast as France confronted the challenges of severe economic indebtedness and reconstruction, as well as new opportunities in the changed European and international landscape in the postwar period. Indeed with the war still very much in course, those leaders began to advocate for the role of tourist commerce in any larger strategy of postwar economic recovery. Among the more influential was Leon Auscher, the Touring Club's vice-president from the war years through the 1920s and a leading voice for joining tourist development to France's larger economic strategies. With France's industrial plant considerably damaged by the war, Auscher argued in 1920, the country could not readily export goods to maintain a favorable balance of payments, and had to devise other means for bringing money into the country. By bringing in much needed money (in particular American dollars), tourism more than most other economic sectors promised to help alleviate France's deficit while the country's industry gradually recovered. As would others throughout the 1920s, Auscher advocated for tourism as a form of *"exportation à l'intérieure"* [exportation to the French interior], vital in bringing money into the country during its period of postwar indebtedness and protracted convalescence. In addition, he argued, France as an attraction had

---

[19]   Stephen Harp, *Marketing Michelin: Advertising and Cultural Identity in Twentieth Century France* (Baltimore: Johns Hopkins University Press, 2001).

the advantage of already being something of a known international "product," with a reputation that already gave it value and appeal within the international tourist marketplace.[20]

Auscher and other French tourist leaders recognized, however, that that market for tourism was a fast changing one, and that securing an advantageous position within it for France would require new resources and initiatives in the aftermath of the war—and more specifically, new and more effective kinds of publicity appeal. The main change they anticipated was an influx of foreign, and especially American tourists to France. To the longstanding allure of France's unparalleled beauty, rich cultural patrimony, and established tourist destinations would be added, in this view, new feelings of goodwill among the populations of France's allies, whose desire to pay homage to sites of shared sacrifice would give way to a fuller stream of tourist traffic in the ensuing years.[21] The discredit Germany and Austria (among France's leading competitors in prewar European tourism) would be bearing before world opinion offered an opportunity for France to win over a greater share of the market for European tourism.[22]

With North and South Americans, as well as Japanese, traveling to Europe in growing numbers in the 1920s, the European tourist market became a more competitive one in which government tourist agencies now had to undertake new and more sustained initiatives of international publicity. The main vehicle for this effort in France was the ONT, which had been enlisted since its founding in 1910 with the task of developing the more rational, systematic, and unified publicity on behalf of tourism in the country that would enable France to compete more effectively with its European counterparts.[23] During the war years the Office constituted a Committee of Tourist Propaganda to study ways of undertaking "an active campaign of French penetration" into foreign tourist markets.[24] Such inquiry continued in the aftermath of the war, as the Office funded targeted studies and individual missions to other countries and

---

[20]   Léon Auscher, *La prospérité de la France par le tourisme* (Bar-le-Duc: Comte-Jacquet, 1920), pp. 3–5.

[21]   Dan Sherman discusses the effort—begun during the war itself—to frame battlefields as tourist attractions and sites of commemoration in *The Construction of Memory in Interwar France* (Chicago: University of Chicago Press, 2000).

[22]   This was the view presented by Touring Club President Henry Defert for example at the group's 1918 Assembly General; Archives Contemporaines [hereafter AC], 53AS9912, "Assembly General and Administrative Council Proceedings," 1918–20, p. 27.

[23]   A large portion of the Office's always-precarious budgets would be dedicated to "propagande"; AC, F14 12357, "ONT: Budgets."

[24]   Archives Départementales du Côtes d'Armor, 8M58, "Propagande en faveur du tourisme," Letter from President of Conseil d'Administration of ONT to Prefect, August 14, 1918.

continents to build the groundwork for more effective promotion of France as a tourist destination.[25] This represented an early and still largely informal version of market research, as a more established French tourist industry attempted to adapt itself to the shift from a familiar to a more varied and still somewhat unknown tourist clientele.

In line with this shift, actual French tourist appeals became more carefully targeted in the 1920s. Like the governmental tourist offices established by its competitor nations on the continent, the ONT dedicated particular effort to appealing more directly to the newly expansive American middle-class market for European travel. The postwar American market seemed to French tourist officials a nearly "unlimited one" as compared to the largely elite clientele that had visited France from the country in the past, and they continued to make primary appeal as well to the more established English market for French travel. Using passport and consular records, the ONT was able to affirm that by the mid-1920s the clientele of American and English tourists coming to France was both expanding and socially diversifying, with a growing proportion of the approximately 675,000 British and 150,000 American tourists visiting France in 1924 for example including middle-, lower-middle-, and even scattered (English) working-class tourists.[26] In addition to the large foreign tourist offices it operated in London and New York, the ONT opened offices in Geneva, Barcelona, Venice, Amsterdam, Berlin, Cairo, and Buenos Aires, in line with the new postwar conviction that effective tourist publicity required a constancy and consistency of appeal.

As they advanced new appeals to foreign tourists, European governmental tourist offices also often undertook new efforts to encourage their citizens to travel within their borders instead of to locations abroad, and French tourist organizers took particular note of American and Italian efforts in this regard.[27] With governments now more actively shaping tourist markets in these ways, French tourist leaders fretted that competing European nations were showing themselves more capable than France of effectively funding and coordinating international publicity appeals, and of using the state to do so. The leading tourist advocate and Savoie-based deputy Antoine Borrel advanced this view most explicitly in making the case for a national publicity budget for France in the

---

[25] See for example Ludovic Gaurier's account of his mission to Latin America and the Antilles, *La propagande touristique à l'étranger* (Bordeaux: Imprimerie de J. Bière, 1919).

[26] AC, F14 12357, "Rapport de l'Administrateur-Directeur de l'Office National du Tourisme," Extrait du Journal Officiel, August 19, 1926, pp. 3–4.

[27] AC, F14 12357, "Rapport du Directeur de l'Office National du Tourisme: Résumé des Travaux en 1922."

late 1920s.[28] He judged Germany particularly effective in its use of well-financed foreign tourist offices (most notably in New York) to organize a continuous and multifaceted appeal to large foreign markets, and in the close coordination of its travel agencies, train companies, and individual cities and towns.[29] As part of its larger commitment to building a tourist Italy that was no longer merely "a honeymoon destination," Mussolini's fascist government likewise dedicated growing budgets both to building tourist infrastructure throughout the country and to revitalizing Italy's traditional appeal to foreign travelers all over the world.[30] Other countries like England, Spain, and Switzerland managed to make progress as well in centralizing and coordinating their publicity appeals to foreigners and dedicating more substantial budgetary outlays to them. By comparison, Borrel argued, French publicity efforts abroad were "derisory," hamstrung above all by the modest and always-imperiled budgets of the ONT and by the high costs of maintaining foreign tourist offices. What was truly called for was not the disparate and largely uncoordinated efforts of *syndicats*, train companies, and larger stations, but rather a "massive publicity" that could speak more effectively and continuously across national lines.[31] While French tourist leaders were on the whole moving toward this embrace of greater centralization and coordination by the later 1920s, the international economic crisis severely damaged the prospects for foreign (and again, most significantly, American) tourism in France. The President of the French Chambers of Commerce estimated that the number of foreign tourists visiting France declined from a peak of nearly 19 million in 1929 to just 900,000 in 1934–35, with the recovery of France's share of international tourist commerce coming only really in the 1950s.[32]

The kindred strategy to modern reorganization that French tourist leaders embraced in adapting to this changing international tourist market was a more forceful assertion of the distinctiveness of the "product" on offer. One notable form this took was the bringing of a new emphasis to the country's

---

[28]   Antoine Borrel, *Il faut à la France un budget de publicité; rapport présenté au Conseil Supérieure du Tourisme, décembre, 1928* (Paris: Imprimerie Nationale, 1929).

[29]   For a fuller account of German tourist development in this period and over the nineteenth and twentieth centuries more broadly, see Rudy Koshar, *German Travel Cultures* (London: Berg, 2000).

[30]   For a discussion of Italian Fascist efforts to mobilize the Italian past for domestic and foreign tourism, see D. Medina Lasansky, *The Renaissance Perfected: Architecture, Spectacle and Tourism in Fascist Italy* (University Park: Penn State University Press, 2005).

[31]   Borrel, *Il faut à la France un budget de publicité*, pp. 5–6; Léon Auscher, *L'Importance économique du tourisme; rapport présenté au Conseil National Économique July 1927* (Paris: Imprimerie Nationale, 1928), p. 6.

[32]   M.L. Bahon-Rault, *Politique consulaire du tourisme* (Rennes: Imp. Ouest-Éclair, 1937), p. 3.

regional diversity in French publicity appeals. Echoing a view that was already becoming prevalent within tourist circles before the war, Vergné recommended the maintenance and/or revival of regional cultural traditions comprising the "originality" of their respective areas as a cost-effective means of luring both French and foreign travelers, while also preserving French national distinctiveness.[33] The leading French regionalist and Touring Club leader Jean Charles-Brun likewise counseled the *syndicats* to propagandize in a "methodical and coordinated" fashion on behalf of the regions, thereby helping to advance the principle of a France defined primarily by its regional diversity and essential unity in difference.[34]

Emphasis on France's regional diversity and surviving (or in some instances reinvented) rural traditions came even more noticeably to the fore of French tourist organizing and publicity appeals in the aftermath of the war, as tourism became one of the leading mediums for regional cultural expression. Advising the *syndicats* on their primary functions in 1920, Touring Club leader Léon Auscher urged them to move beyond merely establishing itineraries in their respective regions by "presenting as geographically and ethnographically homogeneous a face as possible." "Isn't it these two elements," he offered, "that comprise the original physiognomy of an area ... and isn't the main interest of the *syndicat* to reinforce ... what remains of our picturesque particularism?"[35] With the aim both of directing needed resources to often economically hard-pressed regions and establishing French distinctiveness within a shifting international tourist marketplace, French tourist organizers made a more sustained effort to recast France as a place of unparalleled regional variety, where rural traditions were more fully preserved and available than elsewhere. As was the case in politics and culture more generally, rural France became within tourism a kind of foil to an increasingly cosmopolitan Paris in the interwar period, the "truer" France where defining French traditions were much more in evidence than in the capital.[36]

Thus did shoring up traditional regional distinctiveness come to mean, paradoxically, a more effortful integration of provincial France into national and international frameworks of tourist representation. From helping found

---

[33]   Vergne, *Conférence*, p. 16.

[34]   Charles-Brun makes the case for tourism as a form of regionalism in *Le régionalisme* (Paris: Bloud and Cie., 1911); see also his article "Tourisme et Régionalisme," *Revue mensuelle du Touring Club de France*, September, 1910, p. 387.

[35]   Léon Auscher, *Urbanisme et tourisme* (Paris: E. Leroux, 1920), p. 87.

[36]   On the political and cultural resonances of the idea of a "true France" in this period, see Herman Lebovics, *True France: The Wars over Cultural Identity* (Ithaca: Cornell University Press, 1992); and Shanny Peer, *France on Display: Peasants, Provincials and Folklore in the 1937 World's Fair* (Albany: SUNY Press, 1998).

and sustain regional folklore museums throughout the country, to lending direct subsidy to displays of ethnic costume, art, music, and dance in the 1920s and 1930s, and fully reconstituting French folk cultures for European and even global audiences at the 1937 Paris World's Fair, the French tourist economy played a leading role in reframing regional cultures for broader encounter and consumption.[37] Here again, though, it is essential to understand this as a Europe-wide tendency common to all of the major European tourist economies. Whether driven chiefly by the aim of bolstering uncertain regional economic prospects, fostering identification with the purportedly rural origins of national identification or projecting a stylized national image abroad, tourist organizations in France's peer nations likewise dedicated new efforts and resources to the promotional foregrounding of folk cultures in tourism.[38] By the later 1930s, tourism had helped establish a common, trans-European set of protocols and contexts for comfortably encountering local folk cultures as an outsider, contributing to what Orvar Löfgren characterizes (with specific reference to the Swedish case) as the "standardization of cultural difference."[39] The assertion of French regional "originality" was thus not in fact so original, but rather was part and parcel of an emerging European rhetoric of tourist attraction.

Hygiene, Comfort, and Place: Remaking the French Hotel

This same tension played out in the extended campaign to "reform" the French hotel stock along more modern lines, such as to make it more suitable to the diverse clientele an expanded tourist commerce was bringing to the country. The tourist hotel in many ways fully embodies the internationalism and modernity of tourism, providing lodging as it does for a varied clientele of transient consumers, transplanting international urban amenities and norms to often far-

---

[37]   Peer, *France on Display*; see also my article, "Fashioning Heritage: Regional Costume and Tourism in Brittany, 1890–1937," *Journal of Social History* 43/1 (2009): pp. 631–56.

[38]   German efforts on this score were particularly prominent, both within Weimar tourism and under the Nazi "Strength through Joy" tourism program; see Semmens, *Seeing Hitler's Germany*, pp. 81–90, Baranowski, *Strength through Joy*, pp. 99–107, 123–8. Jill Steward suggests that regional tourist promotion could serve very different needs in the Austro-Hungarian empire, fostering ethnic identifications among the empire's increasingly fractious nationalities while also enabling the monarchy to promote itself effectively abroad as a "family of nations" and richly varied tourist destination; see "Tourism in Late Imperial Austria: The Development of Tourist Cultures and Their Associated Images of Place," in Baranowski and Furlough (eds), *Being Elsewhere*, pp. 108–34.

[39]   Orvar Löfgren, "Know Your Country: A Comparative Perspective on Tourism and Nation-Building in Sweden," in Baranowski and Furlough (eds), *Being Elsewhere*, pp. 137–54.

flung rural areas, and acting as a kind of laboratory for many new technologies and practices. As a "home away from home" and place of cross-national and cross-cultural encounter, the hotel is also among the more charged and closely managed tourist environments. Despite its centrality to tourist commerce and experience, the hotel has often been surprisingly absent from accounts of modern tourism and tourist development. French accounts of the tourist hotel tended to view it as a harbinger of modernity, as for example in the French economist and historian Georges D'Avenel's contemporary characterization of turn-of-the-century luxury hotels in Paris and many resort areas as consummately modern in their operation and material organization.[40] Catherine Bertho-Lavenir's more recent discussion in her history of French tourism of the effort to "reform the French hotel" argues along similar lines that the hotel became an important medium through which metropolitan bourgeois norms were spread to the French countryside in the twentieth century.[41] In line with the argument at hand though, what begs further examination is how French tourist organizers endeavored to balance specific national, international, and commercial imperatives in adapting the French hotel to a changing European and international tourist market.

That the existing French hotel stock was largely inadequate to that market and to the changing needs of modern tourists was something upon which many in French tourist circles generally agreed at the turn of the century. The development of elite spa and beach resort tourism in the middle decades of the nineteenth century had given rise to the first significant wave of hotel building in the 1860s, and many of these establishments were by the 1890s pushing at the limits of their capacity to accommodate a growing volume of international tourist traffic. An expanding middle-class clientele for tourism, along with the changing international norms of hygiene and comfort in the later nineteenth century, stirred concerns over the state of French hotels. A main worry was that the stock of French hotels tended overall to divide too rigidly into the luxury installations of Paris and the main beach and thermal resorts on the one hand, and the more traditional and far smaller inns in local areas on the other. If the "hotel-palace" tended to evince a somewhat ostentatious cosmopolitan luxury beloved of nineteenth-century international bourgeois sensibilities, the more traditional *auberge* or inn presented a more humble and sometimes slightly dilapidated aspect that could seem equally incongruent with the needs of the more modern tourist. Where France had a glaring deficit, tourist advocates came to believe, was in *moyen* or middle-level hotels offering reliably modern accommodation

---

40   Georges d'Avenel, *Le mécanisme de la vie moderne*, Série 5 (Paris: A. Colin, 1905), Chapter 19, "Les Grandes Hôtelleries," pp. 1–58.

41   Bertho-Lavenir, *La roue et le stylo*, Chapter 9, "Reformer l'Hôtel," pp. 217–39.

to the larger, international, and more broadly middle-class tourist clientele that would be coming to the fore in the tourism of the twentieth century.

Anachronistic French standards of luxury, it seemed, had to give way to more international and democratic norms of comfort, hygiene, and service. Prior to this dawning age of tourism, one Club leader suggested at the group's 1901 General Assembly, the hotel owner had had to concern himself principally with the solitary commercial traveler, and provide merely a warm greeting and copious table; now, however, that same owner found himself needing to win over a new clientele of tourists, "a great throng of people of middling means," who repaired annually to established tourist resort areas in France or abroad as the only places where they might hope to find the discernibly modern hotels they now required. Bound to its "bad habits, its old equipment, stoves and hanging pots," the French hotel business was still at the dawn of a new century being led by inherited practices and good intentions rather than by clear principle or method. Where Switzerland in particular had succeeded in transforming its hotel business into a modern industry with access to abundant capital and employment of modern management and design techniques, France continued to maintain hotels more appropriate to a passing age.[42]

As in the case of publicity, French tourist leaders made appeal simultaneously to international standards as well as to notions of French distinctiveness in trying to redefine the French hotel. They relied more upon associational initiative, rather than the state or market to spur this move toward new hotel standards. At a time of still-limited state involvement in tourism, the Club used its associational linkages and growing influence to prod French hotels into modifying themselves in matters of design, organization and management—initially through enlisting its own delegates to gather information in their travels on the state of hotels in various regions of the country, and to make recommendations to hotel owners on how to alter their establishments into ones more fully accommodating of tourist needs.[43] If a hotel hewed satisfactorily to the Club's criteria, it earned the right to publicize itself as a "Touring Club Hotel," a guarantee to tourists of specific standards of hygiene, comfort, and service. The Club also debuted a "Chambre Hygienique TCF" or model hotel room at the large hygiene section of the 1900 Paris International Exhibition, promoting it vigorously in subsequent years as a template for the construction or renovation of hotels across the country. The French Automobile Club and French hotel *syndicats* joined as well in advocating

---

[42] AC, F14 12357, "Procès-verbaux," 1901. In the early stages of national tourist development, Switzerland was for French tourist organizers the most compelling model of a country fully outfitting individual regions for tourism, adapting services more closely to the needs of tourist clientele, and building modern hotels.

[43] *Revue mensuelle du Touring Club*, August 1895, pp. 529–30.

for this more modern vision of hotel lodging, one that better adhered to cardinal hygienic principles of light, ventilation, and easy cleaning, as well as to modern norms of basic comfort and to a deliberate simplicity of décor that avoided the excesses of a "false" or "useless" luxury.

The more modern French hotel these tourist leaders envisioned was to be one that would also fit more readily into modern networks of tourist circulation and commerce. Working in league with public authorities, the hotel syndicate in Provence built a "model hotel" in the town of Avignon, for example, that offered not only unimpeachable hygiene and comfort but also a full array of services and orienting materials to enable travel throughout the town and surrounding region.[44] Along similar lines, advocates of hotel modernization encouraged hotel owners to outfit their establishments with new tourist amenities such as darkrooms for tourist photography, as well as expanded garage space and basic maintenance materials for bicycles and automobiles. To encourage renovations as well as more active and professional dispositions in French hotel management, the Touring Club held annual *Concours du Bon Hôtelier* [Hotel Owner Contests] to reward those hotels judged to be doing most to facilitate tourism.

Correcting the inadequacies of France's hotels, however, required in the view of many tourism advocates not simply individual initiative but also a broader reorientation and even reorganization of the French hotel business. It was an objective put forth strongly at the turn of the century not only by the Touring and Automobile Clubs but also by the federation of hotel syndicates from France's main tourist regions, which complained in its journal *L'Industrie Hôtelière* that hotels in the country continued to be seen as small scale or familial businesses that were at best suited to safeguarding charming, if increasingly outdated, traditions of hospitality. Hotel owners above all, it suggested, had to come to view themselves as part of a vibrant modern "industry" and to "be of their century," as the hotel of the twentieth century would have to be markedly different from that of the nineteenth if it were to be able to survive in a more competitive climate of international tourist commerce.[45] The main organizational challenge in doing so—indeed the central one with which French tourist leaders grappled more generally in advocating for tourist development—was finding ways of generating sufficient resources and a more coordinated action on behalf of tourism; and doing so without reliance upon a French state or business community still unconvinced of the profitability and national import of tourist commerce. In this vein, it began to press French hotels at the turn of the century to form into commercial federations as a means of better coordinating their

---

44   *L'Industrie hôtelière*, February 1, 1905.

45   *L'Industrie hôtelière*, April 16, 1908, p. 2; September 22, 1903, p. 3; December 1, 1904, p. 2.

resources and endeavors, and thus better enabling themselves to effect needed improvements. Only the Parisian hotels formed into larger bodies to advocate for their interests before 1900, but succeeding years brought new pressures to constitute commercial organizations that could define and defend the interests of the French hotel sector.

While such reforms had already gathered momentum before 1914, the war years significantly changed the context for discussions of hotel modernization. A main lesson tourist advocates took from the war years was the effectiveness of voluntary consolidation and coordination behind larger shared objectives, and they applied it directly to the question of hotel reorganization. The Touring Club and ONT each established special hotel committees in 1915 to deal expressly with questions of hotel reorganization, and the multiple French hotel syndicates organized nationally into a Chambre National de l'Hôtelerie Française in 1917. As was the case with tourist publicity, such changes were prompted in large measure by the anticipation of a larger and differently constituted tourist market in the war's aftermath. Tourists would be coming to France in greater numbers, and would bring with them new standards and expectations—particularly with regard to hygiene, comfort, and service—that French hotels had to accommodate.

The rebuilding of new, damaged, or outdated provincial hotel stock, as well as the re-staffing of hotels, thus became even more urgent priorities within French tourist circles after the war. The leading figures in the Touring and Automobile Clubs respectively, Léon Auscher and Louis Baudry de Saunier, undertook a nationwide study of France's existing hotel stock and needs, publishing a brochure entitled "Les Hôtels à Créer [The Hotels to be Built]" that advised the construction of medium-sized hotels and inns in areas of projected tourist traffic.[46] Carrying out such a plan meant contending with the longstanding shortage of capital for hotel building, expansion, and renovation, as well as with the need to replace damaged hotel stock in war-torn areas and a largely foreign personnel. Here again, tourist advocates turned readily to France's European competitors for guidance in generating capital for hotel modernization. The ONT's Hotels Committee cited favorably the example of Tyrol, in Austria, where the state provided guaranteed six-year loans at 5 percent interest to enable a spate of new hotel building in the immediate aftermath of the war.[47] Following the example of neighboring countries as well as other sectors of the French economy itself, the Touring Club alongside the Chambre National de l'Hôtelerie Française advocated for the establishment of a "Crédit Hôtelier," effectively a bank that would make

---

[46]　The study was undertaken with the active financial and logistical support of the ONT's Comité de l'Hôtelerie; Léon Auscher and L. Baudry de Saumier, *Les hôtels à créer* (1917).

[47]　AC, F14 12357, "Conseil d'Administration," 1920, p. 9.

funds available to hotel entrepreneurs (especially the owners of small, medium, and seasonal hotels) seeking to effect expansion or renovations of their concerns, particularly in line with new hygienic requirements.[48] French tourist authorities also looked admiringly toward the institution of the "cure tax" commonly levied since before the war at Austrian, German, and Swiss thermal and beach resorts, and were able to pass their own hotel and gaming taxes immediately after the war as a means of generating non-governmental funds (particularly from foreign tourists) to subsidize local hygienic and infrastructure improvements.

As part of this reorganization of the French hotel business, tourist advocates and hotel industry leaders also pushed for a new and more formal kind of training for hotel personnel. Because the modern hygiene and comfort that had to define the new hotel was a complex product, not only of the physical outfitting of the hotel itself, but also the technical competence of the hotel direction and staff, France had to establish special schools to train a new generation of hotel personnel.[49] Whereas in France hotel work continued to carry with it connotations of servility, tourist and hotel leaders lamented, Switzerland, Germany, and Austria in particular had taken great strides to professionalize such work and constitute hotel training schools. Switzerland remained the model in this regard, though Austria also operated 22 hotel schools in Vienna alone, and required that prospective hotel employees undertake an additional three-year apprenticeship in residence at a hotel after graduating to learn hygienic principles of habitation, foreign languages, bookkeeping, and basic gastronomy.[50] Leaders of the Syndicat Général of the French Hotel Industry indeed drew upon extensive study of the Austrian and other models in opening the first French Hotel Industry School at Grenoble in 1910, in line with the larger aim of making hotel work "an honored science" and recognized profession grounded in mastery of varied techniques and modern capacities of adaptation to the fast-changing circumstances of the international tourist economy.[51]

More forceful still was the campaign to fully rid French hotels of German, Austrian, and even Swiss personnel, who occupied a particularly high proportion of positions in Parisian and resort hotels before the war. This effort of "de-bochisation" (*boches* being the main anti-German wartime slur in French) as

---

[48]   On the origin and workings of the Crédit hôtelier, see Pierre Chabert, *Le Crédit hôtelier institué en France par le "warrant hôtelier"* (Paris: Union Nationale des Syndicats Hôteliers de France, 1913).

[49]   *L'Industrie hôtelière*, November 15, 1916, p. 12.

[50]   AC, F14 12357, TCF Congress of 1911, rapport of Dr Lochon.

[51]   *Le pays de France* 2, June 10, 1914, p. 11; *Revue mensuelle du Touring Club*, July–August 1916, p. 106. This is the orientation of Louis Leospo's manual for hotel service training, *Traité d'industrie hôtelière* (Paris: L. Andrau, 1918).

Touring Club leaders referred to it, became a rallying point for the larger ambition of building a more distinctively French tourism. Beginning in 1914, the Touring Club led a boycott of hotels in France that continued to employ personnel that were of neither French nor Allied provenance, and it as well as the Chambre National de l'Hôtelerie Française pushed in the aftermath of the war for a nationwide imposition of limits on foreign (again excepting allied countries) staffing of hotel positions. Even with such measures in place and with scores of newly established French hotel schools now graduating students by 1919, hotels in the country were still often reluctant to hire French personnel exclusively in their establishments, concerned as they increasingly were to adhere to emerging international standards of hotel professionalism.[52]

If new pressures weighed upon the hotels to conform to international standards, others, however, pushed them in the direction of asserting a French or local distinctiveness. Hotels figured prominently in postwar strategies of regional economic revival, cultural preservation, and promotion, as these latter objectives gained a new political foothold both in Paris and within the regions themselves amidst the challenging economic conditions of the early 1920s. Thus alongside the international norms of hygiene, comfort, and modern rational organization that newly weighed upon hotel design and operation, hotels across France were enlisted particularly after the war with the new function of manifesting and preserving distinctive "local color." "The Hotel must vary in line with the *pays* [local area], its climate, sensibilities and traditions," the Touring Club asserted in 1920, and so help to shore up the variety and originality that were paramount within tourist hierarchies of value.[53] To that end, the leaders of the hotel improvement campaign from an early date actively encouraged hotel owners to incorporate regional identifications more visibly into their design and service, with the Touring Club for example according financial support to older inns for the preservation and renovation of the distinctive signs they commonly bore above their entrances.[54] Those undertaking construction and renovation of provincial hotels were encouraged as well to utilize local materials and techniques, and to employ local craftsmen and artists where possible in the remodeling and furnishing of hotels.[55] Partly at the instigation of tourist industry leaders, hotel architects more commonly worked to integrate the design of hotel exteriors

---

[52]   AC, 53AS121, "Écoles hôteliers."

[53]   *Revue mensuelle du Touring Club*, May–June 1920, p. 99.

[54]   *Revue mensuelle du Touring Club*, October–December 1920, pp. 3–4.

[55]   While this tendency would become more pronounced in the interwar period, Edouard Ossent cites the prewar examples of the Hôtel Modern at Tarbes in the Pyrenees, and the Hôtel Cosmopolitain in Contrexeville, among others; Edouard Ossent, *Hôtels et voyageurs au XX siècle* (Paris: E. Eggimann, 1912), p. 7.

seamlessly into their surrounding natural landscapes, to ensure an agreeable "silhouette" for the outside gaze.[56] The notion that the hotel had to function as a space of regional representation and consumption extended inside the hotel as well, to hotel gastronomy. Echoing the opinion voiced by the National Congrès d'Hôteliers [National Hotel Owners' Congress], Touring Club President Abel Ballif called upon hotel owners to eschew the culinary "mélange anonyme" that prevailed at the larger resort areas in the *fin-de-siècle* in favor of helping to "uphold the old traditions of *la bonne cuisine française* (good old fashioned French food)" by serving local dishes and wines and more clearly indicating on their signs and advertisements that they were committed to serving traditional French cuisine.[57]

Such efforts were of a piece with ones to reform or "modernize" the hotel, in that they helped refashion locality in ways that made it more readily available in larger French and transnational contexts. It was this same principle that animated the annual *concours du village coquet* [village beauty contests] the Touring Club began conducting after the war among the towns and villages in a chosen region, to reward those localities most successful in planting trees and flowers, revamping public *places*, and effecting substantial hygienic improvements.[58] The Club handed out diplomas with cash awards to nine different towns distinguishing themselves in "their cleanliness and care in presenting a charming aspect."[59] These kinds of initiatives in interwar rural France extended the scope of French and international tourist circulation in the country by helping to establish a framework of consumer and hygienic modernity within which local places could signify meaning and value to a more diverse traveling clientele. Here again, making localities truly "visitable" within the modern tourist economy hinged upon both national tourist initiatives and conformity to emerging international norms and expectations.

These French efforts to negotiate matters of hotel and publicity modernization reveal the new pressures at play not only in France but across

---

[56] Ibid., pp. 7, 15.

[57] *Revue mensuelle du Touring Club*, April 1910, pp. 145–6. Michelin would of course more famously embrace gastronomic tourism in Paris as well as the French regions as a defining part of its own mission in the interwar period; see Harp, *Marketing Michelin*, Chapter 7, "Defining France: Fusing Tourism, Regionalism and Gastronomy in Interwar France," pp. 225–68.

[58] The *concours* had the additional aim of nurturing among villagers a greater cordiality and openness toward outside visitors, bolstering what the Touring Club called the country's capacity for *tourisme réceptif*. The campaign is discussed in AC 53AS9912, General Assembly proceedings, April 22, 1923, p. 78.

[59] Archives Départementales du Morbihan, 8M131, "Letter from TCF President Henry Defert to President of Conseil Général, April 4, 1923."

Europe in the early twentieth century, as nations now to a far greater degree pursued national objectives in the organization of tourism for a vastly expanded domestic and international clientele. The hotel and the advertisement were, as shown, now enlisted to represent France and French distinctiveness in ways they had not in an earlier age of modern tourism. Yet they also brokered a more complicated interface with a touring public that was not only significantly larger but also in some ways still largely unknown in an age of embryonic tourist professionalization and market research. Even as those became defining features of the more truly popular tourism that emerged in France and across Europe after 1945, however, the balancing of national and international pressures in tourist development would never fully disappear as a central challenge for tourist organizers. Studies of post-1945 French tourism for example have shown that the much greater commercialism and sometimes-uneasy cross-cultural contact that accompanied this shift sparked anxious reaction from cultural observers as well as competing (and sometimes overtly political) strategies for organizing tourism in the country.[60] A France and Europe more fully girded for European and now global mass tourism still grappled with the dilemmas of fully embracing tourist modernity.

---

[60] On competing visions of popular tourism and the ultimate triumph of the market model, see Ellen Furlough, "Making Mass Vacations: Tourism and Consumer Culture in France, 1930s to 1970s," *Comparative Studies in Society and History* 40/2 (1998): pp. 247–86; On American tourism in postwar France and its impact upon international relations and French cultural perceptions, see Christopher Endy, *Cold War Holidays: American Tourism in France* (Chapel Hill: University of North Carolina Press, 2004).

Chapter 8

Made in Ireland?: Irish Tourism in an International Context

Eric G.E. Zuelow

Ireland is an island which stands out like a bastion against the Atlantic waves on the western fringe of Europe. Partly because it is isolated by the sea which surrounds it, it has been able to preserve its own individuality and distinctiveness down the years. But the sea which separates Ireland geographically also links it culturally with the rest of Europe. Ever since man first set foot on Irish soil some eight thousand years ago, many waves of immigrants have come from other lands across the sea to Ireland and have brought with them their own way of life, their mode of building and their own cultural influence. But on reaching Ireland, each wave and each cultural innovation was suddenly, as with a magic wand, transformed and modified into something different, into something which is distinctively stamped with the trademark "Made in Ireland."[1]

The above guidebook description is intended to attract visitors anxious to experience a unique tourist destination, marked by different culture, history, landscape, and people. After all, the search for distinctiveness is a core element of the tourist impulse. While a certain amount of tourism does follow a "beaten track,"[2] tourists nevertheless strive to escape from the everyday world. Prestige is accrued by attaining the furthest possible distance from home, not only in miles "but in cultural terms" as well.[3] There is a curious sense of the discoverer in tourism, a "romantic aura" that finds tourists following, on a kind of spiritual level, in the footsteps of the heroes of exploration: pioneers walking in a track laid by David Livingstone and Edmund Hillary, Marco Polo and Robert Peary. As Hans Magnus Enzensberger put it, "the new human right to distance oneself as far as possible from one's civilization took the shape of the harmless vacation

---

[1] Irish Tourist Board, *Ireland: Heritage of the Past* (Dublin: Irish Tourist Board, 1968), p. 3.

[2] James Buzard, *The Beaten Track: European Tourism, Literature, and the Ways of "Culture," 1800–1918* (Oxford: Oxford University Press, 1993).

[3] Michel Peillon, "Tourism: The Quest for Otherness," *Crane Bag* 8/2 (1984): pp. 165–8.

trip. Yet to this very day tourists insist on the value of the adventure, the elemental, the pristine. The destination has to be both: accessible and inaccessible, distant from civilization and yet comfortable."[4] On these levels, Ireland delivers, says the guidebook. The sea isolates and preserves, freeing the country from the everyday while at the same time preserving elements of the familiar.

It follows that much of the history of Irish tourism involves a concerted effort by tourism developers, local communities, various political factions, and others to portray Irish difference adequately. Following the Irish Civil War (1922–23), when the Irish, largely for the first time, took control of their tourist industry, there was a conscious effort to create a tourist product that truly met the demands of visitors. The principle challenge was to determine just exactly what that product should be.

During the eighteenth and nineteenth centuries, Ireland was paradoxically attractive and off-putting to tourists at the same time. During the first half of the nineteenth century, for example, English visitors came to Ireland to see impressive landscapes and dire poverty. Initially, these tourists hoped to experience the wildness of the Irish west. Over time, travelers became fascinated by the rural poor who lived in squalor, wore clothes that were more holes than cloth, inhabited houses that sat haphazardly in the landscape, and dined upon half-cooked potatoes. English visitors found little difficulty in imagining the Irish to be an "other": geographically close to England, yet culturally distant enough to hail from the Empire's furthest flung colonies. Just as the English dreamed of bringing the glories of civilization to India or Africa, so too they believed that they could reform the Irish, helping "Paddy" to develop his land, his economy, and himself.[5]

After the Famine, English tourism developers led by Frederick W. Crossley, the English founder of the earliest Irish tourism development body, also imagined that they could improve Ireland for tourists. Crossley saw a country with picturesque landscapes every bit as attractive as "the Rhine and Saxon Switzerland." He believed that "With the proper encouragement and enterprise the island might become the dairy farm and pleasure-ground of Great Britain."[6]

---

[4]   Hans Magnus Enzensberger, "A Theory of Tourism," *New German Critique* 68, Special Issue on Literature (Spring–Summer, 1996): pp. 117–35. See especially p. 127.

[5]   William H.A. Williams, *Tourism, Landscape, and the Irish Character: British Travel Writers in Pre-Famine Ireland* (Madison: University of Wisconsin Press, 2008). Also see: Melissa Fegan, "The Traveller's Experience in Famine Ireland," *Irish Studies Review* 9/2 (2001): pp. 361–72.

[6]   Irene Furlong, *Irish Tourism: 1880–1980* (Dublin: Irish Academic Press, 2009), pp. 20–21.

From 1923, however, tourism development was no longer about English entrepreneurs or voyeurism. Although English visitors would undoubtedly view Ireland through their own preconceived lenses, now the Irish had an opportunity to define the color and shape of the glass. While tourist representations were largely English-made before the civil war, afterward the story was far more about native Irish ingenuity and effort. There is scant evidence to support the post-colonial contention that "tourist representations were largely projected onto an Irish screen by English visitors."[7]

In fact, the real challenge facing those involved with tourism development was to determine exactly what image of Ireland to sell. Images of destitution and backwardness had always sold in the past, but was that the image that should be portrayed by a newly independent state anxious to take its place among the nation-states of the world? On the flip side, the image of an industrious island boldly marching toward an industrial future was hardly calculated to attract visitors coming largely from industrialized countries such as England and the United States. Closer to home, questions loomed about whether the partition of Ireland should be shown on maps, whether the Irish Civil War should be remembered, and what traditions best presented Ireland to the world. In short, the process of creating a tourism product prompted a complicated ongoing debate about the nature of Irishness itself. People from across Irish society engaged in a perpetual dialogue about the meaning of Irish national identity so that they could present that identity to the world for tourist consumption. Diverse groups contested the narrative of Irish history, the particulars of Irish landscape, the nature of traditional Irish festivals and fairs, and even whether tourism truly represented a "national interest." The story of post-Irish Civil War tourism, then, is the story of an evolving Irish national identity. It was no longer enough to define Ireland in opposition to England, now Ireland had to be defined relative to the dreams and aspirations of its people.[8]

Having said this, however, just as the above guidebook quote reveals a great deal about the need to sell difference, so too it hints at a reality that might be easily lost: although Irish tourism was the product of hard-working Irish men and women, it also developed within a trans-national and pan-European

---

[7]   Spurgeon Thompson, "The Postcolonial Tourist: Irish Tourism and Decolonization since 1850" (Ph.D. Diss., University of Notre Dame, 2000), pp. 3–4.

[8]   Those interested in the struggle to define Irishness through tourism should see: Eric G.E. Zuelow, *Making Ireland Irish: Tourism and National Identity since the Irish Civil War* (Syracuse: Syracuse University Press, 2009). More detailed information about North/South tourism dialogue is available in: Eric G.E. Zuelow, "'Ingredients for Cooperation': The Role of Irish Tourism in North-South Relations, 1924–1998," *New Hibernia Review* 10/1 (Spring 2006): pp. 17–39.

context. Irish tourism *is* unique. While other countries might claim bog lands, rugged hillsides, green valleys, raucous festivals, tasty cuisine, energetic cities, and peaceful countryside, these ingredients are nowhere combined exactly as they are in Ireland. And yet, as different as it is, Irish tourism remains as much a result of outside influences as it is of entirely indigenous agency. In the same way that tourism inspired a discourse about Irishness within Ireland, so too it brought Ireland into dialogue with tourism developers abroad, with foreign governments, and with tourists from around the world.

On the surface, the struggle over Irishness and a suitably Irish tourist product might seem to be an Irish problem, limited to the Emerald Isle itself, and even more specifically to the 26 counties of the Irish Republic. Yet, the story of post-Civil War Irish tourism development and the negotiation of Irish identity is not a story limited to Ireland. At almost every turn, Irish developers worked within a pan-European and a trans-Atlantic environment. Not only did tourism developers look abroad for ideas and advice but the tourist products that were created, the very markers of a unique identity, were formed within this pan-European milieu. In essence, Ireland was made unique using common tropes and tools gathered from much further afield.

The modern Irish tourist movement came to life in a European-wide context of nascent tourism development. By the *fin de siècle*, tourism promoters launched expansion efforts in various places in both Europe and the United States, often justifying their projects by stressing patriotism. In his groundbreaking book on Spanish tourism during the Franco regime, historian Sasha D. Pack notes that efforts to ease travel on the Iberian Peninsula started as early as the eighteenth century. In 1754 a royal envoy returned to the court of Fernando VI, reporting that Spain was well behind its neighbor, France, in the area of road building and design. The king soon ordered construction of a radial highway system so that travelers might more easily move through Spain. By the 1840s, Spanish travelers abroad still found their homeland somewhat backward. After visiting Belgium, one essayist lamented the poor conditions that travelers faced in his homeland; Spain was lagging behind and would do well to catch-up. During the 1870s, tourist industry groups and local promoters launched a concerted tourism development effort that mirrored similar organizations in France and Switzerland. Finally, at the turn of the century, authors pointed out that Spain could benefit, as had Switzerland, Italy, and France, by developing an extensive tourism sector. Spain's development minister soon launched a "National Commission to Promote Artistic and Recreational Excursions of the Foreign Public." Officials justified the effort by arguing that "those anxious for progress and for our country to figure among the most prosperous, and patriots in general, must second this initiative" to develop tourism.[9] Tourism was a national interest and the various states in Europe looked to one another for examples of how to meet patriotic objectives.

A similar story played out in the United States. Early American tourism developed in dialogue with European models. Early nineteenth-century American tourists were anxious to visit Europe, but also to create attractions that distinguished the United States from the old country.[10] A spate of sites including Niagara Falls, the White Mountains, and Martha's Vineyard emerged to meet this need.[11] By the turn of the century, as in Europe, tourism emerged as a patriotic obligation, a building-block of post-American Civil War national identity building. Railway companies and the nascent national parks service combined forces to offer an image of the United States that featured the sublime and the beautiful on a uniquely American scale. Americans were told to "See Europe if you must, but see America first."[12]

During the early and mid-1920s, Irish tourism promoters, very much aware of the pan-European and trans-Atlantic notion of tourism development as national interest, framed the nascent post-independence discourse in these same patriotic terms. When the Irish Civil War ended in May 1923, the country was in a terrible state. Roads and bridges were impassable. Many buildings were little more than charred rubble. The Irish people, battered by nearly a decade of violence, were divided both by partition and by political fissures between former "irregulars" and those who had accepted the Anglo-Irish Treaty. Tourism advocates found hope in the success that they saw on the European continent and in the United States. One of the first tourism development groups, the Tourist Organisation Society of Ireland, pointed to the Isle of Man, noting that although much smaller than Ireland, "Manxland" attracted three quarters of a million visitors—largely through the use of public funds devoted to advertising and resort development. Switzerland, Egypt, and Wales adopted similarly successful programs.[13] In 1925, the Killarney area attracted a steady stream of well-to-do visitors: "the class that has made Switzerland, and has enriched many resorts in France and Italy."[14]

---

[9]   Sasha Pack, *Tourism and Dictatorship: Europe's Peaceful Invasion of Franco's Spain* (New York: Palgrave Macmillan, 2006), pp. 20–26.

[10]   John F. Sears, *Sacred Places: American Tourist Attractions in the Nineteenth Century* (Amherst: University of Massachusetts Press, 1989), pp. 3–4.

[11]   Ibid. Also see: Dona Brown, *Inventing New England: Regional Tourism in the Nineteenth Century* (Washington, DC: Smithsonian Institution Press, 1997).

[12]   Marguerite S. Shaffer, *See America First: Tourism and National Identity, 1880–1940* (Washington, DC: Smithsonian Institution Press, 2001).

[13]   *Kerryman*, April 26, 1924.

[14]   *Kerryman*, August 15, 1925.

Collectively, tourism promised to help reunify Ireland and "must surely appeal to every patriotic Irishman."[15]

There was considerable pressure to agree with this nationalist image of tourism. In 1924, tourism advocates promised the Killarney boatmen, a group who long made their living by rowing visitors around the Killarney lakes, that motorized craft would never be allowed in Killarney. One year later, urged on by English railway companies, area tourism developers reversed their position, believing that tourists wanted a modern and efficient way to see as much of the region as possible. Not surprisingly, the boatmen protested vigorously, even threatening physical force if motorboats were introduced. Both sides cited patriotic obligations and love of country. Both sides insulted the other and the boatmen even threatened violence. Both sides questioned the other's level of devotion to Ireland and to Irishness. The debate was, above all else about conflicting ideas of Irish identity, one self-consciously modern, the other intensely traditional.[16] Yet the argument was also connected to the larger dialogue about tourism and patriotism. By engaging in this debate, Ireland placed itself firmly into a European and trans-Atlantic context.

Irish tourism developers' first major advertising campaign quickly paid homage to such wider connections and drew directly upon the "See America First" slogan by calling the Irish program "See Ireland First." This scheme consisted of posters, news stories, brochures, tourist maps, and even "See Ireland First" postmarks. Industry officials argued "a healthy option has been created in Ireland this year that the wisest, and certainly the most patriotic, thing Irish people can do is to see their own country in their holiday time."[17] On the surface the program seemed to be all about Ireland, yet underneath it was an adaptation of foreign ideas.

That Irish tourism marketers adapted an American slogan to sell the Irish product is hardly surprising. Developers not only adopted the patriotic language of many tourism promoters, they looked to successful tourism models for ideas and inspiration. Always anxious to attract American visitors, Irish tourism advocates started to engage with their American counterparts almost immediately after the Irish Civil War by sending delegates to the United States.[18] The Irish soon discovered that foreign countries practiced promotion on a much larger scale. At one development meeting held at Killarney, it was reported that the "propaganda" in other countries was "of an intense nature" and that "Ireland

---

15   *Kerryman*, January 26, 1924.

16   For a detailed discussion of the boatmen debate, see Zuelow, *Making Ireland Irish*, pp. 17–21.

17   "Notes and News," *Irish Travel* (August 1926), p. 291.

18   *Kerryman*, January 26, 1924; *Kerryman*, May 2, 1925.

would have to expend a large amount" if it was to attain desired visitor numbers.[19] America stood as a powerful example of what Ireland could be.

Yet the United States was certainly not the only model. In 1927 industry leaders spoke publicly about the national benefits to be garnered from tourism. France pulled in £10 million a year from tourism, the Isle of Man £8 million. Americans spent £120 million a year in Europe. Surely Ireland could earn a substantial percentage of this, but doing so required learning from the competition. J.P. O'Brien, one of the most significant early figures in the Irish tourist movement, thus made regular trips abroad throughout his tenure as an industry leader. These trips seem to have inspired him to think big thoughts about Ireland's potential. When many in Ireland laughed at the prospect of a successful tourist movement, O'Brien spoke in grand terms about turning Ireland into a golf destination—a dream that would only come to fruition after careful study of American "golf courses and club houses." Golf, he said, was "a magnet from the tourist point of view."[20] O'Brien was lampooned for his idea in the Irish parochial press, yet in the long term, Ireland successfully followed the golf tourism model established elsewhere and the sport now stands as one of the country's most successful attractions.

During the 1940s, members of the Irish Tourist Board found something else in Europe to inspire them: state-sponsored leisure policies. Encouraged by a trip to Germany to study the Nazi's *Kraft durch Freude* (KdF) program,[21] the board presented a long memo urging the adoption of an Irish recreational policy which would undermine "the natural tendency, particularly with more hard-working elements of the community ... to use free time for mere idleness." It was essential to ensure "the physical well-being" and "mental development" of the Irish people. Toward this end, the board detailed the lack of recreation facilities in rural Ireland and looked to numerous foreign examples to show what other countries were doing to promote "the *beneficial* use of leisure-time."[22] The idea that the state should help people maximize their spare time was anything but odd during the 1930s and 1940s; the board's report offered a list of 22 countries with such programs alongside the strategies these places employed in urging productive playtime. For example, Irish Tourist Board officials included: Great Britain, which used voluntary organizations

---

[19]   *Kerryman*, December 13, 1924.

[20]   *Killkenny People*, October 6, 1945.

[21]   Shelley Baranowski, *Strength through Joy* (Cambridge: Cambridge University Press, 2004), p. 62.

[22]   National Archives of Ireland [hereafter NAI], Department of the Taoiseach [hereafter DT], S13087A, Irish Tourist Board Memorandum, "Towards an Irish Recreational Policy," February 1944.

supplemented by state subsidies; Germany, which featured state control over organizations alongside compulsory health and physical education; Norway, which featured a "state recreation council"; Czechoslovakia, which utilized state supervision and subsidies to run both official and semi-official recreation bodies; Chile, which used state supervision; and Japan, which made physical education compulsory.[23] While certainly in keeping with a worldwide discourse, the proposal won few friends within Ireland itself. The Minister for Local Government and Public Health, for example, demanded to know "why the Irish Tourist Board considered itself free to turn from those statutory functions which should be its sole preoccupation in order to address itself to a subject with which at best it cannot be more than remotely concerned." He added, rather than "amusing itself in drafting absurd totalitarian schemes," the Tourist Board should strive to enhance Ireland's tourist potential. Renaming the Irish Tourist Board document "Towards an Irish Totalitarian State," the minister demanded to know if the board felt that the Creator should have spent the seventh day doing something other than resting—a clear display of "mere idleness." While the members of the board might have delusions of competency, they had no right to compel the Irish people to play during their time off.[24] More than a mere footnote in the history of Irish tourism development, the "fascist leisure plan" reflects just how intently Irish tourism backers saw themselves within a much larger pan-European, trans-Atlantic, and even global framework which not only ignited the post-Civil War tourist movement, it inspired much of the subsequent development of Irish tourism.

Developing Irish tourism was about more than promotional strategies or widespread ideas about leisure time, the very character of the tourist experience itself was defined partly using outside models. The creation of better hotels, the presentation of Irish heritage, and even the appearance of the Irish landscape itself were all shaped partly through interaction with the wider world.

Hotels

Throughout much of the twentieth century, one of the most significant challenges facing Irish tourism officials was a dearth of suitable tourist accommodations. In 1924, the chairman of the Irish Tourist Association (ITA), the first nation-wide development body, lamented "the shortage of hotel accommodation in the country." Worse, hoteliers were in no position to correct

---

[23]   Ibid.

[24]   NAI, DT, 13087A, Minister of Local Government and Public Health Memorandum, April 29, 1944.

the problem as they lacked the funds necessary to make improvements.[25] As late as the early 1950s, there were only 12 rooms in Dublin considered by the tourist board to be worthy of American visitors. Indeed, the standard for Irish hotels was far lower than found in the United States. In Ireland, a "hotel" was defined by having one bathroom for every 10 bedrooms while in the United States the standard was nearly one to one.[26] This shortcoming was potentially very serious given reports that Americans were anxious to come to Ireland, if only there were suitable lodgings for them on arrival.[27]

　　Despite perceived urgency, tourism developers found it difficult to address the hotel shortage. During World War II, the Irish Tourist Board launched a two-pronged policy to address the problem. On one hand, they inaugurated a hotel ratings scheme that would assure quality for visitors was pushing hoteliers to improve their facilities. On the other hand, the board created a controversial hotel development company. The idea was that no organization was better positioned to correct the hotel shortage than the statutory tourist board. Critics immediately cried conflict of interest. Surely it was wrong for a government organization to grade the efforts of private hotel operators on one hand, often demanding expensive improvements, while on the other hand running hotels that were in direct competition with those same private interests. Many wondered whether the government should be in the hotel business in the first place. Newspaper editorial writers often spoke loudly against the program. Was it right, demanded the *Kilkenny People*, that there were too few houses to hold the Irish people, while the government seemed poised to create "high-class luxury hotels to cater for wealthy tourists who pay flying visits to this country?"[28] Should not the Irish people come first? The *Irish Independent* was equally critical, calling for a reduction in outside visitors in order to assure enough hotel space for Irish men and women. "The Irish people should have first claim on the food and board in this country."[29] Faced with nothing but criticism, the tourist board sold virtually all of its properties by the end of 1949. Ireland, especially in rural and Gaeltacht areas, thus continued to lack adequate facilities. During the 1950s the government attempted to correct the hotels shortage by increasing the number of loans available for development, a policy that was especially prevalent in the Gaeltachts during the 1960s and beyond.[30]

25　*Kerryman*, March 29, 1924.

26　Michael Kevin O'Doherty, interview by author, Dublin, April 29, 2002.

27　*Kerryman*, March 29, 1924.

28　*Kilkenny People*, June 15, 1946.

29　*Independent*, May 1, 1946.

30　NAI, DT, S13087E1, Cabinet Minutes, October 28, 1952.

Hotel grading was often the most contentious tourist board program. While the particulars of hotel grading schemes varied from time to time, there was (and is) almost always conflict between hoteliers who believed their accommodations deserved a top rating and board officials who hoped to either prompt facility improvement by downgrading hotels or who believed that a downgrade would actually increase the amount of business enjoyed by a given establishment. In contrast, hoteliers either wanted to maintain the lowest possible operating costs or simply lacked adequate resources to make the desired improvements.

Given its importance, hotel development sparked considerable international dialogue. According to Michael Gorman, a longtime tourist board official, other countries anxious to establish their own high hotel standards copied the board's hotel grading scheme during the 1960s. Gorman notes "being in Bord Fáilte [Irish Tourist Board] was like being in a university of tourism." Other countries (he did not specify) with less tourism experience were anxious to tap into Ireland's experience and the Irish officials proved to be good teachers by avoiding jargon and otherwise serving as solid communicators.[31]

Yet just as the Irish apparently provided advice to others, so too Irish officials looked abroad for ideas—especially to the United States which was widely believed to have the world's best hotels. In the aftermath of World War II when Marshall Planners combined forces with the ETC and the OEEC to rebuild European tourism (see Introduction), hotel development was an important priority. Among other things, the transnational groups issued a document entitled "Report on the Hotel Industry in the United States" which addressed both investment advice and suggestions for design, decoration, and facilities.[32] Perhaps even more significant, teams of European "experts" traveled to the United States to study the hotel industry there.[33] The Irish both took part in the OEEC trips and engaged the assistance of Robert K. Christenberry, then president of the Astor Hotel in New York City. Christenberry traveled to Ireland to study the industry and subsequently released his report to the Irish government in July/August 1950 detailing elements of the Irish tourist product deserving attention.

Christenberry's report proved to be tremendously important. During the late 1940s, the hotel grading scheme, the ill-fated tourist board hotel program, the personal unpopularity of the director of the tourist board, and several

---

[31]   Michael Gorman, interview by author, Dublin, October 11, 2002.

[32]   NAI, Tourism, Transport, and Communications [hereafter TTA] 3/1/3 vol. 1, OEEC Meeting Agenda, Chateau de la Muette, Paris, December 3, 1952.

[33]   NAI, Department of Foreign Affairs [hereafter DFA], 305/57/128 pt. 1, OEEC Memorandum, December 16, 1949.

other factors combined to transform tourism into a political pariah in Ireland by 1948.[34] Almost immediately thereafter, Marshall Plan administrators, led by Colonel T.J. Pozzi, concluded that Ireland should energetically pursue tourism as a means toward economic expansion. Pozzi did not mince words. He informed Irish officials that tourism must be made a top priority. It was imperative that the Irish "raise the quality of the hotel accommodation ... to the level that will be acceptable to the ordinary United States tourist, and then to construct enough additional accommodation to take a further expansion in numbers."[35] When officials did not address Pozzi's demand, the Irish government was quietly informed that a failure to immediately address tourism development in an effective manner would result in the cessation of Marshall Plan funding for industrial and agricultural projects as well as for tourism. In other words, the United States government mandated that the Irish government get its tourism house in order.[36]

As the government cast about in search of viable strategies to address the tourism question, ministers, and especially future Taoiseach (prime minister) Sean Lemass, settled on the Christenberry Report which offered a variety of suggestions about how to develop tourism infrastructure more effectively. Advice ranged from the development of certain historical attractions such as castles and religious sites to the reorganization of tourism administration to the improvement of sanitation, hygiene, and administration in Irish hotels. Christenberry bluntly stated: "There is not a single hotel that we have gone to which, by American standards, could not have been found in violation of basic sanitary laws in the preservation and handling of food."[37] Almost as bad, untrained, though friendly, staff operated almost all of Ireland's hotels, resulting in inferior service. Hotel staff required professional instruction if Ireland was ever to be a suitable tourist destination. Training schools or on-the-job training was needed.[38] In short, Ireland should follow an American model.

Ireland was far from the only country to find useful examples abroad. French authorities, for example, also looked beyond the frontiers of France for ideas. By the 1960s, French tourism grew far more slowly than the Spanish and Italian markets. Convinced that the problem was a national reputation for being less than friendly, tourism chief Jean Sainteny launched a campaign to recast the

---

[34] For a detailed report, see: Zuelow, *Making Ireland Irish*, pp. 44–55.

[35] NAI, DT, S13087C, Interim Report, 1950.

[36] NAI, DT, S13087C, Department of Foreign Affairs Memorandum, July 27, 1950. See Zuelow, *Making Ireland Irish*, p. 56.

[37] NAI, DT, S13087D, "Christenberry Report," July–August 1950. See p. 31.

[38] Ibid., pp. 34–5.

French as friendly: "There's a big smile on the face of France!"[39] This branding exercise seems suspiciously Irish in character as authorities there worked tirelessly to maintain the long-lasting public impression that friendliness is an indigenous Irish character trait.[40] More than just trying to recast the French as being very much like the Irish, the French government took the initiative to make France more American as well. They attempted to assure fair pricing and to punish businesses that cheated non-Francophone Americans. The move to clean up France's image was given a boost when a French reporter, masquerading as an American, toured the country reporting on how American visitors were treated. The results were gravely distressing. "Be kind to Americans" campaigns saw lovely Anglophone French women employed in information kiosks, and other programs designed to improve France for Americans.[41] There were even efforts to Americanize French hotels. After nearly 10 years of improvement efforts, in 1968 only 20 percent of French hotels had the requisite *en suite* accommodations believed necessary to please Americans.[42]

Heritage

For a small island, Ireland has an extraordinary number of historic sites. As noted above, for thousands of years, men and women arrived in Ireland, supplanted the population they found there, and then made new lives for themselves. These successive waves of immigrants/invaders left behind the telltale signs of their habitation; there are monasteries, castles, round towers, massive stone high crosses, pre-historic passage tombs and stone circles, dolmens and ring forts. Some of these structures, round towers, for example, are virtually unique to Ireland. Even so, the notion that such sites ought to form a substantial part of a tourist's itinerary, should be promoted for their touristic value, and that they deserve to be preserved by the state are all the result of much wider trans-national, and especially pan-European, discourse.

Tourists from across Europe were fascinated by ancient ruins from at least the nineteenth century, finding such sites to be mysterious, romantic, and beautiful. Edmund Burke's notion of the "sublime" was identified with sites such as Stonehenge as readily as it was applied to mountains, beaches, or cataracts. As a

---

[39] Harvey Levenstein, *We'll Always Have Paris: American Tourists in France since 1930* (Chicago: Chicago University Press, 2004): pp. 206–7.

[40] Bord Fáilte Eireann, *Bord Fáilte Eireann Newsletter* (January/February 1957): p. 1–2. For more, see: Zuelow, *Making Ireland Irish*, pp. 113–15.

[41] Levenstein, *We'll Always Have Paris*, pp. 207–9.

[42] Ibid., p. 206.

result, by the late eighteenth century the site was no longer of interest to a limited number of antiquarians it was a "richly brooding icon into which the tourist could read all his fantasies and imaginings."[43] Ireland also featured ancient sites that interested nineteenth-century visitors. Victorians were drawn to places such as Monasterboice, Clonmacnois, Newgrange, and Glendalough. Travel to such sites was more about traveling into the romantic imagination than it was about actual history. Historic sites prompted an emotional response, not an intellectual one.

As European nationalisms grew increasingly exclusive toward the end of the nineteenth century[44] the need to protect distinctive national pasts also increased. Although there are a handful of pre-nineteenth-century preservationist proposals and even papal statutes,[45] state-sponsored monuments acts proliferated at the end of the nineteenth and during the first decades of the twentieth century when most European countries generated either nationalist preservation groups or state-sponsored monuments acts. France passed a hugely influential Historic Monuments Act in 1887 following a growing nationalist preservation movement with roots in the French Revolution.[46]

Illustrating the pan-European nature of this dialogue, preservationists used similar arguments regardless of their country of origin. Victor Hugo declared that "long histories make great peoples," suggesting that physical remains might help remind and educate people about their national past.[47] The great German statesman Otto Von Bismarck insisted that it was of "greatest harm to a nation when it allows the living consciousness of its connection to its heritage and history to fade."[48] University of College Dublin archaeologist R.A.S. MacAlister, arguably the founding father of historic preservation in Ireland, echoed exactly this view when he stressed that preservation and archaeological study represented "a truer patriotism."[49]

---

[43] Ian Ousby, *The Englishman's England: Taste, Travel and the Rise of Tourism* (Cambridge and New York: Cambridge University Press, 1990), p. 95.

[44] Eric Hobsbawm, *Nations and Nationalism since 1780: Programme, Myth, Reality* (Cambridge and New York: Cambridge University Press, 1990), pp. 101–30; and, Michel Winock, *Nationalism, Antisemitism, and Fascism in France* (Stanford: Stanford University Press, 2000), pp. 5–26.

[45] Garald Baldwin-Brown, *The Care of Ancient Monuments* (Cambridge: Cambridge University Press, 1905), p. 128; and, Rudy Koshar, *Germany's Transient Pasts: Preservation and National Memory in the Twentieth Century* (Chapel Hill: University of North Carolina Press, 1998), pp. 29–31.

[46] Baldwin-Brown, *Care of Ancient Monuments*, pp. 73–4.

[47] Ibid., pp. 74–5.

[48] Koshar, *Germany's Transient Pasts*, p. 31.

[49] R.A.S. MacAlister, *Ancient Ireland: A Study in the Lessons of Archaeology and History* (London: Methuen, 1935), p. x.

When the Irish government introduced monuments legislation in the wake of the Irish Civil War (1922–23) officials believed that by "passing such an Act the Irish Free State would take its place among the other nations of Europe." It was not simply that Irish antiquities mattered to Ireland, although they undoubtedly did, but rather that Irish monuments were vital "for an understanding of the early civilization not merely of Ireland but also of Europe."[50] Such legislation would place Ireland at the heart of ancient Europe, while also celebrating the new state's place in modern Europe. It followed that failure to establish monuments legislation would represent not just the rejection of the anguished pleas of a few hyper-educated intellectuals but also the rejection of the widely accepted discourse of modern European nationalisms. Ireland would have been alone in Europe—hardly a viable strategy at a time when the new Irish government hoped to introduce Ireland into the pantheon of nation-states.[51]

More recently, Irish tourism developers remain aware of larger trends. The development of Temple Bar, a tourism center in the heart of Dublin, stands as an excellent example. From the 1960s, the area was slated for use as a transportation hub. Over time, when this project did not take place, residents started to lobby for redevelopment of the area as an arts hub. Finally, by the early 1990s, the government was convinced that turning the site into a "cultural center" was desirable and might ultimately be tremendously lucrative. Government and tourist board grants soon followed and when Temple Bar was unveiled to tourists in the late 1990s, it quickly became one of Europe's leading short-term tourist destinations.[52] Temple Bar features numerous pubs, tourist shops, and other cultural attractions. It is attractive to street musicians, anxious to capitalize on the density of tourists seeking an authentic Irish experience. On the surface, Temple Bar seems to provide just such authenticity. The patina of age is everywhere, from the brightly painted pubs to the cobbled streets to the old-looking street lamps. The site truly looks like a piece of old Ireland—even if it was only created at the end of the twentieth century.

From a trans-national perspective, the touristic experience offered in Temple Bar is replicated in similar heritage zones throughout the world. The area is little different from the Old Port in Portland, Maine, Old Town Montreal, Gastown in Vancouver, British Columbia, or virtually any other urban heritage mecca. As G.J. Ashworth notes, the global heritage industry provides a common set of symbols designed to tell visitors that they are experiencing "heritage." Cobblestones, cast iron lampposts, and apparently vintage storefronts all send a message that is the

---

[50]   NAI, DT, S5004A, Memorandum, Department of the Taoiseach, 1925.

[51]   Zuelow, *Making Ireland Irish*, p. 139.

[52]   Ibid., pp. 90–91. For more, see: Ruth McManus, "Dublin's Changing Tourism Geography," *Irish Geography* 34/2 (2001): pp. 103–23.

same everywhere—in such places, heritage is global, not local.[53] Thus, when Temple Bar Properties, the company behind the development of Dublin's heritage center, undertook the creation of one of Ireland's most significant attractions, there was little truly Irish about it. The story was considerably bigger.

The Land

It was not long after the publication of Burke's *Philosophical Enquiry into the Sublime and Beautiful* in 1757 that visitors anxious to view dramatic landscapes headed to the west coast of Ireland. Almost immediately, places such as Killarney drew praise from scenery-hungry poets and painters. Little had changed in 1924 at the birth of the post-Civil War tourism movement. Travel writers celebrated the landscape and tourism development advocates instructed prospective visitors that Irish scenery was among the most spectacular in the world.

Yet there was another reality to be considered: the landscape was marked by centuries of poverty and emigration. There were few trees and little top-notch farmland. Once deserted by emigrants, cottages quickly fell into ruin, pock-marking both landscapes and townscapes with telltale symbols of failure. This was no small problem. As early as 1925, tourism authorities pointed out that one "eyesore spoils the effects of an otherwise unkept secret [Ireland]."[54] Many proposed solutions over the ensuing 30-plus years. Mandatory destruction of ruins, tree plantings, building restrictions, compulsory painting programs, and more were put forth as possible options. Yet the grim reality was that tourism advocates had few resources to draw upon and the Irish government had little will to impose aesthetic legislation on Irish landowners.

Change finally came during the 1950s with the creation of an annual month-long tourism festival called An Tóstal. Irish homeowners were encouraged to paint their homes, clip their hedgerows, and to plant flowerboxes. A number of local festival committees initiated competitions designed to encourage improvements. Then, in 1958, and building on the success of the local events, the Irish Tourist Board launched the Tidy Towns and Villages Competition. Within only a few years, the rapid success of the annual event inspired new categories, including one for rural farms and another for gardens.

Tidy Towns is extraordinary for the local initiative that it inspired and the event stands as a striking reminder of the significance of horizontal dialogue

---

[53] G.J. Ashworth, "Is Heritage a Globalisation of the Local or a Localisation of the Global?" Paper presented at *Ireland's Heritages: Critical Perspectives on Consumption, Method and Memory*, Castlebar, Ireland, October 19, 2002.

[54] "Notes and News," *Irish Travel* (November 1925), p. 50.

within Ireland, both for the creation of the Irish tourism product and for the perpetual evolution of Irish national identity,[55] but, as above, it was developed within a considerably larger pan-European and even trans-Atlantic discourse about urban aesthetics. There are a significant number of examples of similar improvement projects on both sides of the Atlantic.

During the late nineteenth century, and following the collapse of the whaling industry, the tiny island of Nantucket, Massachusetts, was poised to sink into poverty and obsolescence. Many buildings in the town were starting to fall apart. In 1881, a number of islanders realized that the restoration of remaining seventeenth-century buildings, such as the aptly named Oldest House, might inspire visitors nostalgic for another age. By the 1890s, the restoration scheme was a success and the town, falling into ruins in the 1860s, was reborn as a tourism center. The Nantucket Historical Association was founded in 1894 to assure the preservation of historic buildings and the aesthetic continuity of the village.[56]

At roughly the same time, and perhaps in dialogue with the Nantucket efforts, many towns in Vermont, Maine, and New Hampshire inaugurated an event called "Old Home Week" that was to draw former residents back to the small towns of their youth. Once returned for the festivities, it was hoped that returnees would invest money in their hometowns, perhaps in restoring common lands or in cleaning up cemeteries. Above all, Old Home Week was to inspire a resurgent interest in rural communities, attracting city-dwellers into the countryside where they would find a quaint version of old New England—a New England that would only be possible if abandoned farms were re-inhabited and cleaned up. Programs to inspire just such re-habitation followed in the 1890s.[57]

The *fin de siècle* notion of cleaning up one's hometown was not limited to the United States. In her *Anne of Green Gables* novels, Lucy Maud Montgomery writes about the efforts of Avonlea young people to form an Improvement Society. This organization would remove dead trees, paint barns and fences, and encourage townspeople to tidy up their homesteads. As with all Anne-related stories, the scheme was fraught with dramatic challenges, but Anne and her friends ultimately made quite a difference in their Nova Scotia hometown.[58]

The Irish Tidy Towns competition is probably more directly rooted in twentieth-century European developments, especially in England, France, and

---

[55]   Zuelow, *Making Ireland Irish*, pp. 180–85, 195–201.

[56]   Dona Brown, *Inventing New England: Regional Tourism in the Nineteenth Century* (Washington, DC: Smithsonian Institution Press, 1995), pp. 130–32.

[57]   Ibid., pp. 138–45.

[58]   Lucy Maud Montgomery, *Anne of Green Gables: Three Volumes in One* (New York: Avenel Books, 1986). See pp. 251–5 for an account of the initial formation of Anne's Improvement Society.

perhaps most importantly, Nazi Germany. From the 1920s, Irish authorities kept careful tabs on scenery-related developments elsewhere. Thus, in 1925, one tourism publication pointed to Scarborough, England as an example worthy of study. The Scarborough borough council carefully cared for its townscape by creating parks, walkways, and gardens, by assuring that rubbish was collected, and even by owning and letting a number of neat little beachside bungalows.[59]

Although no records exist, given Irish interest in tourism movements around them, they were almost certainly aware of efforts in France to keep its towns tidy. As Patrick Young notes in Chapter 7 of this volume, the Touring Club of France launched an annual *concours du village coquet* [village beauty contest] after World War I. The program was designed to encourage various French regions to plant trees and flowers and to tidy up public places. There were both certificates and cash prizes for towns "distinguishing themselves in 'their cleanliness and care in presenting a charming aspect.'"[60]

As noted above, German records reveal that Irish tourism officials traveled to Germany during the interwar years to learn about the Nazis' *Kraft durch Freude* organization. While the KdF is perhaps most famous for initiating the Volkswagon, or KdF wagon, and for developing an impressive low-cost travel scheme for working- and middle-class Germans, the organization also devoted an extraordinary amount of energy to improving living and working spaces. Nazi planners were convinced that better aesthetics would produce better and happier Germans. While there was undoubtedly a touristic component to this, everyday life was expected to improve as well. The inclusion of natural light and attractive lunch spots would encourage workers to feel more pride in their country and to work more productively at their jobs.[61] When Irish officials returned from their German tour, they promptly issued a proposal that would have placed the government into the position of administering citizens' free time. Not very much later, and with many of the same staff in place at the tourist board, a program called "Tourism is Everybody's Business" was launched in 1951. The program sought to educate the public about the potential financial benefit of tourism. Citizens were urged to undertake activities that might promote tourism—especially activities that were aesthetically directed. Thus, the tourist board celebrated Arklow where improved street lighting, enhanced signposting, and regular street cleaning were introduced.[62] Tidy Town advocates acknowledged the farmer who "trims a neat hedge" and the "townsman who paints his shop with cheerful good

---

[59] "An Example for Ireland," *Irish Travel*, October 1925, pp. 42–3.

[60] See Patrick Young's "'A Place Like Any Other?': Publicity, Hotels, and the Search for a French Path to Tourism," Chapter 8 of this volume, especially p. 148.

[61] Baranowski, *Strength through Joy*, pp. 75–117.

[62] NAI, DT, S14995A, An Bord Fáilte, *Irish Tourist Bulletin*, August 17, 1951.

taste" as doing their bit for Ireland.[63] Tidiness was everything—just as it was for nineteenth-century Nantucket preservationists, Anne and her friends, and for twentieth-century French and German tourism developers.

Conclusion

While one might conceivably write a history of Irish tourism without placing that story within a much larger transnational context, doing so would conceal the interactions that helped make tourist Ireland what it is. A narrow view of the story would clip out the role of Marshall Planners, ignore the dialogue about the character of hotels, and assume that heritage is a uniquely Irish invention. Worse, a narrow accounting would posit the idea that tourism development itself was entirely an Irish idea, generated by a few tremendously inventive entrepreneurs. It is correct to point out that there was considerable creativity in Ireland and that an extraordinary and widespread attempt was made to build up the tourist industry there. Yet, as shown above, indigenous efforts are not the whole story.

As noted elsewhere in this volume, tourism is inherently about the interaction of peoples from often exceptionally diverse places. They bring with them different experiences and ideas, divergent cultural traditions, and contrary ideas about hygiene, service, and taste. Given this reality, why would anybody expect to find that a national tourist product is entirely the product of homegrown effort? If the character of tourism is one of widespread interaction, does it not follow that tourism development is also born amid a truly transnational dialogue?

In the final analysis, the story of Irish tourism is one of extraordinary horizontal discourse within Ireland, but that discussion involved actors and ideas drawn from across Europe, North America, and possibly even further afield. The initial formation of tourism development organizations, the rhetoric these bodies utilized, and the programs tourism authorities advocated all have roots in these larger conversations. Irish planners did not simply look across the Irish Sea to England, or across the Atlantic to America, they actively sought out ideas wherever such ideas might be found. In so doing, they placed Ireland into a substantial transnational framework of tourism development—a framework that has yet to generate adequate study.

---

[63]   NAI, DT, S14995A, An Bord Fáilte, *Irish Tourist Bulletin*, June 14, 1951.

PART III
The Politics of Transnational Tourism

Chapter 9

Building Tourism in One Country?: The Sovietization of Vacationing, 1917–41

Christian Noack

In 1930, Vladimir Antonov-Saratovskii (1884–1965), an old Bolshevik, lawyer, and high functionary in the Russian Soviet Federative Socialist Republic (RSFSR),[1] wrote a primer on "Soviet proletarian tourism." Antonov-Saratovskii set out to define Soviet tourism in a manner that dissociated it from its equivalent in the capitalist world:

> Capitalist society created another type of travel, so-called "tourism" ... The literal translation of the term conveys the main purpose of these kinds of travel: They must be entertaining, they have to amuse the ruling classes of the capitalist society.[2]

While the middle-class or petty bourgeois tourists in the West were allegedly seeking apolitical distraction, Antonov-Saratovskii emphasized the political significance of tourism in a society building socialism. He argued that tourism:

> educates, it provides a comprehensive idea of the Soviet Union, of her nature and her natural resources, of the peoples that inhabit the country, their economies, habits and cultures in past and present, of the forms of the class war, of the building of socialism and of all that is precious in our country.[3]

Antonov-Saratovskii suggested a multitude of useful tasks to be fulfilled by tourism, ranging from the collection of ethno- and geographic knowledge, to the search for useful mineral resources, to the unveiling of foreign agents. Recreation did not seem to rank prominently among the priorities.

---

[1]   Russian Soviet Federative Socialist Republic (RSFSR) was the official name of the Soviet state between July 1918 and the creation of the USSR in 1922. From then on RSFSR designated Russia, the biggest union republic.

[2]   Vladimir Antonov-Saratovskii, *Besedy o turizme. Azbuka sovetskogo (proletarskogo) turizma* (Leningrad, Moskva: Gosizdat, 1930), p. 9.

[3]   Ibid., p. 27.

Bringing socialist culture and political enlightenment to the most deaf and wild corners of our Union, the tourist should pay particular attention to the less cultured people. Sharing experiences with them, the tourists should above all explain the nationality policy of the party and the Soviet power and, through their behavior, enhance the solidarity between the toilers of all people. ... in accordance to their professional and physical potential, they should help the local dwellers in cultural or technical respects, or with their work force, for example they could repair agricultural machines, communicate popular agricultural findings, cure people and life-stock, install radios, take part in the struggle against agricultural saboteurs [*vrediteli*] and parasites, or help in field work.[4]

Did Antonov-Saratovskii and his comrades in arms succeed in their effort to re-invent tourism as a tool in class war, as an important weapon in a particular Soviet *civilizing mission*? As will be demonstrated in the first part of this chapter, the prospects were favorable at the outset for the creation of a genuinely Soviet variant of tourism. When the Bolsheviks took over in 1917 the Soviet Union was a backward country by contemporary standards and one that had practically no history of domestic tourism. People who were willing to grasp the opportunity and disseminate distinctive socialist variants of tourism and travel would not have met the same sort of resilience that "Sovietization" encountered across East Central Europe after World War II.

Discussion of the attempts at a Sovietization of Russian domestic tourism and travel after the revolutions of 1917 will focus on the 1920s and 1930s. These decades witnessed the most important disputes between the advocates of "proletarian," anti-bourgeois tourism and adversaries with competing agendas within the Soviet system. Against this backdrop, the chapter will explore how far, given the Soviet Union's political isolation, the country can be regarded as resisting contemporary development trends in international tourism. Do we have to take Soviet claims of an anti-Western re-invention of tourism seriously? And if so, how much did negative perceptions of the "bourgeois" tourism blueprint inform the Soviet project of "proletarian tourism?" How successful were attempts to put the Soviet model into practice?

The Backdrop: Pre-revolutionary Russia

When Russia's old regime perished in the 1917 revolutions, the country had already experienced a modest development of domestic tourism. Most

---

[4]   Ibid., pp. 27–61; quote on p. 37.

conventional histories of Russian tourism place the emergence of leisure travel in 1719. In that year, a spa, *Martsialnye vody*, was created by an imperial decree in Karelia, close to the new capital of St. Petersburg. Despite this development, and like their Western counterparts, the Russian nobility continued to prefer the traditional itineraries of the Grand Tour throughout most of the eighteenth century. The first European travel guidebooks appeared in Russian amid this context, and an early Russian Thomas Cook named Veniamin Geish offered the first European package tour for young nobles in 1777.[5] A few pioneering efforts notwithstanding, "taking waters" became a popular pastime for the nobility and educated urbanites only during the nineteenth century. Among the few developed Russian destinations were the North Caucasian baths around Piatigorsk. The numbers of Russian *kurortniki* [spa-goers] grew slowly but steadily, and by the turn of the twentieth century about 75,000 were reported to have visited the country's spas annually.[6]

During the mid-nineteenth century, the propertied classes began to explore the country's Black Sea coast, since construction of new railway lines after defeat in the Crimean War rendered the southern peripheries more accessible. These well-to-do vacationers followed the example of the imperial family who built a lavish summer palace, Livadia in Yalta, in 1834. Beyond the Crimea, Finnish seaside resorts livened up during the summer months—some resorts grew "not by days but by hours."[7] These developments were certainly influenced by contemporary European trends. This is illustrated by the transfer of place names, for example "Russian Riviera," both for the Crimean south coast and the shores of the Black Sea in the Sochi area. Numerous Hotels were likewise baptized "*Russkaia rivera*" or "*Lazurnyi bereg*," the Russian translation of Côte d'Azur.[8] At the same time, the Caucasus mountain range became the Empire's own Alps.

---

[5]   Unfortunately it is not known whether the voyage materialized or not. Gennadii P. Dolzhenko, *Istoriia turizma v dorevoliutsionnoi Rossii i SSSR* (Rostov-na-Donu: Izdatel'stvo Rostovskogo Universiteta, 1988), pp. 12–13.

[6]   Louise McReynolds, "The Prerevolutionary Russian Tourist: Commercialization in the Nineteenth Century," in Ann Gorsuch and Diane P. Koenker (eds), *Turizm: The Russian and East European Tourist under Capitalism and Socialism* (Ithaca: Cornell University Press, 2006), pp. 17–42. See specifically p. 40 note 127.

[7]   A Russian observer in 1892, quoted in McReynolds, "The Prerevolutionary Russian Tourist," p. 34.

[8]   Sochi's comparison with the Italian Riviera and, sometimes, the French seaside resort of Cannes seems to have been authored and popularized by a French traveler, Edouard-Alfred Martel (1859–1938). Martel, speleologist and later chair of the French Geographical Society, published his travel account as *La Côte d'Azur Russe (Riviera du Caucase)* [sic!]: *Voyage en Russie Méridionale, au Caucase Occidental et en Transcaucasie* (Paris: Librairie C. Delagrave, 1908).

This transnational borrowing spelled one of the great challenges for the development of the Russian tourist infrastructure during the late nineteenth and early twentieth centuries. Why should wealthy tourists go for the Russian proxies when they could have the European originals? The Russian elite continued to prefer Carlsbad or Baden-Baden to Piatigorsk or Borjomi, and frequented the French and Italian resorts on the Riviera or the Côte d'Azur. Ironically, Russian destinations saw an influx of vacationers only in the first years of World War I when a new breed of visitor, anxious to experience the breakdown of domestic travel due to protracted warfare, revolutions, and civil war, arrived in growing numbers.[9]

Most of the examples cited above implied stationary forms of vacation and came to be designated with the Russian term *otdykh* [recreation]. In the second half of the nineteenth century these earlier leisure activities were supplemented by more active forms of recreation and sightseeing that were referred to as *turizm* [tourism]. Again, the Russian development did not differ much from what happened in contemporary Europe. Tourism occurred somewhat later, and remained confined to small groups of activists from an urban and educated background. Alpinism, for example, began to inspire Russians by the last third of the nineteenth century. Mountaineers organized alpine clubs in the Caucasus and on the Crimea in 1878 and 1890 respectively.[10] Towards the turn of the century, amateur Russian cyclists and hikers founded various "touring clubs." These organizations soon merged into the first larger national leisure body: the "Russian Association of Tourists" [Rossiiskoe obshchestvo turistov, or ROT]. Against the backdrop of an accelerating pace of urbanization, 13.4 percent of the population in 1897, and an ever-growing network of railroad lines, a modest tourist infrastructure was created in Russian towns. Even so, the bulk of hotels and hostels across the country still catered for itinerant merchants and other commercial visitors rather than for leisured travelers.

As the tourist infrastructure was still in its infancy, the Russian Association of Tourists promoted self-help. They faced significant challenges. Many areas within the Empire were still remote and largely inaccessible by modern means of transportation (trains or steamships). Despite the difficulties, the organization published a journal and road maps. It organized sightseeing tours and accommodation across the country for the adventurous few. Measured by Russia's sheer size the association's activities were hardly more than a drop in the

---

9   McReynolds, "Prerevolutionary Russian Tourist," pp. 32–42. For Crimea see also Andrei Mal'gin, *Russkaia Riv'era. Kurorty, turizm i otdykh v Krymu v epokhu Imperii konets XVIII — nachalo XXv* (Simferopol': Sonat, 2006). For Finland Jurma and Pjajvi Tumoi-Nikula, *Imperatory na otdykhe v finlandii* (Sankt-Peterburg: Kolo, 2003).

10   Dolzhenko, *Istoriia turizma*, pp. 20–40.

ocean. Still, on the eve of World War I, the association counted a membership of 5,000 divided among some 25 local branches across the major cities of Russia.[11]

Commercial tourist enterprises emerged slowly as well. Steamboat companies offered river cruises, and by the second half of the nineteenth century a tour on the Volga had become one of the standard ways to explore the Empire.[12] Travel agencies increasingly targeted Russians planning to travel abroad. From 1867 Leopol'd Lipson's agency in St. Petersburg offered package tours to Europe. He must have been quite successful since his company remained in business for at least two decades. These were pioneering enterprises and hinted at more to come. Even so, the economic potential of tourism was discussed, but not yet realized.[13]

The first decades of the twentieth century saw a boom in short-term and short distance trips when an "excursion" craze seized Russia's schoolteachers. Imperial Russia had no state-run compulsory education system. Education therefore became a part of the civic project propelled by the Russian intelligentsia, and a rising number of schools run by town administrations and the *zemstva*, organs of local self-administration in the countryside, came to supplement confessional schools. Generally, these schools featured a curriculum that combined the transmission of knowledge to the individual pupil with an attempt to instill overarching values of citizenship and patriotism. *Kraevedenie*, a peculiar Russian mixture of area studies and local history,[14] was a central subject to be taught inside and outside the classroom. Russian educational journals consequently encouraged the teachers to take their pupils to towns or district centers in order to show them local museums or cultural monuments. Educators were also encouraged to expose students to their natural surroundings in order to familiarize them with the natural history of their home country. Moreover, the Ministry of Public Education repeatedly declared its support for excursions as part of the school curriculum.[15]

Judging from the publicity in journals and from the role *kraevedenie* and excursions played at teachers' congresses, in quantitative terms the excursion movement exceeded all other forms of tourism in early twentieth-century Russia. Against this backdrop it is little surprising that the Russian Association of Tourists drew its membership from the intelligentsia, mainly from the ranks of schoolteachers.

---

[11]   Dolzhenko, *Istoriia turizma*, pp. 41–5; McReynolds, "Prerevolutionary Russian Tourist," pp. 28–9.

[12]   Guido Hausmann, *Mütterchen Wolga. Ein Fluss als Erinnerungsort vom 17. bis zum frühen 20. Jahrhundert* (Frankfurt: Campus, 2009), pp. 353–429.

[13]   McReynolds, "Prerevolutionary Russian Tourist," pp. 26–7, 40–42.

[14]   Also see Emily D. Johnson, *How St. Petersburg Learned to Study Itself: The Russian Idea of Kraevedenie* (Philadelphia: Pennsylvania State University Press, 2006), Chapters 2 and 3.

[15]   Dolzhenko, *Istoriia turizma*, pp. 46–60.

In conclusion, tourism in Imperial Russia remained a marginal phenomenon that was belatedly "imported" from contemporary Europe. Spas and seaside resorts developed on the southern periphery of the Empire, along the Caucasian mountain range, and particularly in the Crimea. Travel agents and travel companies existed in the larger cities. Urban areas hosted the emergence of a small but very active civic tourist movement, organized in clubs and societies like the Russian Association of Tourists. Yet the bulk of the population had little opportunity to develop a leisure travel habit, except perhaps for short excursions as pupils.

Revolution, Civil War, and New Economic Policies: The 1920s

For the overwhelming majority of Russians tourism was an unknown quantity when the Bolsheviks seized power on October 25 (November 7), 1917 and consigned their less determined socialist rivals to the "dust heap of history." At the start, the victorious revolutionaries had other priorities than musing about mass tourism and travel, as they almost instantly faced substantial and armed resistance inside and outside the country.

Against this backdrop and despite the turmoil of war communism and fratricide, it is rather surprising that, on April 4, 1919, the Soviet government issued a decree "on the Spas of nationwide importance."[16] The timing of this initiative was remarkable indeed, since the Soviets at this particular moment controlled only a tiny fraction of the pre-revolutionary spas. Counter-revolutionary White Army forces occupied the Crimea and the Caucasus region. Finland and the Baltic coast, formally important destinations for the inhabitants of St. Petersburg, had been lost to newly independent states. Nonetheless, the Soviet leadership, and supposedly Lenin himself, perceived *otdykh* [recreation] to be an important enough field for symbolic policies, an issue that would display the regime's care for the welfare of the toiling masses. What role would the first socialist state ascribe to recreation, and how would it organize vacation facilities? Would it continue along the beaten tracks, or would it try to revolutionize the organization of workers' rest and recreation?

The first decree was of limited value for defining the future course of policy. In terms of content, the government nationalized the most important recreational structures and identified measures to protect the natural resources required to run the sanatoria. In its rather technical nature, this decree can

---

[16]   Reprinted in I.I. Kozlov, *V.I. Lenin i razvitie sanatorno-kurortnogo dela v SSSR* (Moscow: Profizdat, 1982), pp. 15–17.

be interpreted as a link in a chain of measures that the Council of Peoples' Commissars had undertaken in building a national health system.[17] Public health did indeed become an important pillar of the Soviet project of modernization. As Michael David points out when discussing the history of Soviet tuberculosis prevention, the health system provided "a mechanism for interaction between state and society, mediated by a small group of experts, with the goal of reforming everyday life to cure and prevent the spread of fatal disease."[18]

After all, the creation of a national health system under Soviet auspices reflected deep-seated ideological beliefs about the interrelations between the human body, work, and recreation that differed surprisingly little from contemporary capitalist ethics. The Soviet Union as the first socialist workers' state defined production as the fundamental basis of all collective and individual wealth. Work was thus seen as an obligation for every citizen. And as work would physically exhaust the human body, the socialist state would have to see to it that the workers would be provided the necessary reproductive rest within the framework of the Soviet economic system.

> Work and recreation are the two functional modes of a developed animal's organism ... sufficient, timely and properly organized recreation is the important and inevitable precondition for the improvement and preservation of [the] human workforce.[19]

This need was addressed through the provision of state-sponsored medical care as well as the allowance of sufficient leisure time. Therefore, at least in theory, the Soviet government from early on guaranteed "healthful rest opportunities" like an eight-hour work day, a weekly day off from work, and annual vacations, two weeks according to the 1922 labor code.[20] Correspondingly, the Soviet interest in recreational facilities was sometimes formulated in quite mundane terms, for example as by a delegate named Mogilevich during the Fifth Congress of the

---

[17]   See Ibid., pp. 9–15.

[18]   Michael Z. David, "Social Welfare or Wasteful Excess? The Legacy of Soviet Tuberculosis Control Programs in Post Soviet Russia," in Thomas Lahusen and Peter H. Solomon, Jr. (eds), *What is Soviet Now? Identities, Legacies, Memories* (Berlin: Lit Verlag, 2008), pp. 214–33, quote p. 231. David explains the reference to "scientific expertise" as a survival strategy for "bourgeois specialists."

[19]   Quoted from entry "Recreation" in *Bolshaia Sovetskaia Entsiklopediia* (2nd ed.), vol. 31 (1955), pp. 383–4.

[20]   Diane P. Koenker, "'The Right to Rest': Postwar Vacations in the Soviet Union," *NCEEER Report*, March 13, 2008. Available online at: http://www.ucis.pitt.edu/nceeer/2008_822-06g_Koenker.pdf [accessed May 1, 2009], quote on p. 1.

Soviet Health Administration in 1924: "The tasks of the health resorts is not the yielding returns, it is exclusively the repair of the toilers' health."[21]

But would this view fully explain why Lenin would have taken a particular interest in the nationalization of the health resorts, as most of the Soviet accounts make us believe? The key to an alternative interpretation can be found in another decree published by the Soviet of Peoples' Commissars on December 21, 1920—immediately after the defeat of the last White strongholds on the Crimean peninsula. The first passage of this decree "on the use of Crimea for the recreation of toilers" deserves extended quotation:

> Thanks to the Red Army's liberation of Crimea from the regime of Wrangel and the White Guards, new perspectives have opened up for the use of the healthy resources of the Crimean coast for the curing of and the restoration of the working capacities of workers, peasants and all toilers from all Soviet republics; and also for workers from foreign countries, sent by the International Council of Trade Unions. The sanatoria and health resorts of the Crimea, earlier a privilege of the higher bourgeoisie, the splendid seasonal homes and mansions, earlier used by the landowners and capitalists, the palaces of the one time tsars and grand dukes shall be put to good use as sanatoria and health resorts for workers and peasants.[22]

The rhetorical confrontation of old and new and the international dimension of the decree display the clearly propagandistic intentions of the document. The following practical instructions contain nothing surprising. Indeed, the People's Commissariat for Public Health was instructed to raise the number of beds in health resorts from 5,000 to 25,000 in the course of 1921, the trade unions were charged with the selection of needy workers in the big industrial centers (with Petrograd, Moscow, the textile belt of Ivanovo, Kharkov', and the Donbass directly mentioned) and other Soviet bodies were exhorted to see to it that the necessary infrastructure for the operation of the health resorts is provided.

Despite the dramatic tone of the above demands, this was still the age of austere "war communism." There was no mention of any "new" or "proletarian" concepts of recreation, or even ideas that would have suited the Soviet toilers, workers, or peasants in any particular way. Following the logic of this document, there was nothing wrong with a Crimean coast spotted with lavish mansions and palaces. The problem was that such places had not been accessible to the masses. As a matter of fact, the early Soviet discourse on public health emphasized

---

[21] E.D. Gribanov, "'Rol' vserussiiskikh zdravotdelov v stanovlenii i razvitii kurortnogo dela v SSSR (1917–1925)," *Voprosy kurortologii, fizioterapii i lechebnoi fizicheskoi kul'tury* [hereafter *Voprosy kurortologii*] 6 (1962): pp. 553–4, quote on p. 554.

[22] Kozlov, *Lenin*, pp. 27–8, quote on p. 27.

the broader social access of medical services as *the* Soviet achievement in the area.[23] Beyond that the Soviet government, for the time being, refrained from re-inventing the wheel.

In fact this policy amounted to the Soviet government protecting and conserving an eighteenth- and nineteenth-century aristocratic or partially gentrified cultural concept: the European spa. During the 1920s the development of the Soviet recreational service, under the auspices of the Ministry of Public Health and the trade unions, was characterized by a high degree of continuity. Existing structures were commissioned and restored. The very few new buildings copied the eclecticism of the *fin de siècle* styles and ornamentations that already characterized the pre-revolutionary spas and health resorts.

Vacationers in those spas required a doctor's certificate emphasizing their particular medical needs to receive a voucher entitling them to a 20–24-day stay. A sojourn in a sanatoria would usually include medical treatment and procedures like taking waters, baths, massages, or particular diets, combined with "cultured" entertainment like concerts, lectures or reading books from the facilities' own libraries.[24] Thus the standard of vacation in Soviet spas was defined at a very costly level; running sanatoria implied the maintenance of a substantial infrastructure for services and medical treatments.

Against this backdrop, the only genuinely Soviet invention was the *dom otdykha*, or "rest home."[25] These facilities were usually located in smaller and simpler buildings. They offered shorter stays (10–12 days) and the regime was more relaxed than in the sanatoria. Still, to be admitted, the vacationers also had to undergo a medical check and needed a certificate testifying to their "exhaustion."[26]

Even if the rest homes were a cheaper and less strict alternative to the sanatoria, the pre-revolutionary idea of the *kurort* still defined their character. Therefore, it seems to be fair to state that the Soviet health resort remained what it had been before the revolution: a *heterotope* in Foucauldian terms, a sugarcoated counter-concept opposed to the mundane routines of the Soviet urban or rural worlds. Rest homes represented an earthly paradise made of pearly white buildings that

---

[23] For example G.A. Nevraev, "Kurortno-sanatornoe delo v strane sovetov," *Voprosy kurortologii* 5 (1957): pp. 3–13, here p. 8; E.D. Gribanov, "'Rol' vserossiiskikh s'ezdov zdravotdelov," pp. 553–4.

[24] For a detailed discussion see Monika Henningsen, *Der Freizeit- und Fremdenverkehr in der (ehemaligen) Sowjetunion unter besonderer Berücksichtigung des Baltischen Raumes* (Frankfurt am Main: Peter Lang, 1994), pp. 56–68.

[25] Postanovlenie Soveta Narodnykh Kommissarov o domakh otdykha, 13 maia 1921g., in: Kozlov, *Lenin*, pp. 33–4.

[26] Koenker, "Right to Rest," p. 5.

leisurely dressed toilers in white summer suits and dresses would enter courtesy of the party's farsighted care.[27]

In numerical terms, Soviet health resorts underwent an altogether unimpressive development during the 1920s. The number of Soviet citizens receiving a state sponsored vacation in the health resorts dropped from 65,000 in 1921 to 28,000 one year later. Subsequent growth was slow. It was not until 1928 that the number of visitors slightly exceeded pre-war (1913) figures, when 580,000 people spent their vacation in recreational facilities housing 80,000 beds (in sanatoria and rest homes).[28]

The temporary decline in vacationers at health spas during the early 1920s must be related to the imminent change of policies that followed the Red Army victory in the civil war. After years of exhaustive warfare and the hardships of war communism the country needed a lull to recover. The so-called New Economic Policy pursued between 1922 and 1928 provided just such a respite. Forced requisitions and a state-run mechanism of distribution allowed for a limited revival of consumer markets. The Communist regime continued to oversee some of the "commanding heights" in the national economy (foreign trade, banking, and large-scale industries), but state authorities pulled back from many activities in the realm of services. The tourism sector was one of these. This change meant that the Soviet health resorts passed to the control of local authorities which sought to reduce expenditure by leasing quite a number of recreational facilities to nongovernmental bodies. To the same extent, the economic situation normalized and affluent customers re-emerged. Workers and peasants therefore shared the spas and seaside resorts with paying vacationers again.[29] Illustrated periodicals like the satiric journal *Krokodil* featured numerous cartoons with portly petty bourgeois NEP-men (and -women) edging the toilers out of the country's sanatoria and seaside resorts.

If the Soviet regime turned out to be highly conservative in the realm of recreation, how did it look upon tourism in the sense of active travel? Would physical endurance and active appropriation of the environment not be more compatible with the ideas and ideals of the new system? Paradoxically, it was not the low-key realm of tourism that the Soviets tried to commission first, even if no Soviet history can do without reference to Lenin's alleged fondness for hiking (supposedly exercised during his exile in Switzerland).

---

[27]   See Michel Foucault, "Of Other Places. Heterotopes," (English translation), at Foucault.Info. Available online at: http://foucault.info/documents/heteroTopia/foucault. heteroTopia.en.html [accessed July 1, 2009].

[28]   Nevraev, "Kurortno-sanatornoe delo," pp. 3–13; Gribanov, "'Rol' vserossiiskikh s'ezdov," p. 554.

[29]   Gribanov, "'Rol' vsesoiuznykh s'ezdov," p. 554.

True, the concept of educational excursions, that particular Russian variety of tourism developed in the early twentieth century, experienced an impressive revival almost immediately after the revolution, the deprivations of the civil war notwithstanding. Prospects might have looked bleak for excursions in material terms in 1918, yet they were politically promising. From the start, the Bolsheviks displayed a strong favor for public educational projects, such as compulsory schooling and adult education, that were designed to eliminate widespread illiteracy. This predisposition potentially implied support for visual methods of teaching, with educational sightseeing being an important example. As a matter of fact, both the veterans of the pre-revolutionary movement and the new educational authorities hurried to revitalize the excursion project that had declined over the war years.

Representatives from Petrograd's academic scene, among them leading advocates of *kravedenie* like Ivan Grevs, Pavel Vittenburg, and Nikolai Antsiferov, were among the first advocates of the revival. As far as Anatolii Lunacharskii, the peoples' commissar for education, was concerned, their arguments were convincing. Lenin's wife, Nadezhda Krupskaia, the gray eminence of Soviet pedagogy during the 1920s, likewise lent support. Renowned Bolsheviks like Nikolai Krylenko, the Russian Soviet Federative Republic's deputy commissar for justice and later general prosecutor, and a fellow jurist and old Bolshevik, the previously quoted Vladimir Antonov-Saratovskii, soon joined the advocates for local studies.

Between 1918 and 1922, a number of "excursion bases" in or near Petrograd were created and sponsored by the government or by local Soviet authorities. Yet under the conditions of civil war their impact on practice is difficult to measure. Tellingly enough, the director of Petrograd's Central Labor School had to petition the government for the provision of "forty pair[s] of hiking boots (for men and women)" for the guides of the excursion section. Another time he asked to borrow two cows in order to provide sustenance to the excursionists.[30]

For a short period this support by the political and academic establishment resulted in dynamic institutional developments. Excursion bases were opened in the major cities and Moscow and Petrograd/Leningrad accommodated several research institutes for tourism development. The Russian Republic's Commissariat of Enlightenment established programs to train excursion leaders. Other *exkursionnye stantsii* were run by the trade unions.[31]

---

[30] Dolzhenko, *Istoriia turizma*, pp. 64–9; example taken from Grigorii Usyskin, *Ocherki istorii Rossiiskogo turizma* (Moscow and St. Petersburg: Gerda, 2000), pp. 90–91.

[31] Johnson, *How St. Petersburg*, Chapter 4; see also Dolzhenko, *Istoriia turizma*, pp. 70–71.

Their life span, as a rule, proved to be quite limited. Again this process of decay in the early 1920s can be related to the policies of "normalization" and re-commercialization of life during the NEP period. This normalization relieved the pressure on society and fewer people may have felt the necessity to engage in local tourism or the preservation of nature and the pre-revolutionary cultural heritage. Probably more important, other commercial leisure opportunities became widely accessible during the 1920s. In the medium term this significantly weakened the excursion movement, even before *kraevedenie* (as a concept) became one of the first victims of renewed communist vigor during Stalin's "revolution from above."[32]

Indeed, during the NEP years the former alliance between local historians and some of the prominent Bolsheviks quickly crumbled. Men like Krylenko supported the revival of the excursion movement, first and foremost, because they were enthusiastic practitioners of tourism themselves. Their idea of tourism, however, was at least as much informed by physical training as it was by spiritual education.[33] *Kraevedenie*, as practiced by the excursion bureaus and bases in Moscow and Petrograd, involved too much talking and too little exercise for them. Beyond that, Soviet tourist organizations seemed to be too preoccupied with pre-revolutionary heritage and local interests. Ideas of revolutionary renewal displayed only limited compatibility with such preservationist orientations; many Bolshevik tourist activists shared the conviction that all remnants of the past had to be destroyed to be replaced by a completely different proletarian culture. The same conflict emerged in the realm of environmental protection, as the "builders of socialism" aimed at a mastery of nature by all available means.[34]

For the time being, however, *kraevedenie* and the excursion movement were not the most urgent concerns for the ideologues. Krylenko, Antonov-Saratovskii, and their like were more angered by what they perceived as a re-commercialization of tourism on the one hand, and by the competition between different Soviet organs in an emerging travel market on the other.

Indeed, the temporary retreat of the state and other party-controlled organizations from arranging vacations on a large scale did not merely create opportunities for a commercialization of the health resorts, it also enabled pre-

---

[32]   Many of its leading proponents were purged as "bourgeois specialists." See also: Johnson, *How St. Petersburg*, pp. 93–6; Usyskin, *Ocherki*, p. 99.

[33]   Krylenko, for example, was a passionate mountaineer who had climbed the Elbrus and who had participated in expeditions to the Pamir. For details see Dolzhenko, *Istoriia turizma*, pp. 94–104.

[34]   On un-proletarian "localism" and "culturalism," see Diane Koenker, "The Proletarian Tourist in the 1930s: Between Mass Excursion and Mass Escape," in Gorsuch and Koenker, *Turizm*, pp. 119–40. See pp. 124–7.

revolutionary societies like the Russian Association of Tourists to resume activity in 1922. Moreover, the Commissariat of Enlightenment displayed remarkable energy beyond the organization of excursions. Backed by the trade unions, the body created a joint-stock company called "Sovetskii turist" (or colloquial "Sovtur") in September 1928. Officially, Sovtur interpreted "tourism" to be an educational activity with some "recreational" intent:

> ... to use the rest and leisure of toilers to broaden their production horizons ... the expansion of the general political horizons of the mass of excursionists and of propaganda about the tasks of socialist construction. These goals should be connected with leisure, educational work should be based on actual emotional perceptions, and the very process of excursions should develop collectivist habits, inculcating in the masses elements of the new cultural way of life, developing the autonomy (*samodeiatel'nost'*) of the masses, tempering them physically, developing the habits necessary for every builder and defender of the socialist country.[35]

In fact, this new company under the roof of the ministry acted as a travel agency that organized commercial package tours and constructed tourist facilities throughout the USSR. What had been self-help in the form of the Russian Association of Tourists before the revolution was now taken up by a state-sponsored, yet commercial, institution. Beyond selling vouchers for tourist trips and accommodation, Sovtur issued guidebooks and distributed train tickets. Shares could be bought for 100 rubles each, and it was the shareholders who were entitled to privileged access to vacationing facilities.[36]

For the proponents of a truly proletarian tourism renewal—a renewal that would open up tourism for the toiling masses—Sovtur's commercialism was clearly anathema. Critics accused Sovtur of failing to address the "autonomy of the masses." Neither would Sovtur accept self-organized, autonomous groups of travelers in their accommodations, nor would it target the masses at all. What Sovtur proposed seemed little different from what tourism was under the old regime and what it continued to be in the capitalist world.

By contrast, advocates for the workers pressed for a re-invention of tourism as a genuinely *proletarian* activity. For them "proletarian" entailed two different meanings. First, active tourists should be workers and not the students and white-collar individuals who had dominated tourist activities in imperial and

---

[35]　Quoted from Diane Koenker, "Who Was the Proletarian Tourist? Class, Leisure and Citizenship in the Soviet 1930s." Unpublished paper presented at the ICCEES World Congress, Berlin, July 25–30, 2005, pp. 7–8.

[36]　V.V. Dvornichenko, *Razvitie turizma v SSSR (1917–1983 gg.)* (Moscow: Turist, 1985), p. 11–12.

early Soviet Russia. Consequently, a truly proletarian culture would be a mass culture and true proletarian tourism had to be *mass tourism*. The industry could not exist for the pleasure of a happy few.[37]

The proponents of "proletarian tourism" were convinced that the active forms of tourism they advocated (and, for the most part, practiced) could be much cheaper and easily accessible. Small groups would travel together, largely independent of developed infrastructures. Stressing the physical, educational, and socializing functions of this type of self-planned autonomous tourism [*samodeiatel'nyi turizm*], they tried to trigger a new concept of tourism and travel that was politically correct, "simultaneously autonomous and collective, self-improving and socially constructive."[38]

Interestingly, their concept displayed only limited influence by workers' tourist movements in contemporary Europe. While self organization and self improvement were certainly shared features in Western and Eastern Europe, the Soviet protagonists of proletarian tourism criticized Western working-class tourist movements for their alleged imitation of petty bourgeois travel habits, and even for what the critics viewed as an ideological void. Antonov-Saratovskii's primer delivered the following caricature of German workers tourism:

> ... workers' tourism is extremely impoverished in its contents; it is even much poorer than "democratic" [petty bourgeois] tourism. Aspects of physical culture are absolutely dominant. This is truly just a trip into freedom [*vykhod na voliu*] to breathe fresh air, to lie in the grass or to stroll through the green hills or forests near the towns. In this case tourism and recreation overlap more than in any other case ... besides some educational moments workers' tourism is penetrated with socio-political tasks, among which one tendency is particularly remarkable: this is the aspiration to travel to the country where there is the dictatorship of the proletariat—in order to go and see for themselves how their brothers, the workers, have taken power into their own hands and transformed a huge country according to the principles of socialism.[39]

Thus there was little obvious international influence in the development of the doctrine, except maybe for the fact that some of the protagonists of proletarian tourism had become tourists themselves while in exile prior to the October Revolution. With the international isolation of the USSR and against the backdrop of factional disputes within the party following Lenin's death in 1924,

---

[37]   Diane Koenker, "Who Was the Proletarian Tourist?," p. 17.
[38]   Quoted in Koenker, "Proletarian Tourist," p. 119.
[39]   Antonov-Saratovskii, *Besedy*, pp. 14–15.

the disagreements over the ideologically correct way to organize Soviet tourism should be interpreted as representations of the underlying clashes between a radical left and a more evolutionary right wing in the party. By the mid-1920s the question was whether the building of socialism required revolutionary cultural change, or whether a more gradual development towards socialism was feasible.

The "proletarians," advocates of revolutionary change, initially attempted to use the Communist youth organization, Komsomol, as their organizational platform. Indeed, in late 1926, *Komsomol'skaia Pravda* printed several programmatic articles that called for contemporary proletarian forms of tourism that would connect with the social developments in the decade since the revolution. In other words, they demanded the creation of real mass tourism. In this context leitmotifs of Antonov-Saratovskii's initially cited proletarian tourism were aired for the first time:

> Our tourism has nothing in common with the bourgeois form. For the bourgeoisie, tourism is amusement, an attempt to flee from the crushing boredom of their parasitical life. Our tourism is one of the stages by which the mass of the people will complete their rise to culture.[40]

Unfortunately, the Komsomol hierarchy was not terribly interested in the matter. This fact did not prevent the tourism enthusiasts from propagating their ideas continuously through the Komsomol press and its publishers.[41] A direct attack on Sovtur, as a state agency, on the other hand, was out of the question.

Against this backdrop the proponents of proletarian tourism had to devise a new strategy. They looked for an alternative springboard and found it in the pre-revolutionary Russian Association of Tourists (ROT). As mentioned above, the association resumed its activities in 1922, albeit on a moderate scale. As the association seemed to cater almost exclusively for the interests of some urban professionals and well-paid civil servants, its class structure provided a perfect ideological battleground in a struggle for proletarian dominance.[42] Komsomol and trade union members were mobilized to flood ROT with new members. In the summer of 1928 these newcomers ousted the former leadership and wrapped up its program. The association was re-baptized the "Society of Proletarian Tourism of the RSFSR" [Obshchestvo proletarskogo turizma RSFSR, or

---

[40] *Komsomol'skaia pravda*, December 17, 1926, cited in Dvornichenko, *Razvitie turizma*, p. 14.

[41] Koenker, "Proletarian Tourist," pp. 121–2.

[42] For the "proletarians," the Russian Association of Tourists was a club of "500 clerks and one worker"—Antonov-Saratovskii, cited in Dolzhenko, *Istoriia turizma*, p. 75. Over time this became "500 members and *not one* worker," see Usyskin, *Ocherki*, p. 107.

OPT], and the proletarian tourists now disposed of the existing assets of the old association, including some hostels in much sought after destinations.[43]

This takeover was only the first step in a mid-term strategy aiming to establish the principle of "proletarian tourism" as binding. The Society of Proletarian Tourism set out to copy the party's and trade unions' organizational structure by establishing factory-based cells across the country. Creating a mass basis in the factories, it was hoped, would prepare the ground for the coming standoff with the state sponsored Sovtur which remained the strategic target. Indeed, with the adoption of the overtly leftist programs of forced industrialization and collectivization by Stalin in 1928 and his propagation of the "revolution from above," the general political outlook seemed more than promising for the "proletarians" in their effort to edge out "capitalist" Sovtur as the most influential player in the field.

The Second Attempt: "Revolution from Above," 1928–36

While the period following the October Revolution had seen a pronounced political interest in recreational facilities as a part of the new social health system, tourism in the narrow sense of the term became the main ideological battleground during Stalin's "cultural revolution." The new leadership of the Society of Proletarian Tourism of the RSFSR was determined to explore the favorable political climate at the turn of the 1930s in an effort to implement a genuinely Soviet concept of travel and vacation and to establish itself as the dominant organization in the field.

Initially the "proletarians" concentrated on creating a massive base of support in the factories, the so-called "tourist cells" or "sections." In 1932, the society allegedly counted 800,000 members and boasted that it had served three million tourists. They claimed that the share of factory workers involved in tourist activities increased from about 33 percent to roughly 60 percent.[44] Against this backdrop the proletarian activists claimed to represent the interests of class as opposed to those of commerce as embodied by their opponents, Sovtur.

> We were for a mass independent proletarian movement; Sovtur was for paid excursions. We were for cells in enterprises, as the basic center; Sovtur was

[43]   V.V. Dvornichenko, *Turizm v SSSR i deiatel'nost sovetskikh profsoiuzov po ego razvitie (1917–1984gg.)* (Moscow: Vyshchaia shkola profsoiuznogo dvizheniia VTsSPS im. N.M. Shernika, 1985), pp. 35–6; Dolzhenko, *Istoriia turizma*, pp. 73–5.

[44]   Koenker, "Proletarian Tourist," p. 122; Koenker, "Who Was the Proletarian Tourist?," p. 17.

for the center to be the excursion base. We were for subordinating managerial (*khoziaistvennye*) services to the political tasks of the movement, Sovtur in practice had raised management to an end in itself.[45]

Amid the heady climate of the "great leap forward," the press was quick to take up the negative cliché of "*sovturovshchina*," summing up Sovtur by emphasizing its alleged leanings toward "capitalism" and its "apolitical" concentration on "organizational work." Yet these polemics could hardly conceal that both organizations were tightly competing in other realms of practical work. This reality is especially true for the development of new tourist routes [*marshruty*], the creation of cheap accommodation (basically tent camps baptized "tourist bases"), and the lobbying for subsidies for low cost travel (train tickets) for tourist groups.[46] Indeed, Sovtur, backed by important state agencies, was much more successful and emerged as the primary provider of services for Soviet tourists, during a time when the country as a whole was ravaged by collectivization of agriculture and the full-blown industrialization program of the First Five Year Plan.

The uneasy standoff between both organizations was solved by decree from above. In March 1930 the Council of People's Commissars, backed by the Komsomol, demanded the merger of Sovtur with the Society of Proletarian Tourism; the new body was called the "All-Union Voluntary Society of Proletarian Tourism and Excursions" [Vsesoiuznoe dobrovol'noe obshchestvo proletarskogo turizma i ekskursii, or OPTE]. Protagonists of "proletarian tourism" received important positions in the new society, and the Peoples' Commissar and proletarian alpinist Krylenko became its chairman.

The forced merger did little to end the war on the tourist front and what at first glance looked like a success of the "proletarians" in the long term turned out to be a pyrrhic victory. The new body took over the "proletarian" label and an organizational principle based on "tourist cells" or "sections" in factories, educational, and administrative bodies. After the imposed union of both associations it quickly turned out that the actual numbers of active tourists was much lower than previously claimed by the "proletarian tourists."[47] Riding the political tide the "proletarians" raced to control the periodicals issued by the "Voluntary Society." Both, the bi-monthly illustrated magazine *Na sushe i na more* ["Over Land and Sea"]—which featured photographs, fiction, exotica, and travel advice—and *Turist-aktivist*—a monthly journal for proletarian tourism activists—provided practical advice and hammered out the guiding principles of proletarian

---

45   *Turist-aktivist* 4 (April 1932): 10, quoted in Koenker, "Proletarian Tourist," p. 122.

46   Dolzhenko, *Istoriia turizma*, pp. 76–9, 105–6; Koenker, "Who Was the Proletarian Tourist?," pp. 8–10.

47   Koenker, "Who Was the Proletarian Tourist?," p. 15.

tourism. Indeed, these years proved formative for the ideological discourse on tourism in the Soviet Union. At least discursively, Soviet tourism was never the same after the "proletarian" offensive of the late 1920s and early 1930s. While the verbal radicalism was toned down after Stalin's death, Soviet instructions, reports, and media coverage of tourism continued to stress the utilitarian and educational nature of tourism up to the very end of the regime in the 1980s.

A 1989 account of Soviet "social tourism" still contemplated the educational tasks of tourism in the USSR:

> ... instructing people in ideological and political respects, morally, in respect to their work and physical fitness ... The accomplishment of useful public work on their tours raises the social importance of autonomous tourism, renders it more interesting, purposeful and positively influences character ...[48]

Yet despite the rhetorical turn, in practice, "proletarian tourism" remained a marginal phenomenon. Neither the "Society of Proletarian Tourism" (between 1928 and 1930) nor the "Voluntary Society of Proletarian Tourism and Excursions" (between 1930 and 1936) succeeded in establishing "autonomous" ["*samodiatel'nyi*"] tourism as a real mass movement. Local cells worked irregularly and ineffectively, receiving little financial support for their efforts. Furthermore, the enormous numbers of "active tourists" reported by the society were achieved by including large numbers of participants in one-day excursions organized in the groups in their count. Society advocates blurred the boundaries between mass excursions, mass picnics, and mass demonstrations in their reports.[49]

Most obviously, Soviet citizens in general, and workers in particular, turned a cold shoulder on the idea of autonomous tourism that was physically straining and difficult to organize. The ideologues of "proletarian tourism" were particularly worried about the lack of involvement of industrial workers. In reality, workers' participation was severely hampered by their lack of either adequate finances or leisure time. With an average two-week vacation, workers would have had trouble organizing and taking self-organized holidays even if

---

[48]   V.A. Kvartal'nov and V.K. Fedorchenko, *Turizm sotsial'nyi: Istoriia i sovremennost'* (Kiev: Vyshcha shkola, 1989), pp. 128–35, quote on p. 133. Another nice example from the 1960s is cited in Paul Hollander, "Leisure: The Unity of Pleasure and Purpose," in Allen Kassof (ed.), *Prospects for Soviet Society* (New York: Praeger, 1968), pp. 418–48, quote on p. 439. For the dominance of "autonomous tourism" and the depreciation of "organized" tourism in publications of the 1930s see Koenker, "Who Was the Proletarian Tourist?," pp. 20–23.

[49]   According to V.A. Kvartal'nov and V.K. Fedorchenko, *Orbity "Sputnika." Iz istorii molodezhnogo turizma* (Kiev: Molod, 1987), p. 24, the voluntary society served 500,000 tourists in 1930, with 95,000 of these embarking on long-distance journeys.

they had wanted to. Therefore "autonomous" tourism remained in the domain of the intelligentsia. Academics, teachers, and students could devote more time to travel during their longer holidays. This reality became particularly visible in mountaineering, which was featured by the tourist periodicals of the 1930s as the highest form of autonomous tourism. Already back in 1928 chairman Krylenko had stated that alpinism was no longer an "idle pass time," but "a weapon of workers' cultural development."[50]

With the workers' lack of enthusiasm for cultural development and self-education becoming more and more obvious, the Soviet press identified tourists by their factory (or school) of origin rather than by their social backgrounds. Class mattered less than the correct practices of "active" recreation. Discursively the proletarian tourist became the *active* tourist, regardless of occupation, sex, or social position.[51]

Still, the Soviet population clearly preferred other types of vacations, from recreation in the health resorts to the organized trips and tours offered in the form of package "tourist routes" that included transportation, catering, and accommodation. Verbal radicalism aside, the "Voluntary Society of Proletarian Tourism and Excursions" continued to manage package tours and to develop tourist infrastructure much in the way Sovtur had successfully done it before. This society expanded the network of tourist facilities and excursions, opened up new routes and destinations, and sold vouchers entitling Soviet citizens to tourist services.[52] If we believe the continuing complaints waged by the "proletarians," the society still viewed "organized tourism" to be the core of its business. Allegedly the society was still doing close to nothing to sponsor "autonomous" tourism, and groups of self-organized tourists were allegedly denied access to equipment, rations, and accommodations on the organization's tourist bases. Thus, the merger did not resolve the conflict between the "revolutionaries" and the "managers," it simmered on within the new organization.[53]

---

[50]   Eva Maurer, "Alpinism as Mass Sport and Elite Recreation: Soviet Mountaineering Camps under Stalin," in Gorsuch and Koenker, *Turizm*, pp. 141–62, see quote on pp. 143, 153–9. See also Koenker, "Proletarian Tourist," pp. 133–4. In a bitter twist of irony Krylenko's political adversaries used the long absence of the People's Commissar for Justice during his trips as an occasion to demand his replacement in 1936. Krylenko was purged and shot in 1938, a fact still not mentioned in Dolzhenko's sympathetic account in 1988! Cf. Dolzhenko, *Istoriia turizma*, pp. 103–4.

[51]   Koenker, "Who Was the Proletarian Tourist?," p. 18. See also Maurer, "Alpinism," p. 144 on "group homogeneity" as an alternative rationale for the selection of workmates for tourist groups.

[52]   Koenker, "Who Was the Proletarian Tourist?," pp. 9–11.

[53]   Dolzhenko, *Istoriia turizma*, pp. 106–7; Koenker, "Who Was the Proletarian Tourist?," pp. 20–21.

The sudden dissolution of the "Voluntary Society of Proletarian Tourism and Excursions" seems to acknowledge this fact. On April 17, 1936 the highest governmental body of the USSR, the Central Executive Committee of the Soviets, "liquidated" the society by decree. All property owned by the society was transferred to the Central Trade Union Council, while the responsibility for tourism and alpinism was assigned to the All-Union Council of Physical Culture, a body directly subordinate to the Central Executive Committee. This split suggests that the Soviet leadership was well aware of the latent conflict within the organization, and hoped to create a more responsive environment for the most physically demanding varieties of tourism within the sport administration.[54]

In fact, however, mountaineering and "autonomous" [*samodeiatel'nyi*] tourism never became an integral element in Soviet physical culture. As in the realm of tourism, these activities constituted a marginal phenomenon organizationally and, moreover, socially. Alpinism and self-organized hiking, cycling, and canoeing remained niche activities popular almost exclusively within the intelligentsia.[55] The attempt to re-create and implement the genuinely Soviet "proletarian" variety of tourism that characterized the late 1920s and early 1930s had thus failed. Even the Stalinist regime seemed to be less worried about ideological purity than about practical performance in the realm of vacationing.

Many Soviet historians interpret the dissolution of the "voluntary society" by the government as an acknowledgement of the limited effectiveness of this form of organization in the development of capital-intensive social tourism.[56] This admission mattered now that state-sponsored and -organized forms of travel became an integral part of the Stalinist promise of a "good life."[57] The "Great Retreat" after the upheavals of the First Five Year Plan featured rewards for all those who worked hard and practiced political conformity, like the famous shock workers. This new philosophy found its universal expression in the 1936 constitution that promised, among other benefits, a "right to rest."

As a result, state spending for different types of social tourism increased significantly between 1936 and 1941.[58] Both branches of the Soviet recreational sector, spas and organized tourism, benefited from these investments. The 1930s

---

[54]   See also Koenker, "Proletarian Tourist," p. 123.

[55]   Koenker, "Who Was the Proletarian Tourist?," p. 17; Maurer, "Alpinism," pp. 155–7.

[56]   Dolzhenko, *Istoriia turizma*, p. 105.

[57]   For consumption see Jukka Gronow, *Caviar with Champagne: Common Luxury and the Ideals of Good Life in Stalin's Russia* (Oxford: Berg, 2003); for public celebrations see Karen Petrone, *Life Has Become More Joyous, Comrades! Celebrations in the Time of Stalin* (Bloomington: Indiana University Press, 2000).

[58]   Koenker, "Right to Rest," p. 3.

were a golden age for the Soviet health resorts in particular. Sochi, a relatively underdeveloped destination in tsarist and early Soviet times, became the Stalinist showcase after 1933. In fact, the Soviet effort to revamp Sochi can be interpreted as a southern extension of Moscow's general development plan. The same architects who planned Moscow's new administrative buildings, living blocks, and skyscrapers designed a number of large-scale and pompous sanatoria and rest homes in the Soviet subtropics for the new elite: party officials and shock workers.[59] While the 1935 development plan and the "Stalinist Gothic" deeply changed the outlook and the character of Moscow, this was much less true for the country's spas and seaside resorts. The massive investment in new Stalinist style sanatoria and health facilities, as at Sochi, did not alter the resorts' general character as surreal alternatives to the mundane world of Soviet everyday life. In the *kurort*, Stalin's "empire" harmonized with the earlier imperial "empire."[60]

Likewise, in quantitative terms, the development of recreation facilities was impressive during the 1930s. The health and recreation system run jointly by the state and the trade unions offered 140,900 beds in sanatoria and rest homes in 1932, 212,000 in 1938, and, allegedly, 411,000 one year later. This growth would have doubled the number of vacationers served by such facilities from 1.9 million to more than 4 million. At the same time, the geographic setting of the Soviet recreational system underwent changes, with new destinations emerging closer to the bigger industrial centers, particularly the new giants in the Urals and in Siberia.[61]

Against this backdrop, the 1936 decision to transfer the tourist infrastructure to the trade unions seems perfectly logical. First, the trade unions always played a certain role in tourism as they did in the recreational sphere. For example, they were co-sponsors in the establishment of Sovtur in 1928.[62] Second, the trade unions featured a similar type of organizational structure to the earlier tourism development bodies; they had bureaus in all enterprises throughout the country that were now primarily organs for the dissemination of vouchers for sanatoria, rest homes, tour bases, and organized trips. Indeed, the new Tourism and Excursion

---

[59]   A.D. Borisov, "Kurort Sochi-Matsesta k 40 letiu velikogo oktiabria," *Voprosy kurortologii* 5 (1957): pp. 47–51, here pp. 49–50.

[60]   Christian Noack, "'Andere Räume'—sowjetische Kurorte als Heterotopien. Das Beispiel Sochi." Paper presented at the colloquium Mastering Space. Raum und Raumbewältigung als Probleme der russischen Geschichte. Historisches Kolleg, Munich, July 13–15, 2006.

[61]   Nevraev, "Kurortno-sanatornoe delo," p. 6. For trade union investment into recreational facilities see V.V. Poltoranov, "Profsoiuzy i sanatorno-kurortnoe delo," *Voprosy kurortologii* 5 (1967): pp. 401–6, especially p. 402.

[62]   Dvornichenko, *Turizm v SSSR*, pp. 27–8, 35.

Authority [*Turistsko-ekskursionnoe upravlenie*], set up by the trade unions in 1936, essentially continued Sovtur's development policies: a concentration on the development of "planned" routes and an extension of necessary infrastructure. In the first two years after the takeover the number of tourist accommodations was almost doubled and the number of organized routes trebled. The same is true for the number of tourists served by the Tourism and Excursion Authorities, amounting to almost 2.7 million Soviet citizens on the eve of World War II. Ambitious plans for further extension were thwarted by the war.[63]

Conclusion

After the October Revolution, Soviet intellectuals looked forward to an opportunity to create new, genuinely "Soviet" concepts of tourism and recreation. They were not wrong to do so. The Soviet Union, with its lack of any widespread travel culture and its international isolation, offered a very real chance to invent and disseminate alternative styles of tourism and recreation.

During the early years of the Soviet Union leading Bolshevik ideologues, including Lenin, showed less interest in a Soviet re-invention of tourism than in a propagandist-style "opening" of the existing spas and resorts to the people. Ironically, this disinterest in creating something new resulted in the conservation of the *kurort*, an eighteenth- and nineteenth-century European aristocratic concept, as *the* model for Soviet recreation. Tourism, as active recreation or touring, played only a marginal role in the early year of the Soviet state. In the big cities, however, a particular Russian variant of pre-revolutionary tourist activity, the educational excursion, experienced a certain revival.

The surprisingly conservative attitude the Soviet leaders displayed toward travel and recreation practices corresponded with their reservations about an iconoclastic revolutionary culture more generally. On the contrary, Lenin's, Trotsky's, and Lunacharskii's cultural outlooks were informed by ideas prevalent among the late imperial intelligentsia that were solidly rooted in noble lifestyles and habits developed during the nineteenth century.

Any iconoclasm in the realm of tourism and travel had to await Stalin's "revolution from above," a combined attack on traditional Soviet economies and lifestyles. Against the backdrop of rapid industrialization and forced collectivization, a group of leftist tourism activists formulated a doctrine of "proletarian tourism" which sought to negate Western bourgeois examples on the one hand, and the developing practices of organized Soviet social tourism

---

[63]   Ibid., pp. 47, 49.

on the other. "Proletarian" tourism was conceived as a mass exercise in socio-political usefulness and individual self-education through low key and self-organized travel off the beaten tracks.

Efforts toward a "proletarian" takeover came to pass in two phases. The initial phase began in the mid-1920s, against the backdrop of general policy disputes following Lenin's death in 1924. The "proletarians" attained discursive sovereignty in the Soviet press and created an organizational springboard by the hostile takeover of the surviving pre-revolutionary Russian Association of Tourists in 1928. The most serious competitor of the re-baptized Society of Proletarian Tourism was "Sovetskii tourist" (Sovtur), a joint stock company set up by several ministries to promote organized package travel and to develop the tourist infrastructure throughout the country. While the newly created "Society for Proletarian Tourism" responded to the contemporary radical agenda of turning the Soviet Union into a real workers' state by promoting mass tourism based on factory cells of tourist activists, the Stalin government was unwilling to sacrifice Sovtur's alternative concept of paternalistic package travel. The latter undoubtedly promised more state and party control over the people's leisurely movements, an aspect that grew increasingly important for a regime that struggled to regain control over the social dynamics it unleashed during the First Five Year Plan between 1928 and 1933.

Against this backdrop, the second phase, which involved the decision to merge both organizations into the Voluntary Society of Proletarian Tourism and Excursion in 1930, seems understandable, even if the underlying conflicts still smoldered. In the media discourse, "proletarian" mass tourism set the tone, while in practice the extension of paternalistic social tourism continued. On that score, Soviet efforts far exceeded results attained through social tourism under fascist regimes, obviously without being directly influenced by Italian or German models. As in these two fascist countries, travel and tourism became an integral part of the social benefit system created to enhance working-class loyalty. The dissolution of the OPTE in 1936 indicated the increased importance of state-sponsored organized travel. Indeed, the trade unions, in full control of tourist infrastructure from now on, and already an important element in the recreational system, invested heavily in the extension of both health resorts and tourist infrastructure.

For Soviet citizens, this situation meant that vouchers for sanatoria or tourist bases would now be distributed by the trade unions' factory cells, and that they would be heavily subsidized by the social insurance system. Self-organized, "autonomous" tourism remained a marginal phenomenon and a playground for the Soviet intelligentsia because contradictions between discourse and practice continued to characterize developments in Soviet tourism until the demise of the system in the 1980s.

Chapter 10

"Tourism and Autarky are Conceptually Incompatible": International Tourism Conferences in the Third Reich

Kristin Semmens

On December 3, 1934, an international conference of hoteliers met in Berlin. One of the keynote speakers was Fritz Gabler, a well-known German hotel owner. His speech, not surprisingly, paid homage to the leaders of the "new Germany," but his concluding remarks may have been unexpected. Though the Nazi regime clearly strove towards self-sufficiency in many areas, "tourism and autarky," he proclaimed, were "conceptually incompatible."[1] He was trying to assuage his fellow hoteliers' fears that the Nazi regime would further restrict tourists' freedom of movement through increased visa regulations and foreign currency constraints, as indeed it soon did. Germany wanted foreign visitors, he explained, and the new government believed that Germans too should get to know foreign lands. But Gabler's statement about the impossibility of autarky in the touristic sphere speaks to more than just the literal crossing of borders by pleasure travelers. No nation's tourism industry has ever stood entirely alone. As this book shows, tourism policies and practices always emerged out of a transnational dialogue between professionals from countries with the most diverse forms of government. Even under Hitler, then, those active in the industry connected with one another, shared ideas, borrowed a concept here and advised on a matter there. This was not and could not be a closed off, self-reliant community.

The contributors to this volume presuppose that European tourism in particular was a product of conversations between nations and that its history must be approached from a transnational perspective. But how, why, when, where, and between whom did those discussions take place? This chapter examines international tourism conferences as one such site of exchange. There has been

---

[1] Fritz Gabler, "Fremdenverkehrspolitik und Beherbergungsgewerbe im neuen Deutschland," speech to the International Hotelier Congress, Berlin, December 3, 1934 (Stadtarchiv Freiburg, XVI/20/9, Heft 1, Jahr 1933/45).

relatively little research into international conferences in Nazi Germany, with the exception of scientific meetings; even less attention has been paid to gatherings of tourism professionals. Since Nazi ideology regularly equated "international" with "un-German," any apparent collaboration between nations is often viewed as a mere smokescreen for the regime's actual belligerent intentions. The regime's oft-expressed belief that world peace might be furthered through such meetings demands some skepticism, but tourism conferences did indeed witness real cooperation and a true transfer of ideas and information.

This chapter examines three specific conferences hosted by Hitler's Germany: the World Congress for Leisure Time and Recreation in 1936, the International Union of Official Tourist Publicity Organizations' annual congress in 1937, and the International Hotel Alliance's annual general meeting in 1938. These conferences can only fully be understood, however, if some background context is first provided. Below follows a discussion of international conferences generally in the Third Reich, a sketch of the origins of the state-run leisure program, Strength through Joy [*Kraft durch Freude*, or KdF], the showpiece of the 1936 World Congress, and finally an overview of the Nazi regime's coordination [*Gleichschaltung*] of what it called "normal tourist traffic": commercial tourism.

In 1934 the German Central Conference Office [*Deutsche Kongress Zentrale*, or DKZ] was established. The ostensible aim of the DKZ was to get Germany to host more international conferences. Clearly these conferences had economic value, but there were also political factors to consider. International conferences were, according to the DKZ, "one of the most effective weapons in the struggle ... [to] eliminate prejudices and hateful lies."[2] Recognizing their potential ideological value, Joseph Goebbels took over the DKZ as a division of his Ministry of People's Enlightenment and Propaganda in 1936. In November that year a formal Führer decree stipulated that no international conference, convention or meeting could take place in Germany without the explicit authorization of the DKZ. The DKZ also played an advisory role with regard to conference planning and maintained an extensive archive about various international organizations. After any international conference concluded in Germany, organizers had to submit answers to a lengthy questionnaire, listing everything from the numbers of foreign participants in attendance to what

---

2   Sheila Faith Weiss, "'The Sword of Our Science' as a Foreign Policy Weapon: The Political Function of German Geneticists in the International Arena during the Third Reich," in Susanne Heim (ed.), *Ergebnisse 22: Vorabdrucke aus dem Forschungsprogramm "Geschichte der Kaiser-Wilhelm-Gesellschaft im Nationalsozialismus,"* Im Auftrag der Präsidentenkommission der Max-Planck-Gesellschaft (Berlin, 2005), p. 8.

kinds of souvenirs the guests took home.[3] Moreover, any German wanting to attend a conference abroad needed the DKZ's permission and its help in obtaining the necessary foreign currency. At conferences in Germany and abroad German participants were expected to adhere to DKZ guidelines about "correct" behavior by avoiding "outspoken opinions," for example, and treating Jewish delegates of foreign countries well "provided they [did] not offend against German hospitality."[4] Representatives of the DKZ were also regularly invited to attend conference receptions or other special conference events.

Although the DKZ paid special attention to scientific conferences, its concerns were wide-ranging, from conferences on bird watching to wine growing, with many devoted to pleasure travel and leisure activities more generally in between.[5] All such meetings presented opportunities for the regime to showcase a new kind of tourism under Hitler: trips arranged by Strength through Joy. It is to the background of this organization that we now turn.

In May 1933 the Nazi regime dissolved the German trade unions and replaced them with the German Labor Front (DAF); six months later its leader, Robert Ley, announced the creation of the DAF subsidiary Strength though Joy. This leisure-time organization had three ideological aims: to solidify the support of the German working class, to strengthen the *Volksgemeinschaft* [racial community] through minimizing class conflict, and to increase workers' productivity in preparation for war. This was to be achieved by raising workers' living standards; not by raising their wages—the Nazis' rearmament drive ruled out that option—but instead by breaking "bourgeois privilege."[6] In other words, KdF strove to grant access to all members of the Volk what had hitherto been the exclusive purview of the middle and upper classes: visits to museums, trips to the theatre, adult education courses, sporting events, and travel for pleasure. The most economically and ideologically valuable of these activities was carried

---

[3]   Hoover Institution Archives, "Germany. DKZ," Box number 309, folder "Touristique (Fremdenverkehr)," n.p.

[4]   Madeleine Herren, "'Outwardly ... an Innocuous Conference Authority': National Socialism and the Logistics of International Information Management," *German History* 20/1 (2002): pp. 67–92, pp. 75, 76.

[5]   The head of the DKZ, Karl Schweig, may have had a personal interest in such matters as he went on to enjoy a successful postwar career as director of the Düsseldorf tourism office (Herren, "Outwardly," p. 69, note 11).

[6]   Gerhard Starcke, "Kraft durch Freude hebt den Lebensstandard unseres Volkes. Der sozialpolitische Sinn der KdF-Gemeinschaft," *Arbeitertum*, February 15, 1936. There is a growing literature on Kraft durch Freude, but the best recent treatment is Shelley Baranowski, *Strength through Joy: Consumerism and Mass Tourism in the Third Reich* (Cambridge: Cambridge University Press, 2004).

out under the auspices of the "gem" of KdF departments, the Office for Travel, Hiking and Vacations [*Amt für Reisen, Wandern und Urlaub*, or Amt RWU].[7]

Both KdF and commercial tourism in Nazi Germany had obvious political functions. Travel at home led to heightened patriotism and decreased tensions based on class, region or confession. Even travel abroad, something the Nazi regime officially frowned upon and generally made very difficult, would lead, so claimed the propagandists, to international peace and cooperation; more significantly, it would deepen Germans' love for their Fatherland.[8] KdF's mandate was to provide such tourist experiences, usually in the form of package tours, at a fraction of the cost of their commercial counterparts. In February 1934 the first "special trains" set off from Berlin to the mountains of Upper Bavaria. By 1939 43 million Germans had traveled with Strength through Joy. Most had taken only day trips or made weekend excursions, but a lucky minority went on overseas cruises aboard KdF's own purpose-built ocean liners. Under Hitler, the Amt RWU became Germany's single largest travel agency, one praised extensively both by Nazi commentators and critics abroad for having solved the "problem" of working-class leisure.

The notion that such a problem existed was taken for granted in many countries—democratic, fascist, and communist—after World War I. In the 1910s and 1920s, several different national and international organizations, such as the International Labour Organization in Geneva, held conferences to address questions about workers' health and fitness—their "nerve" in later Nazi parlance—and the proper use of their free time. Travel was a valid option, but only if it went beyond "mere sightseeing" as organizations such as the British Workers' Travel Association insisted.[9] German participants in these international discussions voiced similar ideas and KdF grew out of shared conversations about labor and leisure. But Strength through Joy also had a closer ancestor: it was closely modeled—"down to the smallest details"—on the Italian Fascists' "After Work" organization [*Opera Nazionale Dopolavoro*, or OND].[10] KdF's original

---

7   Robert Ley, *Durchbruch der sozialen Ehre* (Berlin: Mehden-Verlag, 1935), p. 211.

8   Kristin Semmens, *Seeing Hitler's Germany: Tourism in the Third Reich* (Houndmills, Basingstoke: Palgrave Macmillan, 2005), pp. 11–12.

9   Christine Collette, "'Friendly Spirit, Comradeship, and Good-Natured Fun': Adventures in Socialist Internationalism," *International Review of Social History* 48/2 (2003): pp. 225–44, p. 228. See also Carina Grabacke, "Organised Leisure for the Working Class: European Popular Travel and Leisure Organisations in the Interwar Period." Paper presented at the Economic History Society Annual Conference, March 31 – April 2, 2006.

10   Daniela Liebscher, "Faschismus als Modell: Die faschistische Opera Nazionale Dopolavoro und die NS-Gemeinschaft 'Kraft durch Freude' in der Zwischenkriegszeit," in Sven Reichardt and Armin Nolzen (eds), *Faschismus in Italien und Deutschland: Studien zu Transfer und Vergleich* (Göttingen: Wallstein, 2005): pp. 94–118, p. 94.

name was also "After Work" [*Nach der Arbeit*] and its departments mirrored those of the OND. KdF had the Office for Travel, Hiking and Vacations; OND had the Federazione Italiana del Escursionismo.[11] The earliest KdF propagandists recognized, emphasized, and praised the organization's "Fascist" (i.e. Italian) roots, but the Nazis soon wanted to make Strength through Joy their own. Later literature therefore explicitly stressed the differences between KdF and OND and pointed out the latter's shortcomings.[12] By the time of the 1936 World Congress on Leisure Time and Recreation, where KdF was undoubtedly the star attraction, there was barely a nod to its predecessor: Bodo von Lafferentz, head of the Amt RWU, praised KdF for being "completely novel."[13] In many crucial respects Strength through Joy *was* a "uniquely Nazi" project: in its suppression of the trade unions, in its support for the regime's drive for Empire, and in its racist definitions of community.[14]

While it certainly made the headlines in the 1930s, KdF tourism was not the only or even the predominant form of pleasure travel in the Third Reich. In terms of actual numbers it was only a small part of the story, making up an estimated 10–11 percent of total overnight stays. Given that the Nazis believed all forms of travel could be harnessed to their ideological goals, in 1933 they embarked on a thorough and orderly *Gleichschaltung* [coordination] of German commercial tourism.[15] It was intended to overhaul the organizations responsible for travel both at home and abroad, to rationalize and professionalize the industry and, of course, to bring it more into line with Nazi aims and ideals. A series of tourism laws laid the foundation for what was to follow. On June 23, 1933 Hitler signed the Law for the Reich Committee for Tourism, which established a national body for all tourism matters within the Ministry of Propaganda. Hermann Esser, a Hitler disciple from the days of the Beer Hall Putsch, became the Committee's

---

[11] Alexander Lane, "Neue Ziele der Freizeitgestaltung," *Deutsches Arbeitsrecht* 4/9 (September 1936): pp. 225–9.

[12] Compare, for example, Robert Matschuk's 1933 account, "Dopolavoro, die faschistische Feierabend-Organisation," *Arbeitertum*, December 15, 1933, pp. 6–8, with 1936 articles: Lane, "Neue Ziele"; Max Everwien, "Dopolavoro und 'Kraft durch Freude,'" *Arbeitertum*, February 1, 1936.

[13] B. v. Lafferentz, "Urlaub und Erholung," in Internationale Zentral-Büro "Freude und Arbeit" (ed.), *Bericht: Weltkongress für Freizeit und Erholung — Hamburg/Vom 23. bis 30. Juli 1936/Berlin* (Berlin, 1937), p. 373.

[14] Shelley Baranowski, "Radical Nationalism in an International Context: Strength through Joy and the Paradoxes of Nazi Tourism," in John K. Walton (ed.), *Histories of Tourism: Representation, Identity and Conflict* (Clevedon: Channel View Publications, 2005), pp. 125–43, p. 134.

[15] On the Nazis' coordination of commercial tourism, see Semmens, *Seeing Hitler's Germany*, Chapter 2.

president and as such was directly responsible to the Propaganda Minister Joseph Goebbels. Members of the committee included representatives of various governmental ministries, state governments, and other groups with a direct interest in the promotion of tourism such as Lufthansa. Additionally this first law created state tourism associations to which local tourism societies in turn reported and paid membership dues and from which they received instructions on behalf of the Reich Committee.

Most professionals active in the industry were quickly convinced that the Nazis were good for tourism, applauding guarantees of state interest and public funds and the eradication of overlapping and incompatible organizations. At the time the regime promised that local and regional autonomy would be respected. Not surprisingly those promises were quickly broken by the second tourism law in March 1936, which intensified the Nazification of German tourism: it increased the regime's control over the industry, allowing the recently renamed Reich Tourism Association to regulate downward into the most basic communal cells, the newly established tourism communities.

The changes made to tourism in 1936 tallied with the overall direction of the Nazi state, which that year had begun to tighten the reigns over many sectors of the economy. The limited autonomy which local and regional tourism organizations had once enjoyed now all but disappeared. Yet this rarely elicited any overt protest; in fact most German tourism professionals once again appear to have welcomed the changes. There was also much praise within the industry for the regime's "steering" of international tourism from its efforts to keep Germans at home to its overseeing of the German tourist offices abroad. By 1936, the year Germany hosted the summer and winter Olympics, Germans and foreigners alike were visiting the country's towns and cities in record numbers and the miseries of the Great Depression seemed a distant memory: overnight stays by foreigners were up 40.1 percent compared to the previous year while those by Germans had increased by 13.8 percent.[16]

Success persuaded most tourism officials to accept the more insidious practices of Nazi coordination if they did not already actively support them, such as the dismissal of Jews and the politically "unreliable" and the mandatory appointment of NSDAP members to important positions on tourism society committees. But a pan-European perspective sheds further light on their enthusiasm. In the interwar period throughout Europe there was a shared sense that governmental funding of and even intervention into the tourist industry was desirable. Although the British Department of Overseas Trade insisted that tourism was "a matter for private enterprise," British tourism professionals

---

[16]   "Endgültiges Ergebnis," *Der Fremdenverkehr* 2/37 (19 June 1937): p. 11.

argued that the industry needed the "psychological boost" that state interest and support would give. The British Travel Association itself highlighted how many foreign governments had taken "sole charge" of tourism in a plea to increase its annual state grant.[17] In Latvia too the leading figures of the private tourism industry from all political persuasions welcomed government control; most saw greater state coordination as a "blessing."[18] Amongst fascist and fascist-friendly nations there was also a shared discourse on the potential ideological value of pleasure travel: its ability to foster patriotism and obliterate social differences and thus its important propaganda function. In 1934 Mussolini made the office of the Under-Secretary for Press and Propaganda responsible for tourism. In 1930s Greece tourism similarly became part of the "propaganda machine."[19] These notions shared across European borders explain in large part why German touristic endeavors were so heartily applauded when participants learned more about them at international conferences on leisure, tourism, and hospitality. It is to these that we now turn.

From 23 to 30 July 1936 the World Congress for Leisure Time and Recreation took place in Hamburg. It was a mammoth event. Fifteen hundred delegates from 51 different nations converged on the city just as Germany prepared to host the Summer Olympics in Berlin the following month. The first World Congress sponsored by the American National Recreation Association had taken place four years earlier in Los Angeles alongside the city's hosting of the 1932 Summer Olympic Games. Convinced that there should continue to be "international exchange[s] of experiences in the area of leisure organization," the advisory committee decided upon Hamburg as the next Congress location.[20]

---

[17]   John Beckerson, "Marketing British Tourism: Government Approaches to the Stimulation of a Service Sector, 1880–1950," in Hartmut Berghoff, Barbara Korte, Ralf Schneider, and Christopher Harvie (eds), *The Making of Modern Tourism: The Cultural History of the British Experience, 1600–2000* (London: Palgrave Macmillan, 2002), pp. 133–57, pp. 141, 142, 148.

[18]   Aldis Purs, "'One Breath for Every Two Strides': The State's Attempt to Construct Tourism and Identity in Interwar Latvia," in Anne E. Gorsuch and Diane P. Koenker (eds), *Turizm: The Russian and East European Tourist under Capitalism and Socialism* (Ithaca: Cornell University Press, 2006), pp. 97–116, p. 101.

[19]   Margarita Dritsas, "Tourism in Greece: A Way to What Sort of Development?," in Laurent Tissot (ed.), *Development of a Tourist Industry* (Neuchatel: Éditions Alphil, 2003), pp. 187–210, p. 190.

[20]   Karsten Linne, "'Wir tragen die Freude in die Welt': Der Hamburger 'Weltkongress für Freizeit und Erholung' 1936," *Zeitschrift des Vereins für Hamburgische Geschichte* 80 (1994): pp. 153–75, p. 155. Unless otherwise noted, the following information about the

While foreigners were certainly represented amongst the dignitaries who gathered in Hamburg—the president of the 1932 Congress, the American Gustavus Kirby, became an honorary president in 1936, as did Count de Baillet Latour, the Belgian President of the International Olympics Committee, while the vice-presidents were Belgian, English, Italian, and Chilean—the World Congress was ultimately to be a German-dominated event. Robert Ley, head of Strength through Joy's parent organization, the German Labor Front, replaced Kirby as president. Rudolf Hess, Hitler's deputy party leader, was its patron; Joseph Goebbels was named an honorary president.[21] Sixty-one of the 141 conference papers presented were given by German speakers.

The "wonderful days in Hamburg," as the British contingent later styled them, also witnessed an extravaganza of German nationalism.[22] A number of concerts and exhibitions were staged in Hamburg to coincide with the conference. A mammoth display in the Zoo Exhibition Hall entitled "Leisure Time and Recreation for All" depicted the achievements of German leisure time organizations. The "Olympia Procession of Nations," which extended for seven kilometers, wound its way through the city with 20,000 participants and 165 elaborately decorated parade floats, with the German ones amongst the biggest and brightest. Several different folk festivals entertained thousands of visitors and locals alike. Highlights of these included performances by Schäfertanz [Shepherd Dance], a costumed troupe of German folk dancers much-celebrated for their warm reception at the Albert Hall in London the previous year.[23] Yet alongside seemingly innocuous folk dances there were more alarming displays of National Socialist might, not surprising since the key conference organizer was Walther Rentmeister, a loyal Austrian Nazi who had been a member of the Storm Troopers (SA) since 1926: a "Day of the Associations" offered demonstrations by the SA, SS, and Reich Labor Service; a "Day of the Armed Forces" followed during which soldiers played military music. The costs for such lavish festivities were high. The German Labor Front paid over 2 million Reichsmarks and the city of Hamburg contributed an additional 200,000 RM.

Congress comes from Linne's account, one of very few historical treatments of this major international conference.

[21]   Internationale Zentral-Büro "Freude und Arbeit" (ed.), *Bericht*, p. vii.

[22]   William Carle, "The Wonderful Days in Hamburg," *Freude und Arbeit* 2/5 (May 1937): pp. 70–77.

[23]   Joshua Hagen, *Preservation, Tourism and Nationalism: The Jewel of the German Past* (Aldershot: Ashgate, 2006), pp. 209–10.

The conference itself opened officially on July 23, 1936 with a welcome address by Rudolf Hess who read a telegram that Gustavus Kirby had sent to Hitler to mark the occasion:

> Joy in work and joy in leisure time for all workers overcome internal social tensions and smooth the way for better understanding and mutual respect between the peoples. This ideal, peace at home and abroad, has completely become a reality for Germany through the basic principle of your state leadership, "community before individuals" [*Gemeinnutz vor Eigennnutz*], as much as through the organization, created by you, Mr Reich Chancellor, "Strength through Joy."[24]

The goals of the conference, again articulated by Kirby, were lofty indeed: the disappearance of "hate and mistrust and violence," which would be achieved by solving the leisure "problem."[25] In his remarks, Rentmeister stressed more practical aspects of the conference, which allowed those involved in the various "movements for leisure" to "learn from one another."[26] After the opening ceremony came a week of plenary sessions, executive committee meetings, and paper presentations, grouped into different "commissions" which discussed themes ranging from "women's free time" to the "fundamental relationship between leisure and work." The importance of travel and tourism was frequently touted. For example Commission IV, which had met to discuss topics such as "the weekend" and "vacation and recreation," passed a resolution stating that travel and hiking were amongst "the best forms of vacation arrangement for the less-privileged." It was also "desirable," the group maintained, that workers undertake travel abroad.[27]

The best way to assure that they could and did of course was via programs like Strength through Joy, as German and foreign delegates seemed almost unanimously to agree. The official conference report, German newspapers at the time, and letters of thanks sent afterwards all praised KdF and its paradigmatic role in all areas of leisure organization. Although she acknowledged that "for purely political reasons" it was impossible to construct something "identical" to KdF in her country, the Norwegian delegate, one of very few female participants, suggested that they had "much to learn from the new Germany" and that even "Marxist circles" recognized the "exemplary" achievements of the German Labor

---

[24]   Linne, "Wir Tragen," p. 161.

[25]   Internationale Zentral-Büro "Freude und Arbeit" (ed.), *Bericht*, p. x.

[26]   Walther Rentmeister, "Freizeit in aller Welt," in Internationale Zentral-Büro "Freude und Arbeit" (ed.), *Bericht*, p. 9.

[27]   "Entschliessung der Kommission IV," in Internationale Zentral-Büro "Freude und Arbeit" (ed.), *Bericht*, pp. 34–5.

Front.[28] A Hungarian journalist noted his country would do well to "learn from the German example."[29] Admiration could come from more unexpected quarters too. The French delegate praised KdF effusively for allowing German workers to change their "milieu," even though his Popular Front government held a vastly different conception of leisure from the one predominant at the Congress, one openly critical of the fascist attempt to control workers' free time.[30]

Openly dissenting opinions leave few traces in the official German records, but they were expressed, albeit in muted tones. The Danish delegate for example recalled hearing arguments critical of state intervention into the realm of leisure: "the state should create the possibilities for the useful utilisation of spare time, but ... it should be up to the individual how to use it and organise it."[31] Even Gustavus Kirby's own presentation entitled "Leisure Organization by the Government" suggested that private or non-official posts should take the lead in leisure organization and not the state, although Kirby finished with an unabashedly enthusiastic assessment of KdF: "I know of nothing better," he gushed.[32]

The official report on the Congress was also largely silent about the problems Strength through Joy had actually created in Germany such as the undeniable rivalry between the Office for Travel, Hiking and Vacations and commercial travel agencies. In his talk, the head of the Amt RWU, Bodo von Lafferentz, inserted only a vague rebuff of the suggestion that KdF-like programs damaged "normal" tourism.[33] In a notable contrast to silence on that subject, there was a lot of noise at the conference and in the commentaries on it about how each individual country needed to follow its own path to solve the leisure problem. National Socialism was not, one report stressed, for "export."[34]

---

[28]   Audhild Krohn, "Freizeitbewegung in Norwegen," in Internationale Zentral-Büro "Freude und Arbeit" (ed.), *Bericht*, p. 197.

[29]   Bruno Kaldor, "Ein ungarischer Journalist über deutsche Freizeitgestaltung," in Internationale Zentral-Büro "Freude und Arbeit" (ed.), *Bericht*, p. 380. See also "Kraft durch Freude mustergültig aufgebaut," *Der Angriff*, August 11, 1936.

[30]   Gustave Bonvoison, "Betrachtung zur Freizeitgestaltung in Frankreich," in Internationale Zentral-Büro "Freude und Arbeit" (ed.), *Bericht*, p. 117. On this point, see Gary Cross, "Vacations for All: The Leisure Question in the Era of the Popular Front," *Journal of Contemporary History* 24/4 (1989): pp. 599–621, p. 612.

[31]   Grabacke, "Organised Leisure."

[32]   Gustavus Kirby, "Freizeitorganisation durch die Regierung," in Internationale Zentral-Büro "Freude und Arbeit" (ed.), *Bericht*, p. 106.

[33]   V. Lafferentz, "Urlaub und Erholung," p. 373. On tensions between KdF and the commercial tourism industry, see Semmens, *Seeing Hitler's Germany*, Chapter 5.

[34]   Wolf von Lejewski, "Weltkongress für Freizeit und Erholung," *Arbeitertum*, July 15, 1936, p. 5. See also Carle, "The Wonderful Days," p. 76; "Entschliessung der Kommission II," in Internationale Zentral-Büro "Freude und Arbeit" (ed.), *Bericht*, p. 32.

Yet a closer look at German statements made during the congress itself belied this supposed tolerance of and enthusiasm for individuality. One German delegate was openly critical for example of private organizations taking the lead in leisure organization for they could never be "total" enough and, he pointed out, "leisure arrangement only makes sense if [it is] total"; another emphasized that KdF officials were willing to provide "the minutest details about its work" to anyone who was interested along with reams of KdF material both from an academic and a practical, organizational standpoint.[35] Individual sessions provided another forum in which foreign tourism professionals could learn more about Strength through Joy including its wider significance for other sectors of the economy.[36]

Of course conferences were not the only way to find out about the Nazis' Strength through Joy organization. After the Irish youth leader attended the Congress, the Irish Tourist Board sent a committee to Germany to study KdF more closely the following year, perhaps inspired by what he had reported.[37] Even countries critical of KdF from an ideological standpoint sent their emissaries on fact-finding trips. Although uncomfortable with Strength through Joy being "imposed from above," Hugh R. Wilson, the American ambassador to Germany, praised the "perfect" planning of a KdF trip he took to Helgoland, noting in a memorandum to President Roosevelt that there was "no propaganda on the part of the sponsors."[38]

But conferences remained important vehicles for the dissemination of information about KdF and this one in particular had been a major triumph. Joseph Goebbels recorded his impressions of his closing speech in his diary: "The conference was a raving success. In the conference hall I was received with standing ovations. Many delegates spoke. All are intoxicated by Germany. I speak in high form. ... An undreamt of success. ... Noisy ovations. I am thrown flowers. ... All are totally happy."[39] His inflated evaluation of his own

[35]   Ernst Schaffer, "Weltanschauung und Freizeitgestaltung," in Internationale Zentral-Büro "Freude und Arbeit" (ed.), *Bericht*, p. 170; Horst Dressler-Andress, "Die kulturelle Mission der Freizeitgestaltung," Internationale Zentral-Büro "Freude und Arbeit" (ed.), *Bericht*, p. 73.

[36]   Heinz Zilcher, "Die wirtschaftliche Bedeutung von 'Kraft durch Freude,'" in Internationale Zentral-Büro "Freude und Arbeit" (ed.), *Bericht*, pp. 220–24.

[37]   See Eric G.E. Zuelow's "Made in Ireland: Irish Tourism in International Context," Chapter 8 in this volume.

[38]   For Wilson's memorandum, see: "Summary Report on Strength through Joy," Franklin D. Roosevelt Presidential Library and Museum Website. Available online at: http://www.fdrlibrary.marist.edu/psf/box32/a301j03.html [accessed October 26, 2010].

[39]   Linne, "Wir tragen," p. 168, note 51.

performance notwithstanding, Goebbels' sense about the conference was correct. The 1936 World Congress clearly showed that admiration for the German solution to the problem of workers' leisure time extended beyond Hitler's Reich.

Nazi Germany's achievements in commercial tourism were also the object of envy abroad. Across Europe there was admiration not only for the increase in overnight stays, but also applause for how they had been attained: through the direct intervention of the state, which had coordinated, rationalized and professionalized the industry. Yet German tourism professionals were also more than willing to look beyond their own borders to learn about what worked well elsewhere, especially if it might help them to compete. They liked how the Riviera advertised itself, marveled at the Dutch use of film, and lauded how Italian trains decorated their interior compartments with tourist posters.[40]

European members of the travel industry could inform themselves about the efforts of their competitors in a number of ways. Even while the Civil War raged in Spain for example the newly-created National Spanish State Tourist Department sent an official on a month-long trip across Western Europe; in Germany in particular he was to "visit the state organizations that develop tourism from a commercial point of view."[41] German tourism experts also gained firsthand experience when they traveled abroad. *Der Fremdenverkehr*, the official tourism journal in the Third Reich, made keeping abreast of Europe-wide developments even easier with its "View Abroad" section, which offered a selection of excerpts from foreign newspapers on matters directly relating to tourism. The international conference offered another venue for the exchange of information between those active in commercial tourism. Nazi Germany hosted several important ones between 1933 and 1945. The following focuses on two of them: the 1937 congress of the International Union of Official Tourist Publicity Organizations and the annual general meeting of the International Hotel Alliance in 1938.

According to conference literature the International Union of Official Tourist Publicity Organizations gathered together "the leading men of tourism

---

40   Dufner, "Zur Neugestaltung der Fremdenverkehrs-Belange Badens," May 24, 1933 (Stadtarchiv Freiburg, C4/XVI/20/9); Verkehrsdirektor Denzlinger to Oberbürgermeister Kerber, no date (Stadtarchiv Freiburg, C4/XVI/18/5); Niederschrift über die 45. Sitzung des Verwaltungsrats der Reichsbahnzentrale für den deutschen Reiseverkehr GmbH (RDV) am 6. Dezember 1938, p. 4 (Bundesarchiv Lichterfelde, R 4323, Nr. 2 RDV).

41   Sandie Holguin, "'National Spain Invites You': Battlefield Tourism during the Spanish Civil War," *American Historical Review* 110/5 (2005): pp. 1399–426. Available online at: http://www.historycooperative.org/journals/ahr/110.5/holguin.html [accessed September 14, 2010], quote at para. 20.

propaganda from numerous European countries."[42] The history of this precursor to the World Tourism Organization stretched back to 1925 when representatives of various tourism associations from 14 European nations, Germany amongst them, met in the Hague. Their aims were: "to exchange information on tourism publicity, to obtain international custom concessions for the import and export of tourism publicity materials, and to alleviate frontier formalities or other obstacles in free international tourist traffic."[43]

The Union's eleventh annual congress in 1937 marked the first time that Germany had hosted the event with sessions of the conference taking place in Berlin, Munich, and Friedrichshafen between May 31 and June 7. The Reich Committee for Tourism was the official host and paid for all associated costs of the conference; the Committee's President, Hermann Esser, was designated its formal patron while another of its bureaucrats, Wilhelm Kirchgaessner, was the congress leader in charge of general planning. However, there was not the same kind of German dominance here as there had been at the World Congress for Leisure Time and Recreation. Only two of the 26 delegates from 19 different countries were German. The Union President was the Belgian General Director of the Belgian-Luxemburg Tourism Office in Brussels, M. Pulinx.[44]

The elaborate schedule of events planned for the delegates and the lavish receptions hosted by the highest placed Nazis suggest how politically and economically valuable this conference was deemed to be. For his part Esser endlessly emphasized its meaning for "foreign policy." The conference opened in Berlin with a welcome address from Walther Funk, the Nazi Economics Minister, wherein he laid bare what the regime hoped to gain from the conference: to convince delegates to promote Germany as a travel destination, and thereby become propagandists for National Socialism. Hitler received the Union delegates at his office in the Reich Chancellery and Goebbels welcomed them to the Propaganda Ministry the following day. From Berlin there were excursions to Potsdam to visit Frederick the Great's Sanssoucci palace. Then participants traveled by train to Munich and on to the Obersalzberg for a hike near Hitler's

---

[42]   Hermann Esser, "Zum XI. Kongress der Union Internationale des Organes Officiels de Propagande Touristique, 31. Mai–7. Juni 1937" (Hoover Institution Archives, "Germany. DKZ," Box number 309, folder "Touristique (*Fremdenverkehr*)," n.p.

[43]   J. Jafari, "Creation of the Intergovernmental World Tourism Organization," *Annals of Tourism Research* 2/5 (1974): pp. 237–45, p. 239. See also Maximilian Klafkowski, *Organisationsgrundsätze der Fremdenverkehrspflege in Europa* (Berlin, 1931), pp. 225–34.

[44]   Unless otherwise noted, the following information comes from the DKZ's collection of documents and *Der Fremdenverkehr* clippings about the conference held at the Hoover Institution Archives, "Germany. DKZ," Box number 309, folder "Touristique (*Fremdenverkehr*)."

mountain retreat accompanied by the Führer himself and his deputy, Rudolf Hess, resplendent in lederhosen. The week-long conference ended with sessions in Friedrichshafen and a boat trip on Lake Constance. Clearly this was a group the Nazi regime wanted to impress. *Der Fremdenverkehr* and local and regional newspapers published scores of photographs of Union members at work and play, detailed reports about the delegates' schedules, and in-depth summaries of conference resolutions.

While headlines in German newspapers screamed that this was "a true congress for peace," there were aspects of the conference that sent a different, more bellicose message. The opening session was held in Berlin's Haus der Flieger [House of Flyers] under the gaze of fallen Great War flying aces whose portraits graced the walls. Esser greeted the delegates on the first day with a call to honor the 23 German victims of the "criminal bolshevist attack on the battleship 'Deutschland'" two days earlier.[45] On the second day of the conference delegates laid a wreath at the war memorial on Unter der Linden Avenue in Berlin to the sounds of an SA guard singing Great War songs. In Munich too they visited the Feldherrnhalle where a memorial plaque commemorated the "martyrs" to the Nazi cause who had been killed during Hitler's failed putsch attempt in 1923. As a souvenir of their visit to Munich, conference participants were given a ceramic figurine from the Allach Porcelain factory, which was run directly by Heinrich Himmler's SS.[46]

Though the Union was "international" in name, the delegates in 1937 were all European. Thus the 23 "very difficult and complicated questions" that were on the agenda were ones largely of concern to European countries. One is struck in reading about the conference proceedings by the apparent unanimity of opinion about, for example, the need for an obligatory spa tax in all European countries and internationally standardized tourism statistics. There was also lots of agreement about the major topic of discussion, easing foreign currency restrictions, particularly those put in force by the Nazi government. Many tourism professionals at home and abroad voiced their opinion that such measures hampered their industry. Although Funk made it clear that it was "unfortunately impossible to allow [Germans] unrestricted tourism" abroad, the Swiss representative nonetheless felt the congress had taken a "big step towards the regaining of freedom of movement."

---

[45]   In aid of Franco's Nationalists during the Spanish Civil War, the "Deutschland" had been patrolling Spanish waters when it was hit by Republican air attacks off the island of Ibiza on May 29, 1937.

[46]   For information about Allach Porcelain visit the Allach Porcelain website at: http://www.allachporcelain.com [accessed October 26, 2010].

An even bigger accomplishment was the agreement that travel agencies in all the countries represented in the Union should provide tourist information about the other member nations. Cooperation, not the autarkic self-reliance so regularly praised by Nazi propagandists, was clearly the dominant motif here. Yet it appears that conference delegates also had high praise for areas in which Germany had taken the lead. The spa tax they agreed was "regulated best in Germany"; German tourism statistics were also "exemplary." President Pulinx called Germany a "model land" and a "shining prototype" in the field of commercial tourism. Germany, he continued, had achieved such "pioneering work" because its organization of tourism was "optimal." We should, he concluded, strive to "follow this German example."

That German model was invoked again at another important international conference hosted by Germany the following year. Between 24 and 28 April 1938, the spa town of Baden-Baden welcomed, crowed the local press, the "leading men of the hospitality industry from all the countries of the world" as the International Hotel Alliance gathered for its seventh annual general meeting.[47] The organization had its origins in the International Hotel Men's Association founded in 1869, which brought together hotel owners from across Europe. In 1921, in Paris, representatives of national hotel owner societies and hospitality industry associations established the Hotel Alliance. While its annual general meetings took place every three years, the executive committee met more frequently. In May 1936 Hitler had held a reception for executive committee members meeting in Berlin. Later the British president of the Alliance, Sir Francis Towle, waxed effusive in a personal letter to the Führer, thanking him for recognizing the importance of their organization.[48] But at that Berlin meeting, as at a meeting in Budapest six months later, the German government's attempts to limit travel abroad, such as making expensive travel visas necessary to leave Germany, were explicitly criticized by members of the Alliance: there was, reported one German newspaper, "the widely held conviction" that German-imposed constraints on international tourist traffic represented a very strong "obstacle."[49]

Holding the 1938 annual general meeting in Germany thus offered a way to exert more direct pressure on the Nazi government to ease those constraints;

---

[47]   "Die Alliance intern. de l'Hotellerie," *Badeblatt und amtliche Fremdenliste der Stadt Baden-Baden* 32 (April 23–6, 1938). This and the following newspaper articles can be found in the Stadtarchiv Baden-Baden's file on the Hotel Alliance meeting.

[48]   See related documents in Akten der Reichskanzlei, R769, "Deutsches Verkehrswesen," vol. 2 (Bundesarchiv Lichterfelde), pp. 16, 17, 21.

[49]   Hermann Esser to Joseph Goebbels, December 10, 1936, Akten der Reichskanzlei, R769, "Deutsches Verkehrswesen," vol. 2 (Bundesarchiv Lichterfelde), p. 95.

however, there was likely something to the propagandists' assertion that behind the choice of location lay admiration for the post-Depression health of the German hotel industry under National Socialist leadership. The timing of the meeting was significant as well. Only one month before the annexation of Austria had been achieved. This was then the first time that the Alliance had met in the "new" Germany, the Greater German Reich; the first time since it had become the "most beautiful travel destination in the world."[50]

The 1938 annual general meeting welcomed 200 foreign delegates from 27 different countries alongside 100 German representatives. Even though the Alliance meeting drew more participants than the International Union conference had done, it was not accorded the same political significance if only to judge by the absence of top Nazi bigwigs. The highest-ranking government official to attend was Hermann Esser, president of the Reich Committee for Tourism, although Baden's Reich Governor Robert Wagner did take part in the opening speeches.[51] But the Führer was there in spirit: a new Hitler bust graced the stage of the Kleines Theater where the general assembly met.[52] He was also addressed via a telegram from Alliance President Towle, in which Towle stressed collective ideas about international tourism as a way to achieve worldwide peace and cooperation: "The world's hotel sector earnestly strives together to effect the promotion of international tourist traffic, which to great extent contributes to mutual understanding and therefore broadly to the ... pacifistic goals aspired to by all nations."[53] From less altruistic perspectives, the town of Baden-Baden and the state of Baden viewed hosting the conference as a chance to showcase and market their various touristic delights. Delegates made excursions to the Black Forest, Heidelberg, and Mannheim and enjoyed wines from the region at lavish banquets; singers dressed in local folk costumes performed for them too.[54]

But there was real work to be done as well. The annual general meeting provided an opportunity for those active in the hotel industry to exchange

---

[50]   "Welthotellerie tagt in Grossdeutschland," *Der Fremdenverkehr* 3 (April 23, 1938): p. 1. In 1938 the Austrian International Hotelmen's Association was simply dissolved and merged into the Third Reich's Economic Group for the Catering and Accommodation Industry. On the Nazis' earlier coordination of the hotel industry in Germany, see Thomas Peter Petersen, *Gastwirte im Nationalsozialismus, 1933–1939* (Bad Kleinen, 1997).

[51]   "Ergebnisse der Badener Tagung der Welthotellerie," *Der Fremdenverkehr* 3/18 (April 30, 1938): p. 3.

[52]   "Die Alliance internationale de l'Hotellerie tagte," *Badeblatt und amtliche Fremdenliste der Stadt Baden-Baden*, April 27–30, 1938.

[53]   "Der Kongress der Hoteliers hat begonnen," *Neues Badener Tagblatt*, April 26, 1938.

[54]   "Welthotellerie tagt in Grossdeutschland;" "Festlicher Ausklang der Hotelier-Tagung," *Neues Badener Tagblatt*, April 28, 1938.

ideas and experiences with an eye to furthering international collaboration. As one participant noted, "international cooperation in the hospitality industry is easy, because the problems are almost everywhere the same." Those problems and thus the topics of discussion at the meeting included: the timing of school vacations, the problems of private room rental, hotel reservation systems, the need to combat street noise for hotel guests, and many more. The long list of resolutions passed at the meeting stressed three key goals: international consistency in the listed attributes of various types of accommodation, regulated price quotes and decreased restrictions in international travel, specifically the abolition of travel visas, the easing of passport and customs controls, and the lessening of foreign currency limitations.[55] These central issues and aims were seemingly prioritized at the conference with little effort, no matter that the delegates came from many different countries with very different political systems; such ease thus suggests once again just how transnational the discourse about tourism was at the time.

There was also agreement at the meeting about who was to serve as the next president of the Alliance for the following three years. Fritz Gabler, a German, was the unanimous choice.[56] Gabler, whose thoughts on autarky and tourism opened this chapter, was Germany's leading hotelier. He owned the renowned Hotel de l'Europe in Heidelberg, was head of the national Economic Group for the Catering and Accommodation Industry, and served as chairman of the State Tourism Association of Baden. He was a staunch supporter of the Nazi state, but his cosmopolitan background—he had completed his hospitality studies in Rome and later worked in England and France—convinced him of the need to look beyond German borders, especially to France, for solutions to the hotel industry's problems. Alliance members might have felt that having a German president could make it easier to achieve their goals of convincing the Nazi regime to ease travel restrictions. The Nazi press though depicted Gabler's appointment as president as "proof of the esteem and enthusiasm the German hotel professional awakens in all circles abroad."[57] There was probably some truth to that claim. Declarations that the German hotel industry was viewed as "exemplary" abroad were not simply the stuff of Nazi newspaper headlines. Alliance members conveyed for example their admiration of hotel employees' working conditions under Hitler. But it was also the larger picture— the role of the state—that drew praise. One Swiss hotel owner said he "envied Germany for having statesmen who bring to tourism and the hotel industry

---

[55]   "Ergebnisse der Badener Tagung."

[56]   "Der Kongress der Hoteliers hat begonnen."

[57]   "Ausklang der internationalen Hotelier-Tagung," *Der Führer*, April 28, 1938.

such understanding."[58] Here he echoed Francis Towle's opening remarks at the meeting, wherein he highlighted the difference between the "old" and "new" Germany: now, Towle had said, the state displayed special interest in the problem of travel.[59]

As during the World Congress for Leisure Time and Recreation, there was at least a superficial recognition that the German model could not simply be exported, that one size did not fit all, and that Germany would make no attempt to influence the "thinking and plans" of other peoples. "We in the Alliance," Gabler reiterated, do not think "to disparage the ... idiosyncrasies in travel in different countries." We know, he continued, what a strong impact a people's and nation's "peculiarities" have on its travel industry.[60] Yet even if the German model was not to be replicated exactly, there remained a great deal of interest throughout the 1930s in the Nazis' steering of tourism. International conferences continued to be a means of discovering more about it.

That interest continued even after the outbreak of World War II. Strength through Joy tourism almost immediately ground to a halt, but German commercial tourism flourished in the early years of the war. In February 1941 Slovakia sent leaders of its tourism industry to Berlin "to study the central organizations of the Reich's vast pleasure travel industry, with a view of coordinating Slovakian methods with those of Germany." One month later the directors of nine different tourist organizations from Denmark, Sweden, Norway, and Finland completed a two-week "study tour" in Germany.[61] Germany also continued to look abroad after 1939. *Der Fremdenverkehr*, the Reich Committee for Tourism's mouthpiece, ran a column entitled "View on the World" principally to report on the declining tourist trades in enemy countries: the Riviera's hotel rooms were empty, gloated one edition.[62]

In peacetime, tourism officials had stressed that Nazi Germany had no desire to impose a German touristic model, but the war quickly belied those claims. As the Reich expanded, the German tourism infrastructure was extended with speed and efficiency in one conquered country after another: state tourism associations and tourism communities were created, with Germans sent to staff them, in Alsace, in East Prussia, and even at the heart of the murderous Nazi

---

[58]   See "Deutsche Gaststätten, vorbildlich in der Welt," *Neues Badener Tagblatt*, April 23, 1938; "Das deutsche Hotel als Vorbild des Auslandes," *Der Führer*, April 25, 1938.

[59]   "Die Alliance internationale de l'Hotellerie tagte."

[60]   "Willkommen im Badnerland," *Der Führer*, April 25, 1938.

[61]   RDV (ed.), *News Flashes from Germany by Radiogram from Berlin to the German Railroads Information Office* (New York), no. 69, February 1, 1941 and no. 77, March 29, 1941.

[62]   "Gemauschel an der Riviera," *Der Fremdenverkehr* 6/24 (June 14, 1941): p. 2.

empire, the General Government. Local hotels were taken over, renamed as part of the "Germanization" process, and coordinated with the Reich's hospitality organizations.[63]

Germany continued to host and send delegates to various international tourism conferences during the war as well. In August 1944, however, a total ban on all conferences and meetings not relevant to the war effort was imposed.[64] One year later Berlin and Hamburg, host cities of two of the conferences discussed here, had been devastated by Allied bombs. Baden-Baden now hosted the French occupying forces rather than important hoteliers. Studying international tourism conferences in the Third Reich certainly lays bare the duplicity of the Nazi regime's oft-expressed hope that such meetings would lead to worldwide accord and cooperation. But examining them from the transnational perspective also reveals much more. Conferences, even under Hitler, became vehicles for cross-border conversations, which, though carried out in different languages, were easily understood because notions about the problems of workers' leisure time, the challenges of commercial tourism, and the trials of the hotel industry were shared by many participants. At the World Congress for Leisure Time and Recreation, Germany had offered up Strength through Joy as a model program that many other countries thought worthy of emulation. Yet at the International Union of Official Tourist Publicity Organizations' congress and the International Hotel Alliance's annual general meeting, German delegates were open to an actual exchange of ideas. German tourism professionals clearly wanted to engage in dialogue with their European counterparts, to learn from them even if only to beat them at their own game. The tourism conferences hosted by Hitler's Germany also exposed a surprising commitment to international cooperation that transcended and even at times blatantly opposed the regime's principles and policies aimed at self-sufficiency. "Autarky and tourism" were indeed "conceptually incompatible."

---

[63]   For more on German tourism during World War II, see Semmens, *Seeing Hitler's Germany*, Chapter 7.

[64]   Herren, "Outwardly," p. 90, note 115.

Chapter 11

The Cold War, Mass Tourism and the Drive to Meet World Standards at East Berlin's T.V. Tower Information Center[1]

Michelle Standley

In many regards the Information Center at the T.V. Tower in East Berlin, the capital of the German Democratic Republic (GDR), was not so different from such information centers in other major European cities in the 1970s. Visitors could enter, find maps of East Berlin, get assistance booking a room, purchase tickets to a concert, and pick up a souvenir before heading back out into the city. Similar to information centers in other places, sometimes known as visitor centers, East Berlin's main information center was also located at the base of a major tourist attraction, in this case, the 1,198-foot tall T.V. Tower, or *Fernsehturm* (see Figure 11.1). Communist Party leader Walter Ulbricht inaugurated the tower, which was built in the heart of the city's newly renovated downtown area, Alexanderplatz, days before the GDR's twentieth anniversary on October 7, 1969.[2] During the T.V. Tower's first years of operation Berlin-Information—the organization responsible for promoting the city in the GDR and abroad and for overseeing tourism in the capital—had staff on hand to assist tourists, give out information and sell souvenirs from a humble cart located in front of the tower.[3] In 1972, when builders completed the second and final phase of the tower's construction, the Information Center finally opened its doors to the public. The center was comprised of several rooms: the main entrance, which held such pieces as a three-dimensional map of the new downtown, display

[1]   The Berlin Program for Advanced German and European Studies and The German Academic Exchange Service (DAAD) funded portions of the research for this article. I would like to thank them and Mary Nolan for their support.

[2]   Peter Müller, *Symbol mit Aussicht, Der Berliner Fernsehturm* (Berlin: Verlag Bauwesen, 2000), p. 125.

[3]   Landesarchiv Berlin [hereafter LAB], C Rep. 123, Zg. 1707, Bd. 28, Vermerk ueber die Begehung des Gelaendes des Fernseh- und UKW-Turms zur Gewaehrleistung von Ordnung und Sauberkeit am 31.3.1971, April 1, 1971.

Figure 11.1   The East Berlin Information Center, with its winged roof, rests at the base of the Television Tower, the face of socialist modernity. In the background, to the left of the Tower, stands the newly constructed Hotel Stadt Berlin, another sign of socialist modernity: tourism

windows and mounted books, a movie theater, two discussion rooms, and finally a second level dedicated to temporary exhibitions.

If this brief description adds up to create an image of the Information Center as strikingly similar to those "info points" and visitor centers found at tourist attractions and in city centers throughout Europe, there was a good reason. Berlin-Information, which planned and ran the Information Center, consciously sought to create a typical, "modern" information center and to achieve, what they defined as, "world standards" in display and design technology. This drive to appear "modern" and to meet "world standards" raises several questions. To begin with, why did party and state authorities in the GDR decide to construct an information center, and specifically one that was "modern" and met "world standards?" Secondly, what was, according to Information Center planners, the latest in display and information technology and how did they imagine what "modern" should look like?

Information Center planners drew on numerous strands of inspiration. Yet, no source was more important than international expositions or world's fairs. The Information Center at East Berlin's T.V. Tower, it is argued here, was a modest version of the new type of national pavilions that appeared at the world's fairs held after World War II. From uniformed hostesses dressed to look like airline stewardesses, to interactive audio-visual technology, and an on-site, original film about everyday life in their city to the T.V. Tower itself, the Information Center employed many of the same technologies and methods of exhibition display as those seen at the world's fairs. Like the national pavilions at the world's fairs, the Information Center also sought to convince visitors that the GDR was advanced in terms of technology, science, and industry, as well in terms of the quality of life that it offered its citizens. These numerous similarities in design and purpose should not lead one to overlook the significant differences between the center and the world's fairs. East Berlin's state and party authorities also had their own specific agenda, which they hoped the techniques of display would reinforce. At the Information Center the medium and the message worked together to reinforce the notion that the GDR was a legitimate state that offered an advanced version of socialist modernity, and that, unlike the Federal Republic of Germany (FRG), the GDR had successfully overcome the National Socialist past.

Mass Tourism, the Cold War, and the Postwar World's Fairs

After World War II, the pan-European tourism discourse took a dramatically transnational turn. The Cold War drew European nation-states into an increasingly transnational dialogue over tourist industry practices. On the institutional level, the two superpowers established, or encouraged the establishment of, international organizations dedicated to the promotion of tourism in Europe. US Congress, for instance, established the Economic Cooperation Association (ECA), to deal with Marshall Plan aid. The ECA, in turn, created the Travel Development Section (TDS), with offices based in Paris. The US State Department also "encourag[ed] the creation of the European Travel Commission (ETC), a union of national travel offices from the Marshall Plan countries," to help ensure cooperation between the European countries.[4] The Soviets likewise organized a Socialist Bloc-wide tourism organization.[5] Participation in such organizations provided a means for tourist industry representatives from various European nations to meet, trade ideas, and ultimately to emulate one another.

The Cold War also influenced tourism in Europe in less overt ways. Socialist and capitalist countries used the postwar international trade shows and world's fairs as another platform upon which to stage their rivalries. Competing nations learned techniques of propaganda and effective methods of exhibition display and design, which they could then apply to a different context—on-site tourism promotion. Moreover, as this account of East Berlin's Information Center will show, the influence of world's fairs reached beyond the host cities and official participants. The 1958 Brussels World's Fair and to a somewhat lesser extent the 1967 Montreal World's Fair, established a paradigm in on-site tourism promotion and information dissemination that even countries like the GDR, who did not participate in the world's fairs, could adopt at home. As Wolfgang Clasen, author of the 1967, *Expositions, Exhibits, Industrial Trade Fairs*, noted, the fairs in Seattle 1962, New York 1964–65, and Montreal 1967 all took their cues from Brussels 1958. "In reviewing these exhibitions," he observed, "the critics again and again referred to the World Exhibition held in Brussels in 1958, which was, as it were, taken as a reference in basis and scale."[6]

---

4   Christopher Endy, *Cold War Holidays: American Tourism in France* (Chapel Hill: University of North Carolina Press, 2004), pp. 42–9, and *Der Fremdenverkehr* 8 (Darmstadt: Jaeger, 1950), pp. 6–7. For further information, readers should also consult the introduction to this volume.

5   A survey of German and English language literature reveals no research about this organization. When exactly it was founded and how frequently it met are not clear. What is known is that such an organization existed and that delegates representing the various tourism organizations from socialist countries attended and contributed studies of issues particular to tourism in the Socialist Bloc.

6   Wolfgang Clasen, *Expositions, Exhibits, Industrial Trade Fairs* (New York: Praeger, 1968), p. 7.

The GDR's Struggle for Legitimacy

Traditionally countries who hosted the fair extended invitations to contribute a pavilion to states with whom they had official diplomatic ties. The Belgians therefore did not invite the GDR to participate, as Belgium adhered to the FRG's Hallstein doctrine. The world's fairs were thus closed to the GDR as a forum for international competition. This did not stop the GDR from participating passively, as observers, who could learn from and adopt the techniques of exhibition design to their own needs, and apply them to on-site promotion aimed at tourists and other visitors from home and abroad. By creating a sort of world's fair national pavilion in miniature at the T.V. Tower, the GDR could thereby implicitly communicate the message that the GDR was a legitimate participant in the international competition. As will be shown below, center planners consciously sought to incorporate the latest in exhibition design and technology, albeit tailored to the GDR's own specific needs.

Tourism publicity at home and abroad, as well as tourist services for foreigners in the capital, was part of the GDR's ongoing efforts to win international respect. In the 1960s GDR authorities centered their efforts specifically on overcoming the FRG's Hallstein doctrine and on gaining recognition from the international community as a legitimate state. Berlin-Information's (known as Berlin-Werbung Berolina for most the 1960s) publicity for the capital aimed to help the GDR achieve this goal, in part by simply raising its profile with a polished, modern-looking presence at international exhibits and trade shows. By the time the Information Center officially opened its doors in 1972, the GDR was only months away from gaining the recognition for which it had struggled since its founding in 1949. By late 1972 and early 1973 most major European powers had opened diplomatic relations with the GDR. In September 1973 the United Nations extended membership to the GDR and the FRG. By 1974 even the United States entered into diplomatic relations with the GDR.[7] By the mid-1970s the GDR's years as an international outsider appeared to be over.

When Berlin-Information officials drew up designs and planning for the Information Center the GDR's acceptance into the international community was still in the future. Moreover, far from ceasing its promotional activities, Berlin-Information—in keeping with the wishes of the GDR's new leader Erich Honecker—continued to work towards earning international respect for the GDR as a "model socialist society."

---

[7] David Childs, "The SED Faces the Challenges of *Ostpolitik* and *Glasnost*," in David Childs, Thomas A. Baylis, and Marilyn Rueschemeyer (eds), *East Germany in Comparative Perspective* (London and New York: Routledge, 1989), pp. 1–18, p. 3.

Mass Tourism as Challenge and Opportunity: A New Audience

As part of the international boom in tourism, rates of travel to East Berlin also increased during the postwar period. However, there were some specific causes for increased rates of travel to East Berlin in the early 1970s. To begin with, more East Germans began traveling to their capital. Thanks to the introduction of the five-day workweek in September 1967, GDR citizens had more time to undertake day trips and weekend excursions. Many East Germans came to shop, not to sightsee. This was for the simple reason that one could purchase goods in East Berlin that were scarce elsewhere. This was one of the privileges that the city enjoyed as a frontline of the Cold War.[8]

In the early 1970s East Berlin opened its doors to the outside world, or at least opened a wider space in the metaphoric Wall and in the real border crossings, to allow in an unprecedented number of visitors from their eastern and western neighbors. From the eastern direction, beginning in 1972 visitors from Poland, Hungary, and Czechoslovakia could enter the GDR without visas. This was part of a long-term plan to cultivate ties between socialist neighbors and to provide travel opportunities for their respective citizenry. In the words of a 1975 GDR guidebook to Czechoslovakia, "Within the context of deepening socialist cooperation and integration, many warm, personal friendships between the citizens of our countries have also arisen from [our] close cooperation in the areas of politics, finance, transportation and culture. Therefore the introduction of visa-free travel was a logical decision."[9] Like their East German "brothers" many socialist tourists came to East Berlin to shop. Downtown department stores, GDR authorities noted, could not keep pace with the influx of "shopping tourists." Shopping was not the only attraction that East Berlin offered to citizens of Poland and Czechoslovakia. For many Socialist Bloc visitors the city on the Spree offered a taste of the promised modernized future, with its comparatively more advanced technological and consumer products.[10] In addition to legal

---

8   David Childs, *The GDR: Moscow's Germany Ally*, 2nd ed. (London: Allen & Unwin Australia, 1988), p. 70; Alexander Sedlmaier, "Berlin als doppeltes Schaufenster im Kalten Krieg," in Thomas Biskup and Marc Schalenberg (eds), *"Selling Berlin" Image-bildung und Stadtmarketing von der preußischen Residenz zur Bundeshauptstadt* (Stuttgart: Steiner, 2007).

9   Wolfgang Polte, *Reiseratgeber ČSSR. Landschaften, Städte, Sehenswürdigkeiten, Praktische Ratschläge* (Leipzig, GDR: Urania Verlag, 1975), from inside cover.

10   For more on Soviet tourists "seeing the future" during their travels in the socialist countries of Europe see Anne E. Gorsuch, "Time Travelers: Soviet Tourists to Eastern Europe," in Anne E. Gorsuch and Diane P. Koenker (eds), *Turizm: The Russian and East European Tourist Under Capitalism and Socialism* (Ithaca and London: Cornell University Press, 2006), pp. 205–26.

activities, many visitors, from Poland especially, saw visa-free travel as an opportunity to acquire contraband capitalist goods and to make contacts with visitors from capitalist countries.[11]

From the western direction, the GDR signed a series of treaties with the FRG that made it possible for West Berliners and West Germans to enter with visas.[12] West Berliners and citizens of the Federal Republic made up the largest number of visitors to the GDR from outside the Socialist Bloc. Between 1973 and 1980 an average of just over three million West Berliners visited the GDR annually. Though rates fluctuated, an average of about 2.5 million citizens from the FRG also visited the GDR annually between 1973 and 1980.[13] This represented a substantial increase over the rates of travel during the 1960s.[14] Even if it was not their final destination, many of those visiting other parts of the GDR passed through East Berlin first. After the Basic Treaty came into affect in June 1973, FRG leaders actively encouraged their citizens to travel to the GDR. Presumably this was because leaders were confident that West Germans, who witnessed the contrast between the GDR and the FRG first hand, would return to the FRG fortified in their commitment to the capitalist state.[15]

The tourism boom presented East Berlin's tourist authorities with numerous challenges and opportunities. The increased presence of West Berliners and West Germans created new causes for concern. SED (Socialist Unity Party) state authorities worried that leaders in West Berlin and the FRG would use the eased travel restrictions to sabotage the GDR's efforts to build a stable socialist society. "Class enemies" in the West, GDR tourism authorities argued, used tourism to infiltrate the GDR and to disseminate false information to GDR citizens.[16] SED authorities also worried that increased contacts between citizens of the two Germanys would lead to more opportunities for GDR citizens to flee to the FRG. In addition to these worries, the SED state authorities were

---

[11]   LAB, C Rep. 100-05, Nr. 01496, Einschätzung der bisherigen Entwicklung des visafreien Reiseverkehrs, July 19, 1972.

[12]   M.E. Sarotte, *Dealing with the Devil: East Germany, Détente and Ostpolitik, 1969–1973* (Chapel Hill and London: University of North Carolina Press, 2001), pp. 72, 93–6; and Childs, *The GDR: Moscow's Germany Ally*, p. 86.

[13]   Rates on citizens of the FRG come from Childs, "The SED Faces the Challenges of *Ostpolitik* and *Glasnost*," p. 6. Rates on citizens of West Berlin come from Childs, *The GDR: Moscow's Germany Ally*, p. 90.

[14]   It is difficult to find reliable statistics for the 1960s. Even without the exact numbers there is no question that in light of the Four-Power-Agreement and new GDR citizenship law more citizens of West Berlin and the FRG traveled to the GDR in the 1970s than in the 1960s.

[15]   Childs, "The SED Faces the Challenges of *Ostpolitik* and *Glasnost*," p. 5.

[16]   LAB, C Rep. 737, Nr. 72, Analyse, Modell, Problem, notwendige Entscheidungen, May 25, 1968.

presumably anxious that East Berlin might not stand up to direct comparisons between the GDR and the FRG.

Part of the Information Center's task was to help put a positive "spin" on a perhaps less than positive comparison between socialist and capitalist society, between the GDR and the FRG. Party and state authorities thus looked to the center to communicate to this new and varied audience of domestic and foreign visitors, that the GDR was a legitimate state, that the GDR's vision of socialist modernity was superior to capitalist modernity, and that the GDR had overcome the National Socialist past, inheriting only the positive aspects of the German national past. To communicate this message center planners had to find a language of display and design that their domestic and varied foreign audience alike would understand and respect. To convince visitors that the GDR was modern, it was not enough to say it in audio presentations and explanatory texts, the center had to show it by employing the latest innovations in exhibition display and design technology.

East Berlin as Socialist Utopia: The T.V. Tower and "Action Alex"

The construction of the T.V. Tower and its Information Center fit into a broader scheme to rejuvenate and rebuild the GDR capital, to make concrete—quite literally—the promised socialist utopia. At the Fifth Party Day of the SED in 1958, party leaders announced plans to restore and build up the city's downtown area surrounding Alexanderplatz. "Action Alex," party leaders hoped, would have a "purifying effect" and would finally lead Berlin into the future.[17] The city was indeed in urgent need of reconstruction. Throughout most of the 1950s the old inner city was largely empty, the rubble having long since been removed.[18]

Plans for the key structures were underway by the early 1960s. Most structures were complete within about 10 years: House of Teachers [Haus der Lehrers] (1964), House of the Electronic Industry [Haus der Electroindustrie] (1969), the T.V. Tower (1969), the World Time Clock [Weltzeituhr] (1969), and the Fountain of National Friendship [Brunnen der Völkerfreundschaft] (1970), the Downtown Department Store [Warenhaus Centrum] (1970), House of Travel [Haus des Reisens] (1971), Hotel City Berlin [Hotel Stadt Berlin] (1971),[19] and

---

[17]   Holgar Kuhle, "Auferstanden aus Ruinen: Der Alexanderplatz," in Bernd Wilczek (ed.) *Berlin. Hauptstadt der DDR, 1949–1989. Utopie und Realität* (Baden-Baden: Elster Verlag, 1995), pp. 52–72, p. 53.

[18]   T.H. Elkins with B. Hofmeister, *Berlin: The Spatial Structure of a Divided City* (London and New York: Routledge, 1988), p. 199.

[19]   LAB, C Rep. 100-05, Nr. 1454, Einschätzung der Tourist-Saison 1970 in der Hauptstadt der DDR mit Schlußfolgerungen für die Vorbereitung der Saison 1971, January 8, 1971.

House of Berlin Publishers [Haus des Berliner Verlags] (1973).[20] The structures' names and intended functions (travel, shopping, reading) suggest that in the mid-1960s, when architects designed them, SED state and party authorities hoped that the new downtown would convey to citizens of the GDR and to outsiders that the GDR was on the path to a consumer-oriented, prosperous future.

The aesthetics of the new downtown also communicated this message. Although the various structures had different architects, they all embodied mid-century functionalist aesthetics and building techniques, complete with pre-fabricated concrete slabs, steel frames, and minimal adornment or color. The superlatives, in official promotional material, attached to the department store ("the largest department store in the GDR"), the hotel ("the largest hotel in the GDR"), and the tower ("the highest building in the GDR") suggest that they were meant to showcase the GDR's technological progress and advanced state of development. As an official GDR guide to the city's architecture and urban landscape explained, "The variety of the structures and the different fields of experience make the new 'Alex' not merely one of the most interesting points of attraction in Berlin, it has at the same time become a symbol of socialist reconstruction after the destruction in the Second World War."[21]

The structures' few decorative elements captured the zeitgeist of late 1960s and early 1970s. The sculptures and mosaics suggested that the GDR was building a socialist utopia, a society that was technologically and scientifically advanced, internationalist, and a participant in the age of travel and general mobility. The 17-story House of Travel, for instance, featured a bas-relief sculpture entitled, "Man overcomes space and time" the center of which featured an astronaut surrounded by swirling celestial winds, birds in flight, planets, and a sun. Likewise, designers topped the World Time Clock with a metal sculpture of an atom, linking the GDR with science. Furthermore, the clock itself showed times in different cities around the world; this and the name of Alexanderplatz's main fountain, the Fountain of National Friendship, also underscored the GDR's commitment to the international community of workers. This stress on the GDR's embrace of friendship between nations was also a way to distance the GDR from the hyper-nationalist ethos of the National Socialists.

The T.V. Tower was the crown jewel of the new Alexanderplatz. It is a shiny, stainless steel sphere, with a candy cane-striped antenna that was visible throughout much of East and West Berlin. The tower fulfilled a logistical and symbolic need. SED party leaders wanted to create an architectural landmark

---

[20] Waltraud Volk, *Berlin Hauptstadt der DDR. Historische Straßen und Plätze Heute* (Berlin, GDR: VEB Verlag für Bauwesen, 1977), pp. 216–54.

[21] Volk, *Berlin Hauptstadt der DDR*, p. 218.

that would attest to the GDR's technological and economic progress and fulfill the party's desire for a prestige object.[22] In the words of the GDR authors of *Fernsehturm Berlin*, "It [the T.V. Tower] bears witness to the German Democratic Republic on the threshold of its third decade, and of its high scientific-technological state of development."[23]

Historically, towers have served the dual purpose of function and display of power. But beginning with the construction of the Eiffel Tower in 1889— in time for the city to host the world exposition and to commemorate the centennial of the French Revolution—modern tower building has become nearly a prerequisite for cities seeking international recognition. The iconic value alone of such grandiose structures makes them attractive prestige objects for ambitious politicians and businessmen. Towers also draw tourists and sell souvenirs.[24] Well-known examples include the Seattle Space Needle, built for a world's fair in 1962,[25] and the CN Tower in Toronto, built in 1976.[26] Although it was never built, just the name selected for the planned "Abu Dhabi Tourist Tower," in the United Arab Emirates, for which there was a design competition in 1979, reveals the interconnection between modern tower building and the efforts of city authorities and investors to attract and cater to tourists.[27]

The Socialist Bloc countries of Europe also participated in the great postwar tower-building projects.[28] However, as was appropriate to its position

---

[22]   Müller, *Symbol mit Aussicht, Der Berliner Fernsehturm*, p. 147.

[23]   Ingrid Brandenburg, Rudolf Harnisch, and Alfred Kubeiziel, *Fernsehturm Berlin* (Berlin, GDR: Vertrag für Bauwesen, 1970), p. 9.

[24]   Ferris wheels are perhaps the towers of today. Since the construction of the London Eye in 2000, Chinese authorities have built a similar structure, the Star of Nanchang, and work is underway in Singapore on the Singapore Flyer. If the investment group Great Wheel Berlin Holding has its way, Berlin will soon get its own wheel too. See Möritz Koch, "Berlin dreht am Rad," in *Süddeutsche Zeitung*, December 12, 2006.

[25]   There are some other similarities between the Seattle Space Needle and Berlin's T.V. Tower. As James Lyons explains, "the Space Needle had been the centerpiece of a World's Fair intended by the U.S. government to convey 'the country's achievements in science and space ... [and its] continuing affluence and technological advance'." See James Lyons, *Selling Seattle: Representing Urban America* (London and New York: Wallflower Press, 2004), p. 16 from John M. Findlay, "The Seattle World's Fair of 1962: Downtown and Suburbs in the Space Age," in John M. Findlay (ed.) *Magic Lands: Western Cityscapes and American Culture Since 1940* (Berkeley: University of California Press, 1992), pp. 214–64, p. 214.

[26]   La Tour CN Tower Website. Available online at: http://www.cntower.ca/portal [accessed April 20, 2007].

[27]   Mary Ellen Hulls, *Towers: A Bibliography* (Monticello: Vance Bibliographies, 1986), p. 1.

[28]   After Ostakino, the Riga Radio and T.V. Tower, in Riga, Latvia, is apparently the second largest tower in Europe.

within the Warsaw Pact, Moscow's Ostakino Television Tower loomed largest. Ostakino measures over 1,763 feet and is still the tallest freestanding structure on the Eurasian continent.[29] Builders completed construction of Ostakino, which included such tourist friendly amenities as three observation decks and a three-floor restaurant, in 1967. The tower's design reflected the Soviet preoccupation with space travel in the 1960s. As a 1974 GDR publication, *The Towers and Turrets of Europe*, described it, Ostakino "rises up like a rocket on the launching pad."[30]

Plans for East Berlin's T.V. Tower were already underway before work on Ostakino was complete. Nonetheless, T.V. Tower architects, Fritz Dieter and Werner Ahrendt, could have consulted with Soviet architects. Yet, instead of looking east to Moscow for inspiration, Dieter and Ahrendt turned their gaze west. Dieter and Ahrendt consulted such FRG design and architecture journals as *Der Baumeister* and *Domus*.[31] They also cited Buckminster Fuller's geodesic dome at the Montreal World's Fair as a source of inspiration. In Dieter's words, "While we were designing the sphere, the American architect Buckminster Fuller played a role. He had designed a sphere-shaped pavilion for the 1967 World's Fair in Montreal." The T.V. Tower's dome, with its crosshatch pattern, clearly echoes the honeycombed glass and spherical shape of Fuller's US pavilion at Montreal. For the GDR—still struggling economically and lacking natural resources—this striving to meet standards that were frequently established by wealthier, capitalist countries, resulted in having to import Western technology. To fulfill the architects' vision of a modern tower, the GDR had to import the elevators and the expensive stainless steel for the tower's sphere.[32]

Even before the tower was erected, GDR's tourism publications were already energetically promoting the tower as a socialist icon. The souvenir picture book, *Berlin Heute, Hauptstadt der Deutschen Demokratischen Republik* [*Berlin Today, Capital of the German Democratic Republic*], took the inventive step of leading its readers on an imaginary tour of the tower, going so far as describing in detail what the visitors would see from its yet-to-be-constructed observation deck.[33] The image of the tower appeared in "books and brochures, in film and on T.V., on postcards, even on stamps." Whenever the phrase, "Berlin, capital of the

---

[29]   Center of Moscow Region. Branch of RTN website. Available online at: http://www.tvtower.ru [accessed April 20, 2007].

[30]   Günter Meissner and Heinz Bronowski, *Towers and Turrets of Europe*, trans. C.S.V. Salt (Leipzig, GDR: Edition Leipzig, 1974), pp. 133–6.

[31]   Jörg Burger, "Berliner Fernsehturm: Der Turm der Träume," *Die Zeit* 45 (1999).

[32]   Burger, "Berliner Fernsehturm: Der Turm der Träume."

[33]   Berlin-Information, *Berlin Heute. Hauptstadt der Deutschen Demokratischen Republik* (Leipzig, GDR: Berlin-Information, 1968).

German Democratic Republic" needed a visual emblem, commented author Peter Müller, the tower appeared in some form.[34] Berlin-Information likewise joined the "branding" frenzy. In 1968, one year before the tower's inauguration, it changed its name from Berlin-Werbung Berolina and began using the symbol of the tower as the "I" in "Information."[35]

From the time it opened its doors to the public on October 23, 1969 thousands of visitors flocked to the T.V. Tower. According to Berlin-Information estimates, during its first year roughly 1.5 million guests visited. Berlin-Information officials expected an additional 100,000 the following year. With the successful construction of the tower, party and state leaders had managed to create an enduring city icon for Berlin and to attract thousands of visitors yearly. However, comparatively speaking, building a tower was the easy part. Ensuring that visitors understood its intended symbolism was another matter. The popularity of the tower, combined with the increased rates of tourism, gave the SED state even more incentive to rely on the center to convey the impression that the GDR was on the path to building a socialist utopia.

Berlin-Information or the Center Planners

The same year that party leaders announced plans to renovate and build up the downtown area, the Bezirksleitung der SED established the capital's first tourism organization, Berlin-Werbung Berolina. As noted above it changed its name to Berlin-Information in 1968. The organization grew in size in the years leading up to the opening of the Information Center. Between 1965 and 1968 alone it grew from 120 to 161 employees.[36] As tourism increased in importance, it continuously expanded its duties and services as well. Throughout all of these organizational transitions Berlin-Information remained a local operation. It did not belong to a larger, centrally organized network of GDR city travel bureaus, nor was it directly responsible to a GDR-wide tourism organization.[37] Indeed the GDR lacked such an organization, leading Berlin-Information officials to

---

[34]   Müller, *Symbol mit Aussicht, Der Berliner Fernsehturm*, p. 142.

[35]   For an example see Berlin-Information, *Berlin Heute. Hauptstadt der Deutschen Demokratischen Republik.*

[36]   LAB, C Rep. 737, Nr. 55, Berlin Informationssystem, undated, ca. summer 1965; LAB, C Rep. 737, Nr. 72, Analyse, Modell, Problem, notwendige Entscheidungen, May 25, 1968.

[37]   LAB, C Rep. 737, Nr. 55, Berliner Informationsystem, undated, ca. summer 1965.

complain about the unclear boundaries between the various state and party organizations responsible for domestic and foreign tourism.[38]

Berlin-Information justified its work and shaped its agenda according to SED directives made during the Communist Party plenums. However, Berlin-Information's specific aims and duties came directly from local state and party authorities, the Bezirksleitung der SED and the Magistrat von Gross-Berlin. Although Berlin-Information was able to generate some revenue through the sale of souvenirs, East Berlin authorities "planned [for Berlin-Information] to operate at a loss."[39]

Berlin-Information set up information windows as well as larger booths throughout the city in such places as hotels, train stations, on main streets, and at excursion destinations on the city's perimeter. It also operated numerous "info points" throughout the city. Berlin-Information was also responsible for organizing exhibits to promote Berlin in other cities in the GDR and abroad, as well as within Berlin itself. Frequently this meant making use of its *Campingwagen* to transport materials and serve as a distribution center at yearly events such as Baltic Sea Week in Rostock, the International Gardening Show (IGA) in Erfurt, and the Leipzig Trade Shows.[40] Berlin-Information also set up displays as part of exhibitions in other major cities in the Socialist Bloc, such as Prague, Bucharest, Budapest, and Warsaw. Over time Berlin-Information enjoyed a greater presence in such West European cities as Vienna, Stockholm, Paris, and Milan.[41] Berlin-Information published numerous pamphlets, souvenir books, and calendars, magazines such as *Berlin Journal*,[42] and an inexpensive bi-weekly magazine, *Wohin in Berlin* [*Where to in Berlin*] that listed times and dates of current theater productions, movies, and athletic events.[43]

To carry out its numerous duties, Berlin-Information coordinated with other organizations. For exhibits at the T.V. Tower and abroad, Berlin-Information cooperated with the Ministry for Foreign Affairs [Ministerium für Auswärtige

---

[38] For more information on internal debates in the 1960s about whether or not to establish a GDR-wide tourism organization see the fourth chapter of Scott Moranda's "The Dream of a Therapeutic Regime: Nature Tourism in the German Democratic Republic, 1945–1978" (Ph.D. diss., University of Wisconsin-Madison, 2005).

[39] LAB, C Rep. 737, Nr. 72, Analyse, Modell, Problem, notwendige Entscheidungen, May 25, 1968.

[40] LAB, C Rep. 737, Nr. 55, Berliner Informationsystem, undated, ca. summer 1965.

[41] LAB, C Rep. 737, Nr. 74, Arbeitsprogram der Berlin-Werbung Berolina, February 1, 1967.

[42] LAB, C Rep. 123, Zg. 1707, Bd. 3, Praktikumsarbeit. Thema "Aufstellung einer Kostenanalyse fuer das Berlin-Journal," January 21, 1967.

[43] LAB, C Rep. 737, Nr. 55, Berliner Informationsystemm, undated, ca. summer 1965.

Angelegenheiten] and the League of the GDR for Friendship Among the Peoples [Liga für Völkerfreundschaft]. At the Information Center at the T.V. Tower, Berlin-Information also worked with the GDR Travel Agency [Reisebüro der DDR] to train hostesses. Berlin-Information also exchanged ideas with other socialist countries and to a lesser extent capitalist ones, who had official relations with the GDR. Berlin-Information officials traveled regularly to Poland, Czechoslovakia, and Hungary to visit with their tourist organization counterparts.[44] In their general planning notes for improving their informational brochures, they specifically cite those produced by the Information Center in Prague as worthy of study and emulation.[45]

Berlin-Information officials clearly kept up with tourism promotion and exhibition practices in both the Socialist Bloc and on the international trade fair and exhibition circuit. In discussing plans for improving their exhibits at home and abroad, for example, Berlin-Information officials noted that they sent exchange delegations of employees to study other socialist countries' programs. They also mentioned that they gave employees the opportunity to visit trade fairs and exhibitions "to learn about the global standards [*Weltniveau*] in techniques and methods of promotion and exhibition." In this way, Berlin-Information employees gathered "such sources of information about what was happening in the world [*Weltstand*] in this area as well as information about international tourism literature."[46] Because they were responsible for representing the GDR capital at domestic and foreign trade fairs, Berlin-Information would naturally apply the techniques they honed and acquired through such experience in their planning for the Information Center. This makes it all the more likely that the well-regarded and internationally influential postwar world's fairs in Brussels and Montreal would have had a significant impact on Berlin-Information's ideas about how to construct and run the Information Center.

Welcome to the Information Center

Standing outside the T.V. Tower's Information Center, visitors could not help but be struck by its contemporary architectural style. From the bright white walls and

---

[44]   LAB, C Rep. 737, Nr. 74, Berlin-Werbung Berolina, "International Erfahrungsaustausch," February 23, 1967.

[45]   LAB, C Rep. 737, Nr. 74, Arbeitsprogram der Berlin-Werbung Berolina, February 1, 1967.

[46]   LAB, C Rep. 737, Nr. 72, Analyse, Modell, Problem, notwendige Entscheidungen, May 25, 1968.

large glass windows, to its roof that resembled soaring and descending wings, the center's aesthetics were postwar modernist with a touch of space-age flair. The geometric pattern of the groomed lawn and planters, which lined the pathway to the main entrance, added to the center's orderly and polished appearance. Berlin-Information hostesses, looking like typical airline stewardesses from the late 1960s and early 1970s, were there to greet tourists at the center's entrance.

After the tower itself, the center's main attraction of the Information Center was a large, white three-dimensional model of the new downtown, which included self-service, acoustic narration in 12 languages. Plans for the model were already under way years before the center opened. Before the tour properly began the narrator established two preliminary themes. First, the voice noted that the construction of Berlin reflected the will of the party as expressed at the Eighth Party Day of the SED, "all of our doings and actions serve singularly and alone man's well-being." Second, the reconstruction of Berlin represented a triumph over the damages of the war and the fascist legacy. "First of all, we recall the fascist inheritance." The fascist inheritance, according to the narrator, was Berlin's postwar state of destruction. "In the area of our present capital alone over 185,000 apartments were fully destroyed and more than 400,000 damaged," noted the narrator. Starting with the postwar destruction provided a dramatic contrast to the "new Berlin" that the narrator was about to describe to the visitor.[47] With these key themes framing the narrative—the GDR served the well-being of man and the reconstruction of Berlin represented a triumph over not only the damages of World War II but also over the fascist past—the tour of the "new Berlin" finally commenced.

The tour covered approximately a five and a half mile route, or two or three hour walk, in ten minutes. Lenin Square provided the eastern border of the model, the Brandenburg Gate the western border, the S-Bahn between Friedrichstrasse and Marx-Engels-Platz the northern border, and Leipzigerstrasse the southern.[48] "Dear Guest," the voice on the acoustic guide began, "Berlin-Information welcomes you to the Information Center at the T.V. Tower in the capital of the German Democratic Republic. You are standing in front of a true to life model of the new city center. What a few years ago was still a project has today become reality."

The tour began at the foot of the T.V. Tower. "Our 'tower,'" the narrator commented, "proves itself to be a good 'tour guide!'" Whether discussing Karl-Marx-Platz, as the future home of the Palace of the Republic, Fisher Island, as the site of apartment building skyscrapers, or People's Park Friedrichschain, as a memorial shrine, the narrator found ways to stress the themes introduced at the

---

[47]   LAB, C Rep. 122, Nr. 607, Modellerläuterung, undated, ca. 1973.

[48]   LAB, C Rep. 737, Nr. 72, Analyse, Modell, Problem, notwendige Entscheidungen, May 25, 1968.

beginning of the tour. At the first stop at Rathausstrasse and Karl-Liebknecht-Strasse, for example, the narrator used the surrounding areas to introduce the hallmark of "socialist city planning," harmony between "work, science, culture, living, social life, and recuperation." Two floors of pedestrian passageways, shops, "intimate restaurants," along with fountains and works of art constructed by "trained artists" all led into buildings, squares, and park grounds, noted the voice. Here the narrator painted a picture of relaxed, and "culturally enriching," urban leisure. One can easily imagine a nineteenth-century *flâneur* at home among the shops, parks, and sculptures. However, the narrator interrupted the picture of bourgeois, urban bliss with a reference to the actual conditions of life—childcare and modern, inexpensive apartment buildings. "Notice the new living and business ensemble with the kindergarten and childcare facilities on the terrace," advised the narrator, "in this way one can observe how an area such as this, with its approximately 1,300 apartments and sites for sports and recuperation, makes modern socialist living and life possible."

The narrator returned to the theme of inexpensive, modern housing at several points during the tour. On Fisher Island, for instance, the guide offered extensive details on the cost of rent in East Berlin. On average, the voice noted, rent on Fisher Island cost 1 to 1.25 GDR Marks per square meter. For an older apartment it was less than one GDR Mark per meter. A modern three-bedroom apartment, the narrator continued, cost a mere 4 to 8 percent of a worker family's income. For those with an income under 2,000 GDR Marks the cost of rent was reduced further still. "A good, inexpensive apartment" was a "fundamental concern of our state's social politics," it boasted.[49]

After listening to the narration at the model, guests would then turn their attention to three light boxes, which hung on a wall next to the model. The first box contained a picture of Alexanderplatz in 1945, 1955, and 1971. The second box showed an ensemble of government buildings and the third featured "modern apartment buildings." As a trio the pictures provided a visual testament to the image of East Berlin that Berlin-Information sought to create at the center: Berlin was the seat of a modern state's government, the site of spectacular progress, and home to modern but affordable living conditions.

Adjacent to the light boxes hung an illuminated quote from the first paragraph of the GDR's 1968 constitution that declared, "Berlin is the capital of the German Democratic Republic." Turning 180 degrees away from the light boxes and the illuminated quote, the visitor would then see nine display windows, measuring about 4.5 by 6.5 feet. In each window hung three photographs (two large black and white photographs and one much smaller

---

[49]   LAB, C Rep. 122, Nr. 607, Modellerläuterung, undated, ca. 1973.

one in color) and a short accompanying explanatory text. Two windows were dedicated to "Mitte," or Central East Berlin. The remaining seven focused on other East Berlin neighborhoods. Each neighborhood represented a different aspect of life in Berlin. "Mitte," for example, stood in for the state, high culture, and higher education; Prenzlauer Berg for children and elementary education; Friedrichschain for new construction and triumph over the destruction of war; Treptow for the GDR's gratitude to the Soviet soldiers; Koepenick for leisure and relaxation; Lichtenberg for industry; Weissensee for sports and athletics; and finally Pankow for good healthcare and medical facilities.

After perusing the window displays the visitor would turn to face the exit, to the left of which stood a table with listings of events in the capital. Mounted at eye level to the left of the table were "wall books" that measured 24 × 18 inches. The "books," which perhaps looked more like photo albums, each contained eight double-sided pages with pictures and short explanatory texts. The books focused on two themes: Berlin's development since 1945 and Berlin's role in the history of the German workers' movement.

The last images visitors would have seen before heading left down the corridor, to the movie theater, were three photographs hanging above the mounted books. Since the "books" hung at eye level one can assume that in order to view the faces of Erich Honecker (the current party leader), Walter Ulbricht (the former party leader, who then held the position of honorary "chairmen of the SED"), and Willi Stoph (Politbüro member and prime minister) the visitor would have had to gaze upward to see them.

Visitors would then make their way to the theater to view *Guten Tag in Berlin, der Hauptstadt der Deutschen Demokratischen Republik* [*Good Day in Berlin, the Capital of the German Democratic Republic*]. Just as the display windows used East Berlin's neighborhoods to stand in for certain, idealized aspects of socialist society, the film too presented visitors with a parade of idealized images of everyday life in the GDR: workers in the factories, children at school, party leaders, members of the army, and farmers working for the collective. *Good Day in Berlin* also stressed that leisure was an important aspect of life in the "modern, socialist metropolis." Yet, the movie presented socialist leisure as something productive, not merely recuperative. The film showed citizens engaged in "culturally enriching" activities in the city's "green lungs," or parks. The film then flashed back to images of Berlin in 1945, 1949, and 1961 to show how the past had been overcome, how the GDR had to "defend" itself, how the GDR was gaining international recognition, and how the Eighth Party Day promise "to serve the well-being of man" was being fulfilled. It then showed a few of the sites to see, including the Soviet Memorial at Treptow Park. Finally, it concluded with a triumphal image of the new Alexanderplatz before the final shot of a plane ascending out of Schönefeld.

After studying the three-dimensional model of the new Alexanderplatz, listening to the accompanying acoustic narration through a telephone system, viewing the display windows about Berlin's neighborhoods, and watching *Good Day in Berlin*, visitors would finally have joined the legendarily long lines that led to the T.V. Tower elevators. Handing one of the hostesses their ticket, sightseers would enter one of the two elevators and experience a swift ride to the great heights of nearly 670 feet above the city about which he or she had just learned a great deal. After their tour through the center what did visitors expect to see from the observation deck? The skyscrapers surrounding Alexanderplatz brought to life by the three-dimensional model? The parks and memorials described by the acoustic guide? Airplanes landing and ascending from Schönefeld airport as featured in *Good Day in Berlin*?

The first sight awaiting visitors as the elevator doors opened and they stepped out onto the observation deck was not the "modern, socialist metropolis." It was the class enemy: West Berlin! T.V. Tower architects and engineers had made a mistake and at no point during the planning and building process had anyone noticed.[50] But perhaps it did not matter. After all, if visitors had paid careful attention to the materials on display in the center, if they had properly understood the GDR's mission—to serve the well-being of man—then perhaps it would not have made much of a difference. For visitors would have learned to see like a socialist tourist.

The Medium is the Message

The overwhelming message of the center was that Berlin was the capital of a legitimate state, the GDR. The phrase "Berlin is the capital of the German Democratic Republic" appeared on nearly all of the city's official souvenirs, from matchbooks, to teddy bears, to mugs, and coins. Indeed the phrase appeared in all of the GDR tourism promotional materials, in guidebooks, brochures, and in several places in the center. An illuminated version hung against a wall, with the note that it came from the first paragraph of the GDR's 1968 constitution. It also flashed on the screen as part of the title of *Good Day in Berlin, the Capital of the German Democratic Republic*.

In addition to simply stating "Berlin is the capital of the German Democratic Republic," center planners reinforced this message by stressing that the GDR

---

[50]   Burger, "Berliner Fernsehturm: Der Turm der Träume."

was in an advanced state of modernity, that socialist modernity was superior to that of capitalist modernity, and that the GDR, in contrast to the FRG, had overcome the horrors and guilt associated with the German national past. Center planners employed several methods to communicate these themes. First, they sought to build a center that employed what they defined as "world standards" in display and exhibition design. Second, they employed a team of well-trained, carefully selected hostesses to engage visitors in discussions about the GDR. Third, they constructed a narrative with the audio and visual materials that explicitly supported the center's overall theme that the GDR was a legitimate, modern state worthy of emulation and respect.

In the late 1960s, during the early planning phases, Berlin-Information officials settled on the specific theme, "Berlin: Yesterday, Today, and Tomorrow." The permanent display, the plans noted, would be about "the political position of the capital, its economic and social development and structure, about its modern amenities and its outlook." In other words, the Information Center would provide a general overview of socialist society as embodied by the capital, while at the same time drawing attention to its growth and modernity. The title alone—beginning with the past ("yesterday") and ending with the future ("tomorrow")—gives one a sense of the historical narrative that center planners wanted to construct. The GDR, they suggested, was moving out of the ashes of the German national past toward an ever brighter, socialist future. That center planners wanted the center to embody the spirit of the future is also underscored by the fact that words like "modern," "growth," "development," and "dynamism" appear frequently in the planning notes for the center.

Just as the T.V. Tower architects wanted to meet "world standards" in their design and building materials, Berlin-Information planners were also preoccupied with ensuring that the center's materials and techniques of display met "world standards." As one official noted, visitors wanted not only insight into Berlin's development but they also wanted the information delivered with "contemporary techniques" and "modern means" with such things as uniformed hostesses, electronic and acoustic devices, illumination, panoramas, self-service, and efficient, rational use of the visitor's time: all methods derived from the world's fairs and international trade fair circuit.

Berlin-Information officials were evidently familiar with important developments in museum and exhibition design, specifically with the postwar focus on interactive displays. In his 1968 study of exposition and exhibit design, Clasen noted that the trend was toward dynamic elements, including "projections, shows, live models, tableaux vivants and mirror effects." In 1970 American curator Allon Schoener similarly pronounced that "The trend now is to provide more information than a precise set of facts stated in a logical order ... a museum exhibition offers a mass of images and sounds."[51] This turn toward interactive display was in abundant evidence at Brussels and Montreal. At Brussels the Belgians consciously stressed interaction in their Civil Engineering Building and the US pavilion likewise included such interactive elements as a voting booth. However, it was the Czechoslovak pavilion in Montreal that truly raised the bar with its "Kinoautomat," which featured a film that allowed visitors to decide the ending by pressing a button.[52] The postwar shift toward employing various, interactive media was in part also a response to the work of psychologists in the 1960s, whose research on knowledge acquisition inspired curators to stress interaction.[53]

In keeping with the newfound interest in interactive display techniques, center planners integrated various forms of interactive media that communicated to visitors through active and passive means. On the more active side, the center included a self-service acoustic guide and mounted books, which visitors could flip through. On the passive side, the center featured photographs with captions and a short film. The alternation between passive and active forms of communication had an additional advantage. It was also a rhetorical strategy, designed to communicate to visitors in the most efficient, effective way possible.

Information Center planning notes suggest that Berlin-Information officials paid careful attention to the center's overall strategy of persuasion. Visitors, one report noted, wanted to be persuaded in a "purposeful" and "tasteful" way. The Information Center thus needed to create a "closed system" of persuasion, a system that was "arranged according to political, aesthetic and psychological vantage points."[54] The planning notes do not specify exactly what officials meant by these vague terms. However, Berlin-Information officials noted that they thought that visitors would want to obtain information themselves, using automated "information sources" and other forms of self-service. Such methods of display would also allow visitors to move quickly through the center. Visitors, Berlin-Information officials argued, would want to learn about life in the city

51   Allon Schoener, "'Electronic Participation Theatre': A New Approach to Exhibitions," *Museum: A Quarterly Review Published by Unesco* 23 (1970/71): pp. 218–21.

52   Clasen, *Expositions, Exhibits, Industrial Trade Fairs*, p. 9.

53   Wilcomb Washburn, "Museum Exhibition," in Michael Shapiro (ed.) *The Museum: A Reference Guide* (New York: Greenwood Press, 1990), pp. 199–229, p. 212.

54   LAB, C Rep. 737, Nr. 74, Arbeitsprogramm der Berlin-Werbung Berolina, February 1, 1969.

"in the shortest time possible." The center would therefore have to be planned to help visitors make "the most rational use of time." By paying attention to such concerns as maximizing time, incorporating self-service elements, and employing various media—like audio equipment, photography, and film—center planners could provide additional evidence that the GDR was on a par with the "most advanced" countries.

Center planners thus also incorporated the latest innovations in audio equipment. After the war museum curators and exhibit designers in the United States and in Europe began to introduce more electronic equipment and audio elements. The now ubiquitous personal headset guides, for instance, made their debut at some museums during the 1970s. However, before the age of roving headsets, museums and exhibitions used various versions of the telephone to transmit information in several languages. As early as the 1889 Expo in Paris, the US pavilion included headsets of some sort. At the 1915 world exposition in San Francisco visitors to the five-acre model of the Panama Canal, located inside the US pavilion, listened to telephone handsets while being zipped along a moving platform.[55] The "Germany" exhibition at the 1936 Berlin Olympics also featured a type of "television phone."[56] At Brussels the US pavilion introduced an IBM computer that could answer questions about history in 10 languages. The Soviet pavilion at Montreal also included telephones, as photographs show visitors holding against their ears telephones that were connected to a display.[57]

In short, if center planners wanted to convince visitors that the GDR was modern and capable of at least keeping up with technological developments, they almost certainly had to include some sort of audio equipment, or telephone headsets. Plans for the center therefore included an acoustic guide, which could be listened to through a "telephone system," that would accompany the three-dimensional model of the freshly reconstructed downtown. As an American scholar of museum design noted as early as 1965, "visual communication can be simultaneously reinforced by the spoken word."[58] Thus, as a rhetorical strategy, the acoustic information offered center planners an additional medium through

[55] Anna Jackson, *Expo: International Expositions 1851–2010* (London: V&A Publishing, 2008), p. 80.

[56] John Robert Gold and Margaret M. Gold, *Cities of Culture: Staging International Festivals and the Urban Agenda, 1851–2000* (Aldershot and Burlington: Ashgate, 2005), p. 171.

[57] Photograph in Andrew Garn (ed.), *Exit to Tomorrow: World's Fair Architecture, Design, Fashion 1933–2005* (New York: Universe, 2007), p. 168.

[58] Michael Brawne, *The New Museum: Architecture and Display* (New York and Washington: Praeger, 1965), p. 10.

which to capture the visitors' attention and convey information about the city and about the GDR.

Plans for the center also included visual elements: a panoramic map, large-scale photography, and an original film. Panoramas and three-dimensional models have a long association with world's fairs and with exhibitions. The 1867 Paris exposition included a working model of the Suez Canal. The 1889 Paris exposition featured at least seven major panoramas as well as numerous models. As mentioned above, the 1915 San Francisco exposition featured a five-acre model of the Panama Canal. Two famous panoramas, Democracity (a diorama of a "city of the future") and Futurama (another future city) were part of the influential 1939–40 New York World's Fair.[59] Though not an official fair, the much-admired 1962 Seattle World's Fair, entitled, "Man's Life in the Space Age," had on hand a large panorama of Seattle, built on a scale of 1 to 100.[60] At the 1958 World's Fair in Brussels, the Belgian's Civil Engineering Building also included a large-scale map of Belgium.[61] The US pavilion included two urban planning exhibits, one of which featured a 300 square foot model of Philadelphia "with an automatically generated 'flip over' feature that replaced a blighted ghetto with a planned, modernized city center."[62]

With this in mind, it is hardly surprising that Berlin-Information officials took pride in their own three-dimensional model. Indeed it must have looked impressively large as it was built on a scale of 1 to 500 and measured approximately 26 × 12 feet. As noted above, visitors could experience a "virtual tour" of the new Berlin by taking advantage of the self-service, telephone headsets with summaries of the German narration available in 12 languages.

The center also relied on photographic elements and film. As Clasen notes in his commentary on Montreal, on-site, original films had become so popular that it would have taken 183 days to view all of the films on display at the fair.[63] The film featured at the center was very much in keeping with the films shown by the US military in Korea and West Germany and by the US State Department at various international trade fairs. Films like *The New America*, *Glimpses of the U.S.A.*, and *America the Beautiful* introduced audience members to, and subtly

59   Erik Mattie, *World's Fairs* (New York: Princeton Architectural Press, 1998), p. 199.

60   Ibid, p. 122.

61   Jean-Louis Moreau and René Brion, "Business at the Service of Humanity?" in Gonzague Pluvinage (ed.), *Expo 58: Between Utopia and Reality* (Brussels: Lannoo International, 2008), pp. 119–42, p. 135.

62   Robert H. Haddow, *Pavilions of Plenty: Exhibiting American Culture Abroad in the 1950s* (Washington, DC: Smithsonian Institution Press, 1997), p. 108.

63   Clasen, *Expositions, Exhibits, Industrial Trade Fairs*, p. 9.

promoted, the "American way of life."[64] The Soviets also employed such films and their pavilion at Montreal showed "films about the citizens of the various regions of the country."[65] In addition, the Soviets projected onto a wall moving images of power stations and factories.[66] The Czechoslovak pavilion at Montreal was nonetheless the most innovative by far. Visitors to Montreal were apparently dazzled by the aforementioned Kinoautomat, as well as the Diopolyecran and Polyvision. The Diopolyecran featured a mosaic of cubes with internal light projectors and changing images, while Polyvision was a panorama on modern life projected onto revolving spheres.[67]

Good Day in Berlin showed six times daily in a room that seated over 100 visitors. A superficial glance at the planning notes for the film might suggest that Berlin-Information officials wanted to emulate the classic travel narrative arc of following a visitor on a trip to the city. The opening and closing images showed "modern planes," as the director notes specified, arriving and then leaving Schönefeld airport. However, this was the DEFA director, Ralf Schnabel, paying lip service to the tourism genre. For instead of showing the city through the eyes of a tourist—by emphasizing the city's important sites and places to shop or dine—the film, similar to those films shown at international trade fairs and at Montreal, focused on introducing different aspects of socialist society. Moreover, most visitors to East Berlin arrived by train, bus, and car. The use of airplanes in the film therefore reflected the modern image that Berlin-Information planners wanted to project.

Another way in which center planners sought to meet visitors' expectations about modern exhibitions was by having on hand a staff of attractive uniformed guides, known as hostesses. On site hostesses, at tourist facilities and exhibitions, became standard fare in the early 1950s. The world's fair hosts, at Brussels and Montreal, also employed hundreds of trained and uniformed hostesses.[68] At both fairs hostesses wore tailored suits with coordinated hats and gloves. In addition to the host cities' hostesses, individual national pavilions staffed their sites with guides. At the controversial "Unfinished Work" exhibit, the pavilion sponsored by the United States kept on hand a staff of guides prepared to explain and defend US race relations, a particularly hot topic at the time as Little Rock, Arkansas was on the front page of nearly every major newspaper around the world.

---

[64] Garn, *Exit to Tomorrow*, p. 108; Haddow, *Pavilions of Plenty*, p. 111.

[65] Library and Archives Canada Website. Available online at: http://www.collectionscanada.gc.ca/expo/053302020213_e.html [accessed March 15, 2009].

[66] Clasen, *Expositions, Exhibits, Industrial Trade Fairs*, p. 9.

[67] Jackson, *Expo*, p. 86; and Clasen, *Expositions, Exhibits, Industrial Trade Fairs*, p. 9.

[68] Gonzague Pluvinage, "Expo 58 Hostesses or the 'Nation's Hostesses of Honor,'" in Pluvinage (ed.), *Expo 58: Between Utopia and Reality*, pp. 175–82, pp. 177–8.

At the T.V. Tower and Information Center, hostesses manned the elevators that led to the observation deck and café, and were also present on the deck and at the entrance on the ground floor. Hostesses added an additional visual link between the tower and the aesthetics of mass travel and the space age, as conceived in the GDR during the 1960s and 1970s. Wearing stylish outfits, that included coordinated jackets, vests, miniskirts, together with small hats and pumps, the hostesses resembled airline stewardesses. Greeting guests at the entrance, operating the elevators into the sky, and then serving cold beverages at the café, the hostesses led guests into the future. As stewardesses of the space age, the hostesses suited the overall schema of the new Alexanderplatz. They complimented the bas-relief sculpture, "Man overcomes space and time" that appeared on the newly constructed House of Travel.

Hostesses were supposed to answer general questions about the center, the tower, and the city, and to engage visitors in discussions about socialism and about the GDR. According to a Berlin-Information report, produced before the center opened but when hostesses already staffed the tower and observation deck, hostesses succeeded in making contact with about 10 percent of the tower's visitors. "It can be estimated," noted the same report, that through conversations about problems in the development of socialism in the GDR and in the construction of the capital, certain prejudices that visitors from non-socialist countries have about the GDR are eliminated." To ensure that hostesses were prepared to answer tough political questions about such recurring themes as "freedom" and "democracy" they had to undergo extensive training during the winter months and to pass a written and oral examination. Berlin-Information also held separate training sessions to help prepare hostesses to provide explanations for the three-dimensional model of downtown and for the observation deck. They also provided foreign language courses.

From the extensive training sessions alone it is clear that Berlin-Information officials saw the hostesses as key to the success of the T.V. Tower and Information Center. By taking questions from guests and initiating discussions about socialism and the GDR the hostesses added further, personal testimony to the informational materials on display. The hostesses literally humanized the GDR for visitors and perhaps even softened its image. In addition to bringing a (pretty) human face to socialism the hostesses contributed to creating a certain atmosphere at the T.V. Tower and Information Center. Associated with travel, the service industry and with world's fairs, the mere presence of the mini-skirted guides suggested that the GDR was in dialogue with the modern world.

Conclusion

Berlin-Information officials understood that the medium was only one aspect of the center's overall message. The effort to keep up with world standards in terms of technology and design was a means of capturing the audience's attention, of taking the GDR seriously as a player on the international stage of advanced countries. At first glance the center might have intentionally looked like an ordinary information or visitor center that tourists might have encountered in other modern cities. Nonetheless, in order to understand the motives behind the construction of the center and behind the drive to meet world standards it is necessary to move beyond the mere surface of attractive hostesses, acoustic guides, dioramas, and film. While Berlin-Information officials responsible for designing the center clearly incorporated the aesthetic language of world's fairs and international exhibition practices, they tailored them to fit their own, specific agenda. Center planners were not trying to convince visitors that the GDR was merely another modern country. Rather they were also trying to persuade their diverse audience of domestic visitors from within the GDR and foreign tourists, from the Socialist Bloc and from capitalist countries, that the GDR's version of socialist modernity was more advanced and ultimately more humane than that of capitalist modernity and that the GDR, with Berlin as its capital, had triumphed over history and the horrors of the recent German past.[69]

---

[69]   In its attempt to promote the country as both an "ordinary" modern nation-state and yet singular and even superior to other nation-states, the GDR was in good company. See Eric Zolov, "Showcasing the 'Land of Tomorrow': Mexico and the Land of the 1968 Olympics," *The Americas* 61/2 (October 2004): pp. 159–88 for an account of the Mexican state's discursive strategies for stressing Mexico's modernity as well as its peace-making role, admirable balance of racial harmony, and embrace of its ethnic heritage.

Index

Society of Proletarian Tourism of the
RSFSR (*Obshchestvo proletarskogo turizma RSFSR*, or OPT), 185–8, 193
"soft tourism," 67
Sommer, Roger, 44
South American Travel Association, 7
Soviet bloc
tourism and the, 218, 218 n.5
Soviet Union, 11
"autonomous tourism" in, 189–90
excursion movement and, 181–2
health resorts and, 190–91
"proletarian tourism" in, 183–9
and rest homes (*dom otdykha*), 179–80
and spas, 176, 179–80
Sochi health resort, 173 n.8, 191
Soviet block-wide tourism organization, creation of, 218
tourism education and, 181–3
tourism organization after the First Five Year Plan, 190–91
tourism and recreation policy of, 176–82
trade union control of tourism, 191–2
Sovtur (*Sovetskii turist*), 183, 186–7, 193
Spain
and beach tourism, international, 32–3
Civil War-era tourism, 206
pan-European tourism development and, 4, 154–5
Space Needle, 224, 224 n.25
spas, 20, 118–19, 130–32, 142, 173, 176, 179–80
Staithes Group, 29
Stalin, Joseph, 5, 182, 186
Stoph, Willi, 231
Strength through Joy (See *Kraft durch Freude*)
Swiss chalets, 76–7
Swiss Confederation, 60–61

Swiss Society of Hotels, 70
syndicats d'initiative (France), 133–4, 140, 143–4

Tangier, 29
Taugwalder, Peter, 75
Tell, Guillaume, 68
Temple Bar, 164–5
Terjohi, 27
Third Reich
see Nazi Germany
Thurston, Hazel, 34
Tidy Towns and Villages Competition, 165–8
touring associations, European, 130–31, 130 n.5
Touring Club de France, 129–32, 129 n.21, 131 n.8, 133–6, 140, 143–8, 148 n. 58, 158, 167
"Chambre Hygienic TCF" of the, 143
Concours du Bon Hôtelier of, 144
"Touring Club Hotels" of the, 143
Tourism and Excursion Authority (*Turistko–ekskursionnoe upravlenie*), 191–2
tourism scholarship
Great Britain's dominance in, 3
guest–host relationships in, 13–15
national borders, contained within 3–4, 15
social class emphasized in, 2–3
transnational relationships in, 4–7, 12, 15–16
Tourism and Travel Company (TTC), 108–10, 124
"Tourism is Everybody's Business" program, 167
Tourist Information Center (Budapest), 108–9
Tourist Organisation Society of Ireland, 155
towers, 224–5
Towle, Sir Francis, 209–11